Praise for
Next STEPS in Literacy Instruc

"This timely resource fills the gap between assessment and reading interventions; it's filled with essential information for all reading and elementary teachers."

—Nancy Mather, Ph.D.
University of Arizona

"*Next STEPS in Literacy Instruction* is an excellent example, linked to AIMSweb and DIBELS assessment for reading fluency, for redirecting attention to the 'intervention' in response to intervention."

—Virginia W. Berninger, Ph.D.
Professor of Educational Psychology
Director of University of Washington
Brain Education and Technology Education Site
Eunice Kennedy Shriver Intellectual and
Developmental Disabilities Research Center
University of Washington

"This book lives up to its title and provides the reader with the 'next steps' needed to provide effective literacy instruction to students who require differentiated instruction."

—Sharon Vaughn, Ph.D.
H.E. Hartfelder/Southland Corp Regents Chair
Executive Director, Meadows Center for Preventing Educational Risk
University of Texas

"An excellent resource . . . Teachers will find this book very valuable in helping children become better readers."

—R. Malatesha Joshi, Ph.D.
Professor of Literacy, ESL, and Educational Psychology
Texas A&M University
Editor, *Reading and Writing: An Interdisciplinary Journal*

"A cogent, in-depth guide for teaching not only the major components of reading but also their essential connections for real-world classroom instruction—grounded in rigorous assessment of students' progress along with many evidence based resources for how and what to teach."

—Judith R. Birsh, Ed.D.
Editor, *Multisensory Teaching of Basic Language Skills, First and Second Editions*

"A responsibility I have in my current position is to identify quality professional development materials that will truly impact instruction and empower teachers with the necessary tools to teach to reach their learners. *Next STEPS in Literacy Instruction* does this and more. This text will provide classroom teachers and reading specialists with a variety of critical tools needed to perform reliable assessments and plan differentiated small-group instruction based on the data collected to meet the literacy needs of struggling readers. I highly recommend this book as a wonderful resource and 'tool kit' every classroom should be equipped with."

—Jenny Fisk
K–12 Elementary Education & Reading Specialist

"As schools move toward RTI service models, teachers and reading coaches are seeking guidance for how to best provide effective instruction to their struggling readers. Susan Smartt and Deb Glaser have provided the how-to manual to help answer that question! This book is packed full of excellent research summaries on key issues that will help educators understand why certain instructional procedures should be used. *Next STEPS in Literacy Instruction* is very practical. Every chapter includes specific, step-by-step procedures for implementing proven-effective instructional strategies along with actual scenarios from 'inside a real classroom.' A bonus is an extensive list of additional resources on each topic. Every school seeking answers to how to help every student become a successful reader will find this book to be a valuable resource."

—Jan Hasbrouck, Ph.D.
Gibson Hasbrouck & Associates
Wellesley, MA

"[This book] describes a range of measures for capturing what students know and can do, and a range of activities for what to do when students do not progress as well as expected. As school districts begin serious early intervention efforts in reading, teachers need to know how to and what to teach when assessments identify children who grow slowly in key reading skills. While researchers work on fine-tuning assessment and intervention procedures, Smartt and Glaser show teachers how to begin to match small-group reading activities to assessment results."

—Rollanda E. O'Connor, Ph.D.
University of California, Riverside

"This book includes practical tools and activities that have a strong research base. Teachers will find valuable resources and activities to help them connect their assessment data with the most effective teaching strategies."

—Diane Haager, Ph.D.
Professor, Division of Special Education and Counseling
California State University, Los Angeles

Next STEPS
in Literacy
Instruction

Next STEPS

in Literacy Instruction

Connecting Assessments to Effective Interventions

by

Susan M. Smartt, Ph.D.
National Comprehensive Center for Teacher Quality
Vanderbilt University
Nashville

and

Deborah R. Glaser, Ed.D.
Boise, Idaho

·P A U L·H·
BROOKES
PUBLISHING Co®

Baltimore • London • Sydney

Paul H. Brookes Publishing Co.
Post Office Box 10624
Baltimore, Maryland 21285-0624
USA

www.brookespublishing.com

Manufactured in the United States of America by
Versa Press, Inc., East Peoria, Illinois.

AIMSweb® is a registered trademark of NCS Pearson, Inc.
DIBELS® (Dynamic Indicators of Basic Early Literacy Skills) is a registered trademark of Dynamic
  Measurement Group, Inc.
FAIR is the Florida Assessments for Instruction in Reading.
TPRI® (Texas Primary Reading Inventory) is a registered trademark of Texas Education Agency.

The individuals described in this book are composites or real people whose situations are masked and
are based on the authors' experiences. In all instances, names and identifying details have been
changed to protect confidentiality.

Every effort has been made to ascertain proper ownership of copyrighted materials and obtain permission for their use. Any omission is unintentional and will be corrected for future printings upon
proper notification.

Library of Congress Cataloging-in-Publication Data

Smartt, Susan M.
  Next STEPS in literacy instruction : connecting assessments to effective interventions / by Susan M.
  Smartt and Deborah R. Glaser.
      p.   cm.
  Includes bibliographical references.
  ISBN-13: 978-1-59857-096-0 (pbk.)
  ISBN-10: 1-59857-096-X (pbk.)
 1. Reading (Elementary)   2. English language—Composition and exercises—Study and teaching
(Elementary)   3. Language and languages—Study and teaching (Elementary)—Technological innovations.   4. Web-based instruction.   I. Glaser, Deborah R.   II. Title.

  LB1573.S68 2010
  372.4—dc22   2010004650

British Library Cataloguing in Publication data are available from the British Library.

2022   2021   2020

10   9   8   7   6

Contents

About the Authors

Susan M. Smartt, Ph.D., is Senior Research Associate, National Comprehensive Center for Teacher Quality, Vanderbilt University. She holds a doctorate in school psychology from Tennessee State University and a master's degree in special education and reading from Peabody College of Vanderbilt University. At Vanderbilt, Dr. Smartt engages in research focusing on improving teacher preparation for reading teachers. Dr. Smartt also provides educational consulting services and teacher training to states and local school districts focusing on school reform, reading intervention for low-performing schools, using data to inform practice, developing response to intervention (RTI) initiatives, and implementing scientifically based reading programs.

Dr. Smartt owned and directed a reading clinic for 20 years in which she provided comprehensive psychoeducational assessments and tutoring services. She has been a classroom teacher, a reading coach, a reading specialist, a principal, a university faculty member, and a researcher. Her publications include authorship and coauthorship on journal articles, edited volumes, and books on research-based reading intervention and policy initiatives. She travels the country extensively, presenting workshops for classroom teachers and administrators.

Deborah R. Glaser, Ed.D., is a national education consultant, trainer, and author based in Boise, Idaho. Glaser received her doctorate in curriculum and instruction with specific focus on reading and school reform from Boise State University. She is a professional development provider with expertise in reading assessment and a vast knowledge of instructional methods derived from trusted research. During Dr. Glaser's many varied years in education, she has experienced both classroom and learning disability instruction and served as Director of Education of the Lee Pesky Learning Center in Boise, where she oversaw the development of remedial programs for individuals with dyslexia. She has assisted universities with the development of research-based reading curricula and established training and consultation programs to support the success of state and national reading initiatives. Dr. Glaser was an advisor to Idaho's Legislative Reading Committee and a principal author of Idaho's Reading Initiative.

Dr. Glaser is a national trainer of the distinguished teacher curriculum authored by Louisa Moats, *Language Essentials for Teachers of Reading and Spelling (LETRS)*. She consults with national policy institutes regarding quality reading instruction and teacher preparation, and assists schools and districts with implementing scientifically based reading programs and strengthening practitioners' collaborative efforts toward improved instruction and student reading abilities. Dr. Glaser is author of the LETRS Modules, *ParaReading: A Training Guide for Tutors* (Sopris West Educational Services, 2005), and *LETRS Foundations: An Introduction to Language and Literacy* (co-authored with Louisa Moats, Sopris West Educational Services, 2008).

For more information about having *Next STEPS in Literacy Instruction* workshops, train-the-trainer opportunities, or consultation in your school or state department of education conducted by the authors, you may e-mail them at info@nextstepsreading.com. You may also contact Brookes On Location at http://www.brookespublishing.com/onlocation/index.htm for custom-designed *Next STEPS* workshops presented by the authors.

Preface

The preface of a book stands sentinel at the beginning of the text. The preface is written last but sets the stage for readers because the concluding word reveals one last reflection on the exhaustive, cumulative labor and abundant knowledge gained by its authors that serves to illuminate the subject matter and its interpretation. Furthermore, in education, even the final word is replaced tomorrow with new knowledge—another step—to inform our pedagogy.

So it is with *Next STEPS in Literacy Instruction: Connecting Assessments to Effective Interventions.* When we began *Next STEPS* several years ago, our intention was to provide clarity to the issue of how to use and interpret the two most prevalent fluency assessments at the time, DIBELS and AIMSweb. Since initiating our work, however, we've added interpretation of two additional assessments, the TPRI and FAIR, also designed to help inform literacy instructional decisions for classroom teachers; literacy coaches; school psychologists; special education teachers; intervention teachers; paraprofessionals; and, generally, any members of the school support team. After examining the initial screening data derived from these four assessments, the message was clear; there was work to be done. The process of using the data was complex and not easily assimilated.

As *Next STEPS* expanded, we remained steadfast in our initial goal: to help educators plan and organize small, intensive reading groups and, even more important, to seek to clarify effective teaching behaviors that lead to higher levels of reading achievement. Each of these topics can be isolated for study, but in actuality, they exist in a relationship of integrated application in successful programs. *Next STEPS* breaks them down into separate topics for study, discussion, and consideration before bringing them back together to present an amalgamation of best practice.

Since the inception of *Next STEPS,* response to intervention (RTI) has taken the country by storm. Developed as an approach to better integrate general and special education, as an alternative to traditional flawed special education eligibility guidelines for learning disabilities (the discrepancy model), and as a conduit through which science will inform our reading assessment and instruction, RTI has the potential to upgrade our reading paradigm! However, there are many assumptions surrounding the ease with which schools will be able to implement the deeply layered and complex components of RTI.

RTI represents a complex framework of assessment, intervention, progress monitoring, and decision making that requires high levels of expertise and knowledge to implement effectively. Without a firm grounding in assessment and research-based instruction and intervention coupled with persistent professional development for teachers and school leaders, RTI implementation efforts risk a surface application, eventual failure in meeting intended goals, and missed identification of students with true learning disabilities and dyslexia.

A *Next STEPS* goal is to provide a beginning process to reinforce RTI efforts in classrooms by guiding teachers to a clearer understanding of identification of students at risk for learning difficulties. Furthermore, monitoring students' progress, planning purposeful small reading groups that are dynamic as time passes, providing targeted and persistent practice, and applying ever-increasing knowledge to make instructional decisions that will lead students to higher levels of reading achievement is a tall order for teachers. These efforts are lost if our approaches resemble a surface treatment. When students are not making gains, it is imperative that, first, we determine that the core curriculum is research-based and implemented with fidelity and, second, that
responses to instruction include school-based team decisions to involve wide expertise in making assessment and instructional decisions for our students.

We leave you with *Next STEPS,* which are beginning steps for some and continuing steps for others. You are each on your own professional step of understanding, knowledge levels, and experience. *Next STEPS* will continue your growth and development. Allow your professional development through *Next STEPS* to be full of questioning, seeking answers to ensure that all children, regardless of ethnicity, rich or poor, young or older, learn to read and thus achieve their next steps in life.

Acknowledgments

We wish to acknowledge one individual and many others who collectively assisted us with raising *Next STEPS* from infancy through its several growth periods and finally to its published form.

First and foremost, we acknowledge an extraordinary individual, the graphic designer of our working drafts, Karen Hayes in Nashville, Tennessee. Karen's ever-present positive attitude and belief that we could design or create anything graphically sustained us through many challenges. Her tireless determination never failed to help us meet deadlines because she, too, believes that every child can learn to read. She was a force that turned our ideas into a reality, and we will forever be grateful to her for sharing her talent with us.

Second, we acknowledge the innumerable teachers who encouraged us to take *Next STEPS* to its logical next step as a published text. Thousands of teachers trained in Next STEPS expressed the desire for more information about *how* effective teachers teach and *what* effective teachers do in their classrooms to ensure more students gain from their instruction.

We acknowledge our professional colleagues across the country from Florida to Massachusetts, from Texas to Connecticut, to Idaho and beyond, whose research and valuable contributions to the field of teaching reading informed every *Next STEPS* chapter.

We acknowledge the outstanding editorial and design staff at Paul H. Brookes Publishing Co., who were consistently professional, with a twist of humor and a personal touch mixed in. They were always willing to provide assistance and support when uncertainty was looming. What a team!

To

Our husbands, Andrew and Steve,
whose constant support and voices of reason encouraged us
through the challenges of the birth of Next STEPS

Our grown children,
Joshua and David,
who remind me often of life's truly important priorities

and

Stephanie and Stuart,
who show me the unexpected inner strength that each of us is given
to persevere when the challenges appear insurmountable

To each other,
for the tenacious support that sustained and lifted each of us
to our own next step in communicating our passion
about reading to our teacher colleagues everywhere

And finally, to the Next STEPS *community of teachers,*
we dedicate Next STEPS *to you who make it possible for all children to learn to read.*

I

Introduction

Introduction to *Next STEPS*

Next STEPS in Literacy Instruction is a learning tool and guiding resource for schools that use data-based decision making—or more specifically, formative assessments—or for those who are dedicated to taking reading instruction to the next steps necessary for prevention of reading difficulties and the remediation of our struggling readers.

Next STEPS is designed to help teachers learn better *how* to teach, and it provides clear direction for *what* to teach so that they reach more students. Preparation for small-group reading intervention is enhanced by the clever and powerful lesson design included in *STEPS:*

1. **S**et-up: Review and warm-up
2. **T**each: Model and explicit teaching
3. **E**ngage: Practice with feedback
4. **P**ractice Activity: Practice skill through activity
5. **S**how You Know: Monitor progress

Next STEPS is for teachers who want to

*   Implement scientifically (or evidence)-based reading assessments to identify and monitor at-risk students
*   Use data to create small instructional reading groups
*   Make data-informed interventions when necessary to obtain the highest levels of early reading achievement
*   Teach reading based on the latest research findings
*   Learn how to teach reading using effective teaching methods

TODAY'S READING TEACHER

Compelling, scientifically derived research has resulted in access to innovative reading assessment and instructional tools. When applied, these tools provide unparalleled reading achievement for students who previously struggled with the reading process and failed to become proficient readers. The professional demands placed on today's teachers require them to be mindful of this research, proficient with the application of research findings, and up-to-date with their instructional decisions. As a result of these expectations, educators need straight-forward guidelines and efficient tools to support the demands of teaching struggling readers to read.

WHO ARE STRUGGLING READERS?

Struggling readers often come from backgrounds that afford little enrichment, verbal interaction, or print resources in the homes. Frequently, these children participate in the federal free and reduced lunch programs at school. They typically score below the 40th percentile on national achievement tests in reading and are considered high risk for reading failure in school. However, children with this profile of low socioeconomic status and a history of low reading test scores do not necessarily make up the only group of struggling readers. Other preschool or early elementary students who have not acquired basic language skills, who lack the phonological awareness needed as the foundation for early reading success, or who have weak background knowledge and vocabulary skills may also be considered at risk for reading failure. A fifth grader who reads on a third-grade level, for example, is also considered a struggling reader. Struggling readers are represented by many faces and ages. However, in general, a struggling reader is one in elementary school who is not learning to read at the expected rate and who requires systematic, explicit, intensive instruction in the scientifically based elements of reading as the core of reading instruction to catch up minimally to grade-level achieving peers and maintain that momentum.

RESPONSE TO INTERVENTION

Today's reading teachers and administrators have been taking notice of and feeling pressure to implement RTI. Educational policy now requires schools to have a plan in place to ensure that struggling readers receive the services they need to improve their reading abilities. RTI is a shared responsibility of all reading teachers. Classroom teachers, special education teachers, and other specialists work together to use assessment—coupled with analysis of that assessment, instruction, and progress monitoring—based on the skills that students need. They also endeavor to employ regular, systematic intervention to make sure that students grow and succeed. In RTI, data-based decisions form the foundation for instruction, and instruction is dynamic, reflecting changes based on the student's response to instruction. Knowledgeable and supported teachers are in the best position to make these ongoing decisions. *Next STEPS* provides a tool for learning how to use formative assessments to guide these instructional decisions.

Many schools implement the Three-Tier Reading Model to manage reading group intervention (Vaughn Gross Center for Reading and Language Arts, 2005). Formative assessments fit nicely with the Three-Tier Reading Model, providing a system that assists with the multiple decisions teachers make around forming and monitoring small-group instruction. *Next STEPS* is used by many teachers to help design the overall focus and routines of Tier II and Tier III small-group instruction.

Next STEPS provides a clearly developed and organized resource for all educators involved in the assessment, instructional planning, and teaching of elementary readers. Using formative assessments or data-based decision making measures as a foundation for their RTI model, teachers, reading coaches, school psychologists, and administrators will appreciate *Next STEPS* for the following features:

- Simplified yet rigorous instructional routines
- Teaching methods that get results, with minimal effort and planning
- Synthesis of research on teaching struggling readers to read
- Annotated resource lists of teaching resources coordinated for each fluency
- Guidelines for student performance analysis using fluency-based measures and other formative assessments
- Grouping procedures for establishing assessment-responsive reading groups

Next STEPS provides trustworthy answers to the questions formative assessment users ask, such as, "What do I do next?" As Torgesen and Miller (2008, p. 16) said, "Simply having assessments in place will have little impact on teaching or student learning if no one has the time or expertise available to turn the raw assessment data into usable information."

DATA-BASED DECISION MAKING

The term *data-based decision making* may be considered the umbrella term for the overall systematic empirical use of data for making management and instructional decisions on the local, district, and state levels in schools. In narrowing the concept, schools look more specifically at student outcome data to determine program effectiveness and areas in need of improvement. Within student outcome data, there are two distinct types of assessment data that teachers are faced with every year:

1. Summative assessments, which are traditionally given at the end of year and designed to measure what the student has learned
2. Formative assessments, which are designed to inform the instructional process throughout the year

Formative assessments form the foundation of *Next STEPS*. For purposes of simplification, the formative measures discussed in this book are divided into two categories:

1. Fluency-based measures, such as Dynamic Indicators of Basic Early Literacy Skills (DIBELS, 6th Edition; Good & Kaminski, 2002; DIBELS Next, 7th Edition; Good & Kaminski, 2010) and AIMSweb (Pearson Education, 2008)

2. Assessments for learning, such as the Texas Primary Reading Inventory (TPRI; Texas Education Agency and University of Texas System, 2006; McGraw-Hill); and Florida Assessments for Instruction in Reading (FAIR; Florida Department of Education, 2009).

Fluency-Based Measures

Fluency-based measures began when a group of innovative researchers recognized education's need for assessments that could provide valid and reliable measures of skills directly related to what was being taught, as well as provide information to guide instruction. Curriculum-based measurement (CBM) was the focus of their research (Deno, 1985; Shinn, Good, Knutson, Tilly, & Collins, 1992). These fluency-based measures were founded on 1-minute measurements of a student's rate and accuracy while orally reading grade-leveled passages. The results of many years of study on the relationship between early oral reading fluency and future ability to read and comprehend served to strengthen the use of fluency-based measures to indicate reading proficiency, predict future reading ability, and to monitor the progress of student reading achievement (Fuchs, Fuchs, Hosp, & Jenkins, 2001).

AIMSweb and DIBELS are two widely used fluency measures. *Next STEPS* references these two measures (along with two other formative assessments, TPRI and FAIR) during discussions about analysis and lesson planning. Fluency measurement and other forms of formative assessment continue to evolve as a science and practice, with new indicators being developed. However, the basic skills as outlined by the five components of reading—phoneme awareness, phonics, fluency, vocabulary, and comprehension—continue to drive the development of these assessments. *Next STEPS* is founded on the five components, so its relevance to teaching the struggling reader will continue to support the use of fluency measures and assessments for learning as the assessments evolve.

AIMSweb

AIMSweb (published by Pearson Assessment, http://www.aimsweb.com) offers a data collection service that downloads data from both DIBELS and AIMSweb users and prepares a variety of useful reports for classroom teachers and administrators. It offers several fluency measures for K–8 reading, spelling, math, and writing skills. AIMSweb offers PalmLink software for those who wish to capture the student data on their Palm handheld personal digital assistants (PDAs) and then synchronize the data with a computer or directly with AIMSweb. The following AIMSweb measures are referenced in *Next STEPS* and available on the PalmLink software:

- Letter naming fluency
- Phoneme segmentation fluency
- Letter sound fluency
- Nonsense word fluency
- Oral reading fluency
- Maze fluency (currently must be administered and scored by hand)

DIBELS

DIBELS (Good & Kaminski, 2002) and DIBELS Next (Dynamic Measurement Group, 2011) are collections of reading fluency measures for K–6 that are available through the University of Oregon (http://dibels.uoregon.edu, which also provides a data collection and reporting system to subscribers). DIBELS assessment kits and replacement student booklets can also be ordered through Sopris Educational Services (http://www.sopriswest.com). Schools and teachers may be interested in facilitating DIBELS testing by collecting data on a Palm PDA and later downloading the data to the designated source (e.g., school, district, or state). The following DIBELS fluency assessments are referenced in *Next STEPS:*

- First Sound Fluency (replacing an earlier assessment, Initial Sound Fluency)
- Letter Naming Fluency
- Phoneme Segmentation Fluency
- Nonsense Word Fluency
- Oral Reading Fluency
- Retell Fluency
- Word Use Fluency (no longer available in DIBELS Next, 7th Edition)

ASSESSMENT FOR INSTRUCTION

In contrast to the fluency-based measures, on assessments for learning, such as the TPRI and the FAIR, students are not timed on most measures. The primary focus is more on accuracy than fluency or automaticity. In addition, TPRI and FAIR include diagnostic measures designed to allow teachers to follow up with students whose scores on the initial screening measures indicate the probability of low to moderate success on end-of-year tests. The diagnostic tests cover a broad range of developmental reading skills at each grade level. Both measures provide linkage to curricular and intervention support for teachers.

Texas Primary Reading Inventory

The TPRI (http://www.tpri.org) is a screening and diagnostic tool designed for use in kindergarten through third grade. A quick screener assists teachers with identifying students whose basic reading skills are not well established. The inventory tool provides a more detailed picture of how the skills are developing to help teachers devise instructional responses to the students' strengths and needs. Progress monitoring is built into the assessment options. Like DIBELS, the TPRI and TPRI Progress Monitoring Assessments (Progress Monitoring Emergent Reader [PMER], Progress Monitoring Beginning Reader [PMBR]) can also be administered by using a Palm PDA. Reports are generated electronically and are available almost immediately for teachers, parents, principals, and district and state administrators. The following skills are assessed with the TPRI:

- Book and print awareness
- Letter and letter/sound knowledge
- Phoneme awareness
- Decoding
- Word reading
- Listening and reading comprehension
- Reading accuracy and fluency

Florida Assessments for Instruction in Reading

FAIR is a comprehensive assessment for Grades K–12 initiated by the Florida Department of Education, Just Reads Florida, and developed at the Florida Center for Reading Research (Florida Department of Education, 2009). This assessment provides student-specific information to inform instruction rather than the summative student learning profiles provided by more traditional end-of-year tests (e.g., Florida Comprehensive Assessment Test [FCAT]; IOWA Test of Basic Skills [ITBS]). The goal of FAIR is to provide teachers with assessment tools that support decision making for reading instruction. FAIR incorporates all of the research-based integrated components of reading including phonemic awareness, phonics, vocabulary, fluency, and comprehension. Teachers are given screening, diagnostic, and progress monitoring information through four types of assessment on FAIR: broad screen, broad diagnostic inventory (BDI), targeted diagnostic inventory (TDI), and progress monitoring tasks. While all students are screened three times a year (September, January, April), only those who demonstrate a high probability of having difficulty reaching targeted learning objectives complete additional diagnostic tasks in order to isolate specific areas of concern for focused intervention. Progress monitoring of oral reading fluency is available for Grades 1–5 in 1-minute probes equated for passage difficulty. FAIR includes the following tasks:

- Print awareness (optional)
- Letter naming and sounds (letter name knowledge/letter sound knowledge)
- Phonemic awareness (blending and deletion)
- Letter sound connections (initial and final)
- Word building
- Multisyllabic words
- Word reading
- Listening comprehension
- Reading comprehension (computer adaptive for Grades 3–12)
- Vocabulary
- Spelling (Grade 2 only)
- Computer-based mazes (Grades 3–12)
- Computer-adaptive word spelling (Grades 3–12)

ROUTINES OF EFFECTIVE TEACHING

Teachers often find that their core and supplemental reading programs do not completely meet the needs of struggling readers in their classrooms. Although core and supplemental reading programs remain the first choice for providing additional support and practice, alternate resources can fill a need to strengthen instruction. In their pursuit for magic methods and the answer to how to teach struggling readers to read, teachers have filled their bookshelves with resource books brimming with multiple and appealing activities from which to choose. Although instructional activities can contribute to a viable plan for teaching young students reading skills, the use of unrelated activities without a connection to goals for learning is no longer an acceptable method of intervention for struggling readers.

Teachers need clearly outlined routines to guide them in their use of data when identifying goals for learning, planning their reading instruction, and finally selecting the activities that may play an integral role in the well-defined learning opportunities students require in order to become successful readers. Teaching struggling readers begins with identifying a primary purpose—the skills that students need to learn (assessment/screening); then as a secondary response, teachers can plan activities within explicit and systematic routines and lesson plans to teach those identified skills.

NEXT STEPS DESIGN: HOW WE TEACH TO REACH

A systematic process is defined in *Next STEPS* to help teachers teach efficiently. The process begins by identifying skills or components as weak or missing. Next, targeted planning and teaching of those isolated skills is initiated, with components often taught in small-group lesson formats. Finally, the components that have been identified as weak and separated for instruction are put back together and integrated into the complete reading process, usually in the form of reading connected text, checking for comprehension, and explicitly teaching new vocabulary.

Most formative reading assessments measure the five critical components of early reading—the vital early readiness and reading skills that allow teachers to then identify students who may be at risk for reading failure. Finally, by assessing and using progress monitoring measures, teachers can intervene with planned, purposeful, small-group lessons, re-teach when necessary, and adapt the reading program to better meet the needs of the struggling reader. All of these efforts work together toward the goal of increasing the overall level of reading proficiency for all struggling readers.

According to Torgesen and Miller (2008, p. 18), "Classroom teachers need very frequent assessments to help both themselves and their students understand the necessary 'next steps' in learning to improve their literacy skills." Through analysis of assessment data, teachers can identify which components to teach. Some teachers prefer to call these components the *Big Ideas;* others call them the *Fab Five* or the *Five Critical Components of Reading Instruction.* No matter what label is chosen, the content of early reading instruction (the "WHAT to teach") should focus on identification and integration of the following:

- Phonemic awareness
- Phonics
- Fluency
- Vocabulary
- Comprehension
- Written and Oral Language

THE IMPORTANCE OF PROFESSIONAL DEVELOPMENT

Teaching reading is like "rocket science" (Moats, 1999). Mastery of the deep knowledge and acquisition of a skill set that identifies an expert teacher requires a professional lifetime of study and practice. *Next STEPS* is a tool—a resource that has the potential to take teachers to higher levels of expertise in their work with students. Ongoing study through professional development, constantly updated and based on current well-founded results, is a necessary companion to instructional resources like *Next STEPS.*

Schools are successful when administrators and teachers work together to develop a professional development plan in which grade-level meetings, conference attendance, in-service and summer workshops, professional learning communities, and collaborative problem solving are all focused on gaining the insight and knowledge that will create expert teachers and successful students.

We are pleased to contribute to the work of reading teachers everywhere with this resource. May the *Next STEPS* taken by teachers become the next steps toward each child becoming a reader.

Steps to Reading Success

Teaching Struggling Readers to Read

WHAT WE TEACH

Each of the components that we teach—phoneme awareness, phonics, fluency, vocabulary, and comprehension—is the focus of a chapter in *Next STEPS in Literacy Instruction*. Descriptions of how the components are assessed and how to teach them within a small-group reading lesson are provided.

HOW WE TEACH

How do we motivate students to be involved in learning? How do we motivate students to be engaged in the reading process? By being the best teachers we can be! Essential instructional elements and teacher behaviors that lead to motivation to read are identified in *Next STEPS* (see Figures 2.1 and 2.2). Along with lots of active student involvement, these can make a big difference in how motivated both students and teachers are.

HOW WE TEACH TO REACH

Since the National Reading Panel completed their work in 2000 (NRP, 2000), volumes have been written about the five essential components of reading instruction: phonemic awareness, phonics, fluency, comprehension, and vocabulary (Birsh, 2005; Haager, Klingner, & Vaughn, 2007; McCardle & Chhabra, 2004; McCardle, Chhabra & Kapinhas, 2008; Vaughn & Linan-Thompson, 2004). Reading teachers, coaches, and specialists are familiar with the idea that in order for all students to learn to read by the end of third grade and to continue developing as readers throughout the grades, reading instruction should be systematic and explicit in all five critical components. In-service training and professional development have been focused on helping teachers gain understanding about the five components and what to teach.

TEACHING STRUGGLING READERS TO READ

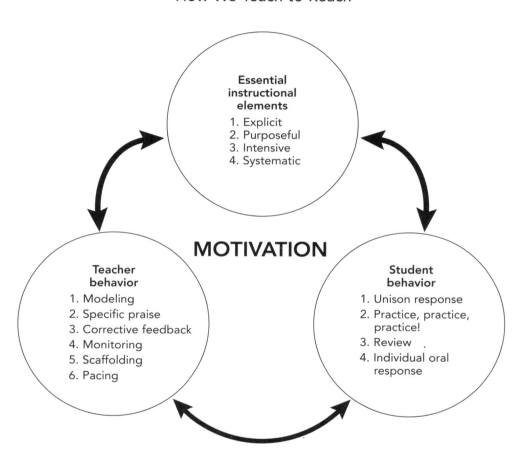

What We Teach

| Phonemic awareness | Alphabetic principle | Fluency | Comprehension | Vocabulary |

How We Teach to Reach

Essential instructional elements

1. Explicit
2. Purposeful
3. Intensive
4. Systematic

MOTIVATION

Teacher behavior

1. Modeling
2. Specific praise
3. Corrective feedback
4. Monitoring
5. Scaffolding
6. Pacing

Student behavior

1. Unison response
2. Practice, practice, practice!
3. Review
4. Individual oral response

Figure 2.1.   Teaching struggling readers to read: What we teach, how we teach to reach, and motivation.

However, given this focus on the components of what to teach, little guidance is provided about how to teach reading based on the converging scientific research published since the 1980s. What does research say about effective methods for teaching struggling readers to read? What is the role of the teacher? What behaviors can teachers develop in students to enhance student learning and ensure greater success? These questions will be answered by *Next STEPS*.

WHEN WE TEACH TO REACH

Teacher behaviors that lead to higher levels of learning have been isolated and are well defined. Read through each of the behaviors, descriptions of the behaviors, and examples that are presented in Table 2.1. Whew; that is a lot for teachers to remember to do! Begin by creating awareness of these behaviors one at a time. Use Table 2.2 to reflect on the presence of these teacher behaviors after you teach a small-group lesson. Choose one behavior to master and then move on to

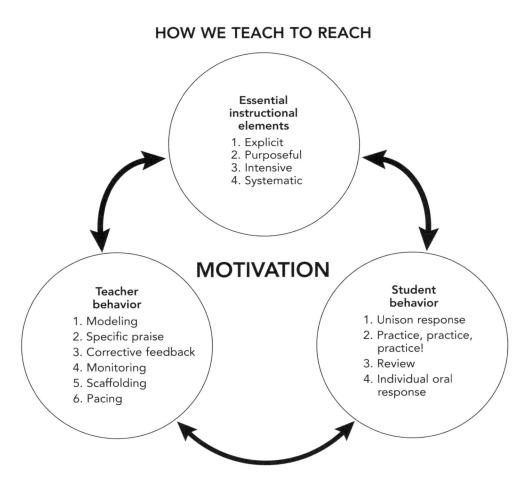

HOW WE TEACH TO REACH

Essential instructional elements
1. Explicit
2. Purposeful
3. Intensive
4. Systematic

MOTIVATION

Teacher behavior
1. Modeling
2. Specific praise
3. Corrective feedback
4. Monitoring
5. Scaffolding
6. Pacing

Student behavior
1. Unison response
2. Practice, practice, practice!
3. Review
4. Individual oral response

Figure 2.2.   How we teach to reach. Essential instructional elements, student behavior, and teacher behavior are all instrumental in changing student motivation.

Table 2.1. Teacher behavior examples

Behavior	Description	Examples
Modeling	Teacher demonstrates and describes a new concept. Each step or part of a new concept or strategy is explicitly shown and explained to the students. Show and tell works best.	*Phonics:* Teacher points to the letters *m-a-n* and says, "Students, watch. My turn to sound out this word: 'm-a-n.'" *Comprehension think-alouds:* The teacher says, "When I read this part of the story, I thought about the time I went to a farm and saw cows, pigs, and chickens."
Specific praise	Praise that describes what the students did rather than generic, unspecified praise	Teacher says, "Awesome! You heard each of the sounds in that word and showed them to me."
Corrective feedback	Response to student errors that leads to teaching to mastery. Steps include model, lead, test, firm up, and delayed test. Corrective feedback can be provided, not only for reading skills but also for reading strategies as well.	Teacher points to *a* and says, "What sound?" Student responds, "/o/". Teacher *models* correct sound, "/aaa/." Teacher *leads* correct response with students, "Say /aaa/ with me." Teacher *tests*, asking students to answer on their own: "What sound?" Teacher then *firms up*: "Say it again. What sound?" In the final step, *delayed test*, the teacher points to *a* and says, "What is this sound?"
Monitoring	Checking to make sure students are giving correct oral responses. When students practice incorrect or confused responses, they may learn incorrectly. Reteaching will be necessary and time consuming.	Teacher says, "Students, which word rhymes with *toy: cat* or *boy?*" One student in the group says, "Cat." Because the teacher was carefully monitoring, she knew to provide more practice for this student. Students are reading orally in pairs. The teacher monitors by walking around the room, asking students to reread sections, to retell what they have read, or to decode difficult words from the selection.
Scaffolding	Providing support for learners to help connect what they know and can do to the new information they are learning. With instructional scaffolding, students have higher rates of success when learning new material. As students progress, the scaffolding, or teacher support, is gradually pulled away or decreased (Hasbrouck & Denton, 2005).	Before reading new and potentially difficult material, the teacher does an echo read with the students. This allows students initial success and strong support as they are introduced to new material. Teacher says, "Let's sound out this word together, 'm–a–n.' Now you do it." Teacher gradually decreases the support with each subsequent step so that students are gradually reading the words independently the "fast way" (Kame'enui, Carnine, Dixon, Simmons, and Coyne, 2002, p. 68).
Pacing	Presenting the material in a lively, energetic, brisk manner that keeps students' attention engaged. Minimize downtime after students' responses.	For young children giving sounds for letters, expect 55–60 responses per minute without interruption. Practice about 3–5 minutes on letter-sound tasks, then give about 15 seconds of praise (e.g., verbal, high fives), then move on to phonemic awareness activities.

another. Master teachers use these teacher behaviors automatically, applying them without conscious attention to using them.

Teachers may use Table 2.2 to assess how well they demonstrate the teacher behaviors that are linked to accelerated student learning. This table will guide teachers in determining which skills they are comfortable using and which skills they need to concentrate on improving. Reading coaches or principals working closely with classroom teachers may also find this table to be helpful. It can be used as a tool for guiding reading session observation and establishing personal goals for improvement in their work with teachers.

Student behaviors that lead to higher levels of learning have also been isolated and are described in Table 2.3. Read through each behavior and ask, "What am I doing to elicit these student behaviors?"

Table 2.2. Teacher behavior reflections

Behavior	Reflection
Modeling	Did I demonstrate, or show students, how to do something?
	Did I explain to students how to do something as I demonstrated, or why?
	Did I break the skill down into simpler steps, showing and explaining the process or concept to the students?
	Did I specify the student behavior in the praise I provided?
Specific praise	Did I provide feedback that isolated the student performance or skills I was teaching?
Corrective feedback	When students made mistakes, did I respond with the following steps? 1. Model the correct answer or process. 2. Lead students to repeat the process correctly with me. 3. Test if students could answer on their own and repeat again (firm up). 4. Check again for correct response after a brief period (delayed test).
Monitoring	Did I observe student responses carefully and identify students who responded correctly and those who did not or hesitated?
	Did I make a note of student weaknesses in order to recheck learning or reteach?
	If students were reading in pairs or independently, did I briefly check their skills by listening to them, asking them to read isolated words and text, monitoring comprehension, and providing feedback or praise?
Scaffolding	Did I anticipate difficulty with a task and provide support through access to previous learning?
	Did I provide support by doing the task with the students and then slowly releasing the responsibility for students to do it independently?
Pacing	Did I maintain a brisk, lively pace?
	Did I prompt for student responses several times per minute (more student voice than teacher voice)?
	Did I minimize downtime between student responses?

Table 2.3. Student behavior examples

Behavior	Description	Examples
Unison response	All students respond at the same time, resulting in a high level of student engagement. This also allows for participation of students who might not typically get a chance to respond.	Teacher says, "Everyone get ready. What is the first sound you hear in *map*? Where do you hear the /p/ sound in *map*: at the beginning, middle, or end of the word?" Teacher says, "Get ready to read these words," then points to each word in a column, allowing a brief time for thinking between student unison responses.
Practice, practice, practice!	Practice is important for all learners, but especially for struggling readers to help develop accuracy, fluency, and automaticity. Frequent, distributed practice is best. This means that several times throughout the day, students are asked to practice the skills they are learning. 1. Provide ample concentrated practice directly after new concepts are introduced. 2. Practice new learning along with previous cumulated learning. 3. Practice applying new skill in real reading and writing. Supplement practice with activities if the core reading program does not provide enough practice.	Following a phonics lesson, students read a list of words to their partners, then they read them independently. Finally, they read them in a story. Before the students go to recess, they read the words. They then read them again at home that evening and again the next day. Wow! That is a lot of practice! Practice with vocabulary would look like this: 1. Students read and hear the words along with a teacher-provided, brief, student-friendly explanation within the story context. 2. Students read the words in the story, then give examples of the meanings from their personal context. 3. Next, they write answers to questions using the words. 4. They use the words at home that evening and report on their use the next morning at school. 5. They create a page for each word in their vocabulary journal. Multiple exposures = increased practice!
Review	Review should be built into daily lesson plans to ensure continued retention and connection of old with new information. Distributed, brief, and frequent reviews and reviews at the beginning of reading lessons work well.	Reteaching and clarification may be part of the review. The teacher says, "Students whose names begin with the sound /m/ may line up first. Students whose names end with the sound /d/ may line up next." The teacher says, "Raise your hand if you can tell me a word that means hard working…. *Industrious!*"
Individual oral response	This is typically used when the group has mastered a new skill. Teacher attempts skills that were troublesome during unison responding exercises to check individual learning levels. Teacher uses a random order for calling on students to help maintain their attention. Teacher can point to the word or give the question first so that all students will figure out the answer, then call on one student. If several students make errors, then insufficient practice was provided during the group response section of the lesson.	The teacher says, "What is the beginning sound in *boat*? [pause] Mary?" The teacher says, "What is an antonym for *wealthy*? [pause] James?" The teacher displays the front flashcard of a pack while the students look at it and prepare to read it. The teacher calls on one student to read it and continues working through the pack. The students do not know when it will be their turn, but are urged to be ready.

Student Behavior (that leads to improved student engagement)

Teachers understand the truth in the following statements:

- Engaged students are learning students.
- Practice makes permanent.
- Increased academic engaged time equals higher levels of learning.

However, achieving classrooms of highly engaged students can be challenging. The guidelines in Table 2.4 can be successfully introduced into small-group lessons. Consider asking a colleague or reading coach to observe students during small-group time using this list. Use the observation results to help plan stronger lessons focused on increased student participation.

Essential Learning Elements

Instructional (or learning) elements also have been isolated and described. Read through each element in Table 2.5, its description, and examples provided. Consider whether these elements are a part of your reading lessons every day.

MOTIVATION

Motivation guides, inspires, provides direction, and stimulates us to engage in activities that may be difficult. Where does motivation come from? How do we cultivate hope in students to motivate them to learn from us and engage in reading tasks? How do teachers maintain hope and motivation to learn and apply

Table 2.4.   Student behavior (engagement) reflections

Student behavior	Reflection
Unison response	Did students participate in the lesson through choral-unison responses when prompted?
Practice, practice, practice!	Did students practice a new concept with teacher monitoring directly after learning it?
	Did students practice frequently during the reading period and then again distributed throughout the day?
	Did students practice new learning in varying contexts?
Review	Did students practice previously learned concepts through teacher-directed review?
	Did students have opportunities to review and use learned material independently?
Individual oral response	Did individual students respond to teacher prompts?
	Did all students have opportunities to respond individually?
	Did students wait and then respond when the teacher gave the prompt to respond?

Table 2.5. Essential instructional elements

Element	Description	Examples
Explicit	Explicit instruction is direct, explained, straightforward, and clear cut. Struggling readers may often be confused about what it takes to learn to read and need to be taught the skills, concepts, or strategies needed for success in understandable, precise terms. Guessing is not an option!	The teacher says, "Students, the sound of these letters is /oe/," as she points to the two letters *oa.* "When you see *oa* together in a word, you will usually say /oe/. What sound do these letters usually make? Let's read some words that have *oa* in them." "There are many English words that share the morpheme *-ject.* Knowing the meaning of *-ject* helps us figure out the meanings of words with *-ject.*"
Purposeful	Purposeful lessons are planned with a clear, targeted focus. Teachers teach specifically what students need to learn based on assessments including progress monitoring. Additional instruction and practice is planned and provided by the teacher in small groups and learning centers when needs are identified by assessment and monitoring results.	At a first-grade team meeting in January, after the benchmark assessment was given and results were available, the following conversation may be overheard: *Teacher 1:* "I have seven children in my class who cannot recode or blend the sounds. They didn't reach benchmark on the Nonsense Word Fluency measure of DIBELS." *Teacher 2:* "I had five who can't recode also." *Teacher 3:* "Me too; I had eight. Let's look at their student booklets and see how they did on phoneme segmentation. Then we can plan some lessons that focus on helping them transition from segmenting to decoding and recoding."
Intensive	*Intensive* refers to supplemental reading instruction that is provided in small groups for an extended period of time each day. Intensive is the first of two descriptors used by the National Reading Panel to describe the type of reading instruction needed to ensure that all children learn to read by the end of third grade. Students are actively engaged in learning, practicing, reviewing, and applying the five components of reading. Struggling readers tend to learn better in small groups of three or four students (Torgesen, 2000).	The struggling readers in Miss Anderson's class receive whole-group instruction and an additional 30 minutes of targeted small-group instruction. In addition, they see the Title I teacher in the afternoon for follow-up review and fluency practice on the skills they learned in Miss Anderson's class. That is intensive! The Three-Tier Model for grouping students (Vaughn Gross Center for Reading and Language Arts, 2005) provides guidelines for providing intensive instruction.
Systematic	Systematic instruction asserts that there must be a plan (a clearly defined sequence) for teaching children how to read. Scaffolding often accompanies systematic instruction, which implies chunking instruction in small, digestible bites in a logical progression (Marzano, 2009).	In systematic phonics instruction, all of the major letter-sound correspondences are taught in a clearly defined sequence. Students learn short and long vowels, vowel and consonant digraphs (*oi, ea, sh, ck*), and blends, (*st, br*) progressing to more complex vowel patterns such as *aw, eigh, eu, ow,* and *ou.*

Activity

Review a core or supplemental reading program for the essential instructional elements in Table 2.5. Label sticky notes to identify each element as **explicit, purposeful, intensive,** or **systematic.** Place the notes in a week's lesson to show where the element is incorporated. For example, if the reading program provides a review of the phonic element taught in a previous lesson, a *systematic* note would be placed next to that lesson reference. Does the program adhere to these essential instructional elements? What needs to be done to strengthen the program's application?

teaching behaviors that work? Richard Lavoie (1998) said, "Motivation is the most misunderstood concept in education today. Students are only motivated to do what they are capable of doing!" Motivation plays a role in outcome for both students and teachers.

If students are going to be motivated to read, we have to teach them how to read. Adults are motivated by success, by fulfillment, and by what they are capable of doing. In the classroom, this helps us to appreciate that we have a commitment to teach students the skills needed to read, to provide ample opportunities for them to practice the skills to mastery levels, and to engage students in multiple and varying experiences with high-quality literature while modeling an appreciation and application of the skills we teach. Read through this excerpt and note the complexity of the teaching reading task:

> **Children do learn to read if they don't lose hope.**
>
> Teacher on the International Reading Association's Reading Teacher Listserv (rteacher @bookmark.reading.org)

Agreement by experts in recent, comprehensive reviews of reading research is substantial: A successful teacher of beginning reading enables children to comprehend and produce written language, exposes them to a wide variety of texts to build their background knowledge and whet their appetite for more, generates enthusiasm and appreciation for reading and writing, and expertly teaches children how to decode, interpret, and spell new words from a foundation of linguistic awareness. The successful teacher adapts the pacing, content, and emphasis of instruction for individuals and groups, using valid and reliable assessments. The teacher's choices are guided by knowledge of the critical skills and attitudes needed by students at each stage of reading development. Beginning reading skills are taught explicitly and systematically to children within an overall program of purposeful, engaging reading and writing. (Learning First Alliance, 2000)

Researchers studying successful school environments have identified the following key components that are present in motivated classrooms (Eaker, DuFour, & DuFour, 2002):

> • • • • •
> **Success is the motivator; ability is the key.**
> • • • • •

- *Routines:* Activities done with regularity to provide students practice with new skills
- *Repertoire:* The range of techniques, skills, and approaches teachers use to stimulate their students
- *Caring:* A teacher's sincere concern for the welfare of students
- *Expectations:* The belief that all students can do high-quality academic work
- *Rigor:* Student performance that is precise, exact, and meets or exceeds high standards
- *Small scale:* Small enough in size for students to receive adequate individual attention

Watch for the presence of these factors throughout *Next STEPS.*

To keep students learning and motivated to expand their worlds through reading, we have to teach them how to read. Simply supporting them in the learning process is not enough. Students need a teacher who understands how to teach, how to create the best environment for learning, and how to teach them the skills that will motivate them to apply their learning for a lifetime.

CREATING SMALL GROUPS FOR INSTRUCTION AND DECIDING WHAT TO TEACH

The small-group design provides an ideal setting for targeting skill instruction and is a critical ingredient of response to intervention (RTI) and the Three-Tier Model. Forming groups of students whose learning profiles share similar needs can help teachers address the urgency to "catch them up." Deciding on group composition and what to teach is made easier with the information we gain from fluency or CBM measures and other formative assessments. This section models a step-by-step process exposing the internal thinking

> • • • • •
> **To keep a lamp burning, we have to keep putting oil in it.**
> Mother Teresa
> • • • • •

that teachers use when interpreting their class reports from DIBELS, AIMSweb, TPRI, FAIR or other similar formative assessments.

● ● ● ● ● ●

Activity

Compare your thinking with Miss Mayfield's assessments in Figure 2.3. Look at the instructional recommendations in the right column. At first glance, Miss Mayfield is pleased. Many students are reading at Benchmark level and are therefore on track to reading success. Nine students are rated as Strategic (needing additional instruc- 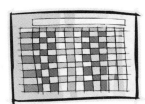 tion), and one student is rated as Intensive. The Instructional Recommendations classification is assigned to students, with a heavier weight on the measure determined to be the most important skill at the time the assessment is given. During the first-grade class's winter assessment period, Reading Curriculum-Based Measure (R-CBM) or Oral Reading Fluency is considered to be the strongest predictor of all of the measures given, so student performance on this measure drives the instructional recommendation determination.

Now look back through the assessments listed on the top of Figure 2.3. Analyze basic skill levels, decoding (Nonsense Word Fluency), and phoneme awareness (Phoneme Segmentation Fluency) to determine if there are any student needs that may require additional intervention or assessment. This analysis also provides an overview of the instructional focus for the small-group instruction (hint: Benchmark score is listed at the top of each column).

Using the worksheet in Figure 2.4, write each student's name on a sticky note, placing the student in the appropriate instructional group based on his or her raw scores, and add any additional information about the student's skills. Place the sticky notes on the form and move them around as the groups become more clearly identified. Next, complete the following steps.

1. *Form an intensive group* (the lowest performing students). Keep this group small, with three to four students. Some teachers may have more than one of these groups. In an RTI school, all school resources work together to brainstorm solutions and creatively plan to provide instruction for these students.

(continued)

(continued)

In Miss Mayfield's class, Bo, Will, Karen, and Cesar have similar scores on R-CBM and should be assigned to Group 1 (Intensive). They have well-established phoneme awareness and all have similar decoding needs. Emily is the most intensive student, with very low skills. Miss Mayfield will include her in this small group to teach phoneme segmentation and decoding, but Emily will require one-to-one instruction or another small group during the day. Her progress will be closely monitored. She also receives special education support services intermittently throughout the day.

Group target skills: Decoding and lots of practice reading decodable text, rereading text from core reading lessons, and sight word practice

2. *Form the highest performing group.* In Miss Mayfield's class Sarah, Jo, Frank, Maya, and Cindy have established decoding and phoneme awareness skills and are reading above and well-above average. They should be assigned to Group 3 (Benchmark) because they will benefit from the extension lessons provided in the core reading program. Tarique and Susan can fit in this group too, but they need the explicit phonics lessons that Miss Mayfield teaches during whole-group reading as reflected by their not-yet-established decoding skills. Miss Mayfield is going to monitor Tarique and Susan's decoding skills through weekly, lesson-based decoding checks.

Group target skills: Practice and advance reading skills through lots of opportunity to read, extension lessons in reading program, and explicit phonics instruction, especially for Tarique and Susan. All students benefit from explicit phonics lessons at this reading level; therefore, phonics lessons should continue even though the screening scores suggest "Established" skills development in the alphabetic principle for five of the students. (Sarah, Jo, Frank, Maya, and Cindy).

3. Place the remaining students into groups and determine if any changes need to be made to the group composition. Mike, Bob, Buddy, Leo, and Nancy show some variable decoding skill fluency but similar oral reading fluency skills. They should be placed into Group 2. Miss Mayfield will continue to provide phoneme segmentation practice during whole-group instruction to reinforce these students' need to strengthen phoneme awareness. She will build decoding skills, making sure knowledge of sound-letter correspondences and sound blending are well developed. She will monitor the progress of Leo and Nancy on Nonsense Word Fluency for their overall decoding skills development.

Group target skills: Practice and improve reading skills through phoneme segmentation and decoding instruction combined with abundant repeated reading of decodable connected text.

An example of a completed small-group worksheet is provided in Figure 2.5. A worksheet for a weekly small-group lesson plan is provided in Figure 2.6.

Class Report—First Grade (Winter)

Name	Phoneme Segmentation (Benchmark: established Score 35+)			Nonsense Word Fluency (Benchmark: established Score 50+)			R-CBM Oral Reading Fluency (Low risk Score 20+)			Recommended Instructional Level
	Score	%ile	Status	Score	%ile	Status	Score	%ile	Status	
Sarah	53	5	Est.	68	88	Est.	85	100	WAA	Benchmark: at grade level
Jo	53	56	Est.	128	100	Est.	73	94	WAA	Benchmark: at grade level
Frank	48	25	Est.	83	94	Est.	53	88	AA	Benchmark: at grade level
Maya	58	88	Est.	55	75	Est.	35	81	AA	Benchmark: at grade level
Cindy	71	100	Est.	55	75	Est.	28	75	AA	Benchmark: at grade level
Tarique	61	94	Est.	40	56	Emerging	26	69	Average	Benchmark: at grade level
Susan	56	81	Est.	46	63	Emerging	25	63	Average	Benchmark: at grade level
Mike	45	13	Est.	37	50	Emerging	16	56	Strategic	Strategic: additional intervention
Bob	31	6	Emerging	50	69	Est.	14	50	Strategic	Strategic: additional intervention
Buddy	49	31	Est.	33	44	Emerging	13	44	Strategic	Strategic: additional intervention
Nancy	55	75	Est.	25	19	Deficient	11	38	Strategic	Strategic: additional intervention
Leo	49	31	Est.	22	13	Deficient	7	25	Strategic	Strategic: additional intervention
Bo	46	19	Est.	20	6	Deficient	7	25	Strategic	Strategic: additional intervention
Will	53	56	Est.	27	31	Deficient	6	13	BA	Strategic: additional intervention
Karen	50	50	Est.	26	25	Deficient	6	13	BA	Strategic: additional intervention
Cesar	49	31	Est.	29	38	Deficient	5	6	WBA	Strategic: additional intervention
Emily	9	<1	Deficient	13	<1	Deficient	4	<1	WBA	Intensive: substantial intervention

Figure 2.3. Miss Mayfield's Class Report: First grade (winter session). (Key: %ile = Percentile, Est. = Established, WAA = Well above average, AA = Above average, BA = Below average, WBA = Well below average)

Small-Group Worksheet

Teacher's name: _____ Date: _____

Groups	Individual needs	Instructional focus
Intensive group		
Strategic group		
Benchmark group		

Figure 2.4. Small-Group Worksheet.

Small-Group Worksheet

Instructions: Place student names on sticky notes to allow for changes. Use target scores to help define group placement and instructional need for both individual and group.

Groups	Individual needs	Instructional focus
Intensive group Cesar Karen Will Bo (Emily)	Emily needs phoneme awareness, decoding plus another small group during the day for more individualized instruction.	Decoding plus lots of practice reading decodable text
Strategic group Leo Nancy Buddy Bob Mike	Monitor and practice phoneme segmentation to strengthen phoneme awareness, decoding. Leo and Nancy need phonics screen to determine specific areas of weakness for targeted instruction.	Explicit phonics instruction after screening to determine specific weaknesses, repeated reading decodable text
Benchmark group Sarah Tarique Jo Susan Frank Maya Cindy	Tarique and Susan need explicit phonic instruction and practice decoding unfamiliar words.	Practice. Advance reading skills through many opportunities to read, extension lessons in reading program and explicit phonics instruction to continue growth.

Figure 2.5. Miss Mayfield's Small-Group Worksheet.

Weekly Small-Group Lesson Plan

Date: _____

Student names		Monday	Tuesday	Wednesday	Thursday	Friday	Notes/ Observations
Benchmark		Instructional focus:	Instructional focus:	Instructional focus:	Instructional focus:	Instructional focus:	
		Activities/ strategies	Activities/ strategies	Activities/ strategies	Activities/ strategies	Activities/ strategies	
		Materials needed	Materials needed	Materials needed	Materials needed	Materials needed	
Strategic		Instructional focus:	Instructional focus:	Instructional focus:	Instructional focus:	Instructional focus:	
		Activities/ strategies	Activities/ strategies	Activities/ strategies	Activities/ strategies	Activities/ strategies	
		Materials needed	Materials needed	Materials needed	Materials needed	Materials needed	
Intensive		Instructional focus:	Instructional focus:	Instructional focus:	Instructional focus:	Instructional focus:	
		Activities/ strategies	Activities/ strategies	Activities/ strategies	Activities/ strategies	Activities/ strategies	
		Materials needed	Materials needed	Materials needed	Materials needed	Materials needed	

Figure 2.6. Weekly Small-Group Lesson Plan. (Instructional focus considerations: PA Phonemic awareness, P Phonics, V Vocabulary, F Fluency, C Comprehension, L Language: _____, O Other: _____.)

Next STEPS in Literacy Instruction: Connecting Assessments to Effective Interventions by Susan M. Smartt and Deborah R. Glaser
Copyright © 2010 by Paul H. Brookes Publishing Co. All rights reserved.

● ● ● ● ●

Activity

Using Figure 2.7, paste the comments on 3″ x 5″ index cards, punch a hole, and then put them together with a small metal ring, somewhat like a "cheat sheet" to carry around or keep in your pocket to remind you what to do for interventions when students are not at benchmark (i.e. showing weakness) in the areas assessed.

For extra practice forming small instructional groups, use the data in Figure 2.8 (Miss Springfield's class report) to form groups, determine students' instructional focus, and complete a progress monitoring plan. Use the worksheet in Figure 2.4 to answer the following questions:

- Who will be placed in the lowest group? In the highest performing group? In the middle group?

- What are the instructional plans for the lowest group? For the highest group? For the middle group?

Another helpful tool used in grouping students for small group instruction is the Student Sorting Steps, known by some as the Stem and Leaf. This tool was created by the Regional Professional Development Providers under the direction of the Massachusetts Department of Elementary and Secondary Education (see Figure 2.9). It is essentially a spreadsheet prepared for the three benchmark periods: beginning, middle, and end of year for kindergarten through Grade 3. The sheets are color-coded to reflect Intensive, Strategic, and Benchmark levels of performance in each of the fluency measures assessed for that particular grade level at that specific time of year. Prior to participating in small-group or grade-level planning meetings, teachers can write the names of their students in the correct placement or list based on their Benchmark scores. By having all of their students' names grouped by skill performance level, teachers can more clearly begin making plans for small-group instruction and deliberate educational focus.

THE SMALL-GROUP LESSON

Now that you are acquainted with teach to reach, motivation, and small-group formation, it is time to put it all together into a usable, efficient, and proven lesson format.

Instructional Responses
Initial Planning Guidelines

Instructions: Cut out each box, glue on an index card, attach all six cards with a metal ring, and use as a quick guide when planning small-group instruction.

Letter Naming Fluency (LNF)

If students are not at Benchmark levels:
1. Teach letter names.
2. Teach phoneme awareness.

Phoneme Segmentation Fluency (PSF)

If students are not at Benchmark levels:
1. Teach phoneme segmentation.
2. Teach phoneme blending.
3. Teach letter sounds.

Letter Sound Fluency (LSF)
First Sound Fluency (FSF)

If students are not at Benchmark levels:
1. Teach letter sounds.
2. Teach phoneme awareness.
3. Teach decoding.

Retell and Maze Comprehension

If students are not at acceptable levels:
1. Assess language and listening skills; model think-aloud processes of proficient readers
3. Read to students and model think-aloud processes of proficient readers
4. Teach vocabulary implicitly and explicitly
5. Prepare background knowledge using vocabulary
6. Use prior-during-after reading strategies

Nonsense Word Fluency (NWF)

If students are not at Benchmark levels:
1. Teach letter sounds.
2. Teach phoneme awareness.
3. Teach decoding.
4. Use decodable text.

Oral Reading Fluency/ Reading–Curriculum Based Measurement (ORF/R-CBM)

If students are not at Benchmark levels:
1. The response will vary depending on accuracy levels and rate.
2. Refer to the ORF Decision Tree: Assess, diagnose, and teach targeted skills to automaticity.

Figure 2.7. Fluency template with instructional responses for initial planning guidelines.

Name	Benchmark 40+ Letter Naming Fluency	Benchmark 35+ Phoneme Segmentation Fluency	Low risk 25+ Nonsense Word Fluency	Recommended Level
Tulip	37	50	40	Benchmark
Daffodil	45	10	37	Benchmark
Daisy	55	38	32	Benchmark
Lavender	54	50	58	Benchmark
Phlox	41	38	30	Benchmark
Sweet Pea	55	71	42	Benchmark
Lily	40	50	38	Benchmark
Lilac	41	57	41	Benchmark
Orchid	35	41	64	Benchmark
Sprout	46	0	2	Strategic
Azalea	16	32	37	Strategic
Iris	18	68	28	Strategic
Blossom	2	2	0	Intensive
Sprig	20	48	20	Intensive
Bloom	10	4	16	Intensive
Flower	8	42	4	Intensive
Bud	5	0	7	Intensive
Rose	18	22	15	Intensive
Amaryllis	6	0	8	Intensive

Figure 2.8. Ms. Springfield's class report, kindergarten (spring).

Winter DIBELS

First Grade Instructional Grouping

Teacher: _____

Score	Phoneme Segmentation Fluency	Nonsense Word Fluency	Oral Reading Fluency	Instructional Focus/Providers
60+				
60+				
60+				
59,60				
57,58				
55,56				
53,54				
51,52				
50				
49				
47,48				
45,46				
43,44				
41,42				
40				
39				
37,38				
35,36				
33,34				
31,32				
30				
29				
27,28				
25,26				
23,24				
21,22				
20				
19				
17,18				
15,16				
13,14				
11,12				
10				
9				
8				
7				
6				
5				
4				
3				
2				
1				
0				

☐ Low risk   ☐ Some risk   ☐ At risk

Figure 2.9. Sample page from a set of Stem and Leaf charts, typically prepared for the three benchmark periods (not shown): beginning, middle, and end of year for kindergarten through Grade 8 (available from http://www.hillforliteracy.org/component/content/article/47). Teachers add student names to the cells. (*Sources:* Hanson Initiative for Language and Literacy [HILL]; Massachusetts Department of Education, Office of Reading; and Reading First Implementation Facilitators)

STEPS to Success with Struggling Students

Next STEPS aims to introduce, organize, and guide teachers to develop lessons that incorporate Teach to Reach elements within a step-by-step process. This section explains each step of the lesson process by answering the following questions:

- What is it?
- What does it look like?
- What does it sound like?

The goal of learning provides the basis for the decision of what to teach at each step:

1. *Set-up:* Prepare for learning through review of previously learned material.
2. *Teach:* Model and explain new learning using teacher voice.
3. ***Engage student responses:*** Use oral responses.
4. ***Practice activity:*** Guide with immediate feedback and scaffold.
5. *Show you know:* Assess quickly as students demonstrate new knowledge.

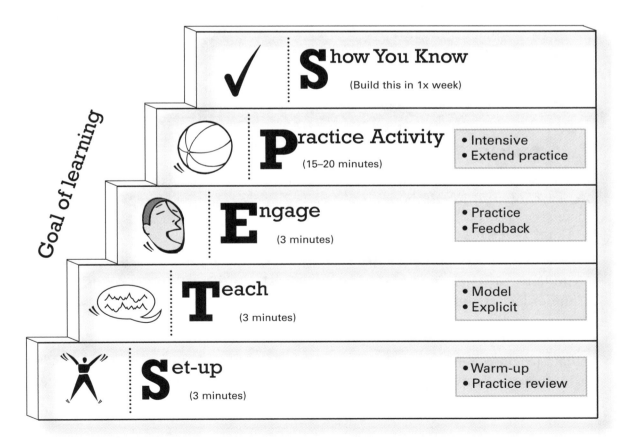

Set-up

What Is It?

This brief 3- to 5-minute first step is the primer for the lesson. Just like starting an engine before beginning on a trip, you want to jumpstart the students for learning. Target the material used for set-up. Choose previously learned material for this all-important review and practice.

What Does It Look Like?

Students are motivated through active involvement at a high rate of success, for example, by playing with flashcards, reading sentences, standing when a certain sound is heard in a word, quickly writing letters when sounds are given, or acting out vocabulary words from previous lessons.

What Does It Sound Like?

Students are familiar with the content, so set-up mostly consists of oral responses at a quick pace, with little teacher direction.

 Teach

What Is It?

This step is the kernel of the lesson, in which the teacher explicitly teaches the new content through modeling.

What Does It Look Like?

The teacher may point and direct attention to the content to be learned; instruct students to watch as the teacher models what students are learning; or scoop under letters, point to words, and highlight words or parts of words to be learned.

What Does It Sound Like?

The teacher demonstrates and the teacher's voice dominates. For example, the teacher may say, "My turn. Listen. These letters *ou* mostly make the sound /ow/. Watch me sound out these words with *ou*, /ow/."

Engage

What Is It?

In this step, students apply and practice the concept just taught with the teacher. Students practice orally through applying what they just learned from teacher modeling. This is the first of many opportunities students will have to practice and build automaticity with the skill.

What Does It Look Like?

Students are engaged in the process through independent responses or paired responses. Students may take turns as the teacher points to words on a white board, a pocket chart, or a deck of flashcards. The teacher provides corrective feedback and scaffolds the process as needed.

What Does It Sound Like?

Student voice is dominant through unison responses and oral reading of words and text. Although there is more student voice than teacher voice in this step, the teacher provides specific praise to motivate students. The pace is quick, with multiple student responses.

 ## Practice Activity

What Is It?

Students require multiple opportunities to practice new skills to attain automaticity, which is the subconscious application of reading skills such as phoneme awareness, decoding, vocabulary, and comprehension strategies. *Next STEPS* activities can assist with providing additional, frequent, and varied practice opportunities.

What Does It Look Like?

Teachers plan activities (or use the reading program lesson) that support the targeted goal for learning. Activities are active processes that apply a variety of learning tools; they provide ample opportunities for students to match, create, read, write, and respond while strengthening learning. The teacher monitors and scaffolds activity practice.

What Does It Sound Like?

In this step, student voice and multiple responses are featured. Students move from teacher support to independent application. They practice by reading connected text, sentences, paragraphs, decodable text, and controlled text. The teacher provides corrective feedback and specific praise.

 Show You Know

What Is It?

During this closing step, students are asked to demonstrate their learning. Teachers want to know, "Did the students master this skill?"

What Does It Look Like?

Students read a list of words, segment sounds, spell dictated words or sentences, produce word meanings, or complete a timed progress monitoring measure. Teachers keep data on student performance to help them plan future lessons.

What Does It Sound Like?

Students independently demonstrate how well they have learned the target skill, either orally or through spelling. Students read words, phrases, sentences, or connected text. They may write words or sentences from dictation. Figure 2.11–2.13 are STEPS Lesson Plan forms that teachers can use to plan instruction.

Students may be asked to complete a timed progress monitoring measure for this part of the lesson, which the teacher can then use for a Progress Monitoring Map, which will be explained in more detail later.

LINKING *NEXT STEPS* TO RESPONSE TO INTERVENTION

Next STEPS is a resource to help teachers interpret the screening assessment, plan and teach reading skills, and monitor their students' response to intervention.

Struggling Readers

RTI is the model or framework for modifying instruction based on early screening evaluation that identifies students who may be at risk for academic failure and behavioral concerns. RTI regulations mandate that teachers use research- or evidence-based strategies and validated instruction at all levels of instruction: whole group, small group, individual, and during Tier I, II, or III instruction.

Next STEPS
Lesson Plan

Week of: _____

Students: _____

Targeted learning focus: _____

Step	Activities
Set-up Practice/review Quick practice of skills students have mastered 3 minutes	Use one of these opening activities to get the students warmed up: • Flashcards: choral and individual responses • Reread word lists • Reread decodables or controlled text • Act out vocabulary words • Match comprehension strategies with skills
Teach Model explicitly Model and teach new concept 3 minutes	Show students new phonic element. Tell students the new information. Demonstrate how to use the new concept or strategy. Use instructions such as, "My turn," "Watch me," "Listen."
Engage Practice with feedback Teacher-led practice 3 minutes	Suggestions for practice with feedback: • Flashcards • Read a list of words displayed on a pocket chart • Retell comprehension strategy in own words • Connect vocabulary words with context
Practice Activity Intensive, extended practice of new skill 15–20 minutes	Choose Next STEPS activities. Use core or supplementary reading program activities to extend application of new skills and learning: • Phoneme-grapheme mapping • Word building with magnetic letters • A variety of segmentation phoneme awareness activities • Word sorts • Fluency training: Oral timed reading, independent and with partners • Write answers to questions about the story using vocabulary words
Show You Know! Quick check of mastery Once per week or every 2 weeks	Suggestions for mastery check: • Spelling dictation • Dictate a sentence for students to write • Read a short list of the target words • Progress monitor with a fluency measure (DIBELS)

Figure 2.11.   *Next STEPS* Lesson Plan (sample).

Next STEPS
Lesson Plan Form

Week of: _____

Students: _____

Targeted learning focus: _____

Step	Activities
Set-up Practice/review Quick practice of skills students have mastered 3 minutes	
Teach Model explicitly Model and teach new concept 3 minutes	
Engage Practice with feedback Teacher-led practice 3 minutes	
Practice Activity Intensive, extended practice of new skill 15–20 minutes	
Show You Know! Quick check of mastery Once per week or every 2 weeks	

Figure 2.12. *Next STEPS* Lesson Plan (blank form).

Step	Date: ___	Date: ___	Date: ___	Date: ___	Date: ___
Set-up *Practice review* *Quick practice of skills students have mastered* 3 minutes	Read words from last week's lesson, with long sound of a. Use flashcards.	Read long a sound words on pocket chart.	Kids stand up when they hear long sound o in words. Use: oat, foam, soap, vote, mom, moon, shout, baby.	Read sentences with words that have the long a vowel spellings. Use sentences from the reading program.	Independent and choral read of long o words we have been working on written on the white board.
Teach *Model explicitly* *Model and teach new concept* 3 minutes	Introduce oa with the long sound of o. Teach decoding with oat, boat, coat, foam.	Teach decoding with o-e using vote, toe, hoe, home.	Teach decoding of a mix of oa and o-e words: road, toast, hope, choke.	Read sentences from the story with oa and o-e words. Model expression and fluency. Instruct students to follow along as teacher reads. Point to words.	Repeat explicit decoding process for oa and o-e. Decode words from the sentences on white board.
Engage *Practice with feedback* *Teacher-led practice* 3 minutes	Point to the words and assist students to decode and blend to read the new words. Add soap, bloat, and roam.	Point to words and assist students to decode and blend to read the new words: hole, vote, home, joke, cone.	Students read a list of words from the white board: drove, oat, joke, roast, coat, stove, those, throne, pole, stone, groan.	Read sentences from story that have the oa and o-e words.	Students silently decode and say the words that fast way: drove, oat, joke, roast, coat, stove, those, throne, pole, stone, groan.
Practice Activity Intensive, extended practice of new skill 15–20 minutes	Use letter tiles and dictate words for students to build and then read: oat, boat, float, foam, soap. Dictate and read.	Use building words activity with o-e words: hole, home, cone, joke, pole. Dictate and read.	Dictate words. Students write them and cut them out to do a word sort. Use words from the *Engage* part of the lesson.	Repeat word sort from yesterday. Sort and read. Do concept sorts.	Read the decodable text. Echo Read and then take turns.
Show You Know! Quick check of mastery Once per week or every 2 weeks					While students are reading story, monitor progress Nonsense Word Fluency with Susan and Joseph.

Figure 2.13. *Next STEPS* Lesson Plan (sample form).

RTI is the framework and *Next STEPS* is the application (see Figure 2.14). *Next STEPS* answers the questions, "What do I teach on Monday morning?" and "How will I teach?" Teachers first conduct screening assessments, then analyze the assessment data to form small groups, plan research-based instruction focused on the identified student needs, teach or remediate, and administer progress monitoring assessments over time. Progress monitoring data help to keep teachers informed not only about their individual student's reading growth but also about the effectiveness of the specific reading strategies and programs the teachers have implemented in their classrooms.

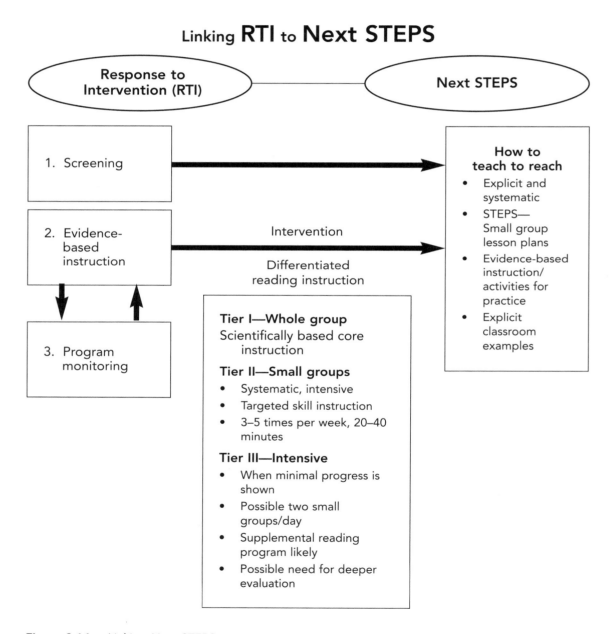

Figure 2.14.   Linking *Next STEPS* to response to intervention (RTI).

RTI, as part of the Individuals with Disabilities Education Improvement Act (IDEA) of 2004 (PL 108-446), is an alternative method for making special education referrals and one part of the evaluation process for determining specific learning disability eligibility. Educators can only make these important decisions regarding students' educational programs when research-based instruction is used as the intervention component of RTI. Initial decisions regarding which intervention or what type of instruction to select for a specific student's intervention are based on the student's performance on Universal Screening (Benchmark) measures. The student's response to intervention is carefully monitored and adjustments to instruction occur as necessary. When students fail to make expected gains, a referral for an in-depth evaluation and subsequent intervention through special education professionals may be made.

Evidence-Based Intervention

Both instruction and intervention in the RTI model are required to be based on scientific research or evidence. In this book, the term *evidence based* will be used to represent both terms. When teachers or administrators are determining whether programs, materials, strategies, or activities are evidence based, several guidelines and resources may help. First, teachers should determine if the approaches and material they are considering have been used in an intervention study that resulted in statistically significant outcomes aligning with their students' specific learning needs. In other words, do the chosen instructional materials for a Tier I, Tier II, or Tier III instruction or intervention program have a strong research base? Materials or programs for consideration should demonstrate the following characteristics (Smartt & Reschly, 2007):

- Treatment integrity or fidelity (lessons were observed for fidelity)
- Appropriate dependent measures, with reading as the outcome measure
- Statistically significant results that are practically significant in the classroom
- Replicability, as multiple studies verify effects
- Comparable student population to local schools
- Strong internal validity showing that the intervention actually made a difference
- Rigorous experimental designs
- Random assignment
- Subjects described in detail
- Contrasting intervention conditions

Another method for identifying an evidence-based intervention program was described by several well-respected researchers (Scammacca, Vaughn, Roberts, Wanzek, & Torgesen, 2007). Their paper reviewed 12 high-quality research studies in an effort to synthesize the relative effectiveness of interventions for struggling readers. Several supplemental early reading intervention programs grew out of these studies, including *Early Reading Intervention* for kindergarten and first grade (Mathes, 2005) and *Responsive Reading Instruction* for kindergarten to second grade (Denton & Hocker, 2006).

Although there is no single reading program that meets the needs of all students, a group of essential elements make a difference in the likelihood of success when teaching young struggling readers. When searching for evidence-based intervention programs, teachers use the following elements as guidelines:

- Explicit instruction (i.e., makes the thinking process public)
- High level of student–teacher interaction with opportunities for feedback and practice
- Frequent opportunities for small-group instruction
- Systematic instruction in phonological awareness, decoding, and word study
- Guided and independent reading of increasingly more difficult texts
- Writing exercises
- Opportunities to engage students in discourse and in practicing comprehension strategies while reading text

Two Response to Intervention Models

Once teachers have completed the screening process, sorted their data, and created small groups of students for focused systematic and explicit instruction, the self-questioning process resumes: "What intensive strategies can be used to solve the problems or reduce the severity of struggling readers?"

The answer to this question may become clearer after schools decide which RTI model is right for them. While there are many models to consider, the two most prominent models are *standard protocol* and *problem solving*. Those who advocate the standard protocol approach tend to use a standard research-based protocol or a stand-alone program for students who require individual interventions. One of the best known standard-protocol reading programs is Peer-*Assisted Learning Strategies* (PALS), which has programs designed for students in kindergarten through high school (Fuchs et al., 2001; Fuchs & Fuchs, 2005; Fuchs, Fuchs, & Kazdan, 1999; Fuchs, Fuchs, Mathes, & Simmons, 1997). If phonemic awareness is an identified weakness, the standard research protocol might include *Phonemic Awareness in Young Children: A Classroom Curriculum* (Adams, Foorman, Lundberg, & Beeler, 1998). For Tier II, reading tutoring with a small group of students may be considered an appropriate intervention (McMaster, Fuchs, Fuchs, & Compton, 2005; Morgan, Fuchs, Compton, Cordray, & Fuchs, 2008).

Using the problem-solving model, a team convenes to make instructional decisions that result in a unique, individualized plan for every student. Some school districts may determine that a combination of both models fits their needs best. For any RTI model, the intervention must comply with these descriptors:

- *Research based:* incorporates instructional principles that have proven successful using controlled research studies
- *Validated:* features a set of practices that have proven successful using controlled research studies
- *Effective:* emphasizes instruction, for example, in the five essential components of reading (phonemic awareness, phonics, vocabulary, fluency, and comprehension) that is systematic and explicit, with plenty of opportunities for teaching, reteaching, teacher modeling, practice, scaffolding, and application of skills in a meaningful context

RESPONSE TO INTERVENTION AND BENCHMARK ASSESSMENT

Benchmark assessments (also known as *Universal Screening*) are given to all students three times per year: fall (beginning), winter (middle), and spring (end). Students who do not score at the low-risk or established level are identified through the benchmark assessment and receive additional individualized reading instruction. *Next STEPS* assists teachers with planning intervention that is specific to students' identified needs. These students can then be closely monitored through progress monitoring. In progress monitoring, a 1-minute fluency measure or another form of formative assessment is given to students regularly to assess ongoing growth.

RESPONSE TO INTERVENTION AND PROGRESS MONITORING

Once screening, analysis, planning, and instruction are in place, progress monitoring of student response to the intervention becomes a critical component of the instructional plan. Teachers need to know if their instruction is working. They need timely and frequent feedback on the effectiveness of their instruction through the growth of their students' reading skills because every day counts when striving to "catch up." According to Hasbrouck and Denton (2010), struggling readers have to "learn faster than the average student." Just as a runner who is behind in a race must run faster to catch up, so must the struggling reader learn faster. Learning faster requires more instruction (extra intervention in Tier II and Tier III), more efficient instruction (better informed and supported teachers), and more opportunities for practice (smaller instructional groups and more frequent instructional sessions).

Progress monitoring informs the teacher's ongoing decisions about instructional content, frequency of instructional sessions and progress monitoring assessments, and size of instructional group. A very positive benefit of RTI is that lesson content is adapted to better meet the needs of individual students.

Several progress monitoring measures are available, based on the age of the student. AIMSweb provides progress monitoring for early literacy measures: Letter Naming, Letter Sound, Phoneme Segmentation, and Nonsense Word Reading. Oral Reading Fluency (R-CBM) begins in the middle of first grade and is an exemplary progress monitoring tool for all elementary and middle school grades. DIBELS provides progress monitoring in First Sound Fluency, Phoneme Segmentation, Nonsense Word reading, Oral Reading Fluency, and Word Use Fluency. TPRI also provides progress monitoring for the Basic Decoding and Phoneme Awareness skills, Oral Reading Fluency, and adds Listening and Reading Comprehension.

Whichever progress monitoring measure is being used, plan on using it at least once every 2 weeks. For students receiving intensive intervention, progress monitoring once a week is recommended. Some teachers use it once a month for feedback with students whose needs are less severe. Fluency measures are sensitive to the smallest increments of change, so if students are producing more sound segments or reading more words per minute, then teachers know that instruction can continue as planned. However, if students are not responding to intervention or the number of responses per minute is decreasing, then the instructional process needs to be examined and changed.

See the example of a progress monitoring chart in Figure 2.15. What can be said about this first-grade student's response to intervention? This student is making remarkable progress, with performance above the expected trajectory. This student's teacher can be assured that instruction is effective and that no changes in intervention are necessary at this time (mid-March). When the student's performance yields 4 Xs above the Aimline, it is time to consider moving the student into a different ("higher") instructional group.

The graph in Figure 2.16 shows a history of intervention changes over time as the student failed to respond to intervention. The solid line (Aimline) shows the trajectory needed to make adequate progress. The data points are words correct per minute. What can be said about the effectiveness of the program changes that were made? What can be said about this student's response to intervention? With each program change, the student shows improved growth. The progress monitoring is beginning to demonstrate a regular pattern of growth and the teacher can be assured that the current intervention is working well.

What to Do if Growth Isn't Happening

When students are not demonstrating growth on their progress monitoring charts, instructional changes must be made. Make one change and continue to monitor progress. If, over the course of three monitoring assessments, the data do not show positive movement toward the solid trajectory line, (e.g., 3 data points above the Aimline), then make another intervention change. Here are some guidelines to help make intervention decisions:

Progress Monitoring: The Teacher's Map

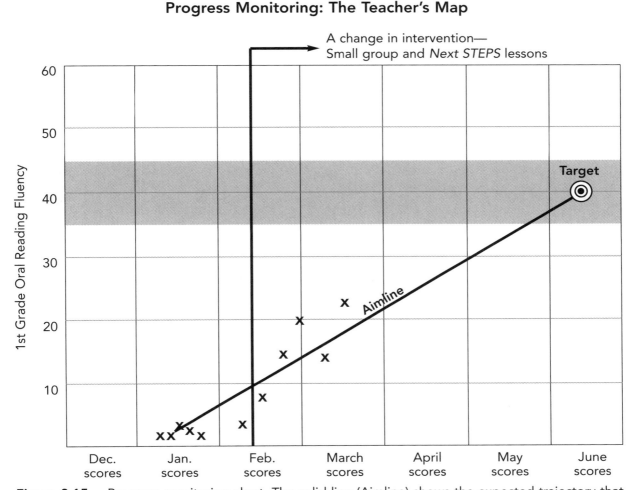

Figure 2.15. Progress monitoring chart. The solid line (Aimline) shows the expected trajectory that the student will need to follow in order to reach Benchmark (or low-risk) levels. The Xs show the student's performance on the progress monitoring measures over time.

1. *Change instruction.* Are the learning activities (strategies), the instructional level, and process providing the right amount at the right level? Is the instruction systematic and explicit with sufficient practice? Does the student have the necessary precursor skills?

2. *Change group composition.* Are there issues with discrepant performance levels within the group that do not allow students to be instructed with appropriate level materials? Are there too many students in the group, not allowing for enough individual responses or corrective feedback from the teacher?

3. *Change materials.* Are the materials and/or program used for instruction appropriate? Were they designed for this same or a similar population of students?

4. *Change amount of instructional time.* Does the student need more time and practice with the material to make gains? Should the student's time in a

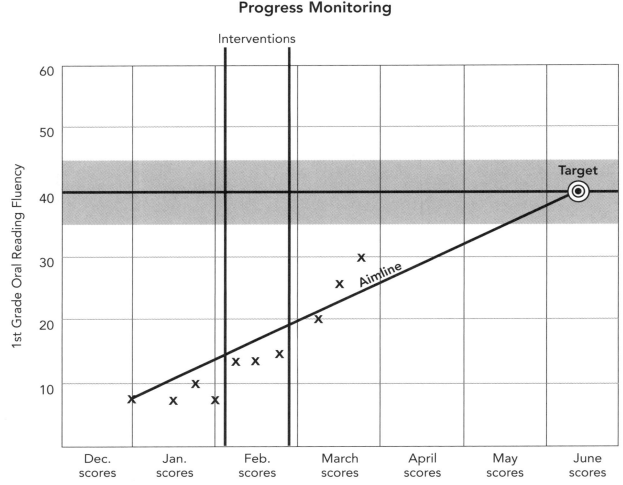

Figure 2.16. The graph shows a history of intervention changes over time as the student failed to respond to intervention. The solid line (Aimline) shows the trajectory needed to make adequate progress. The data points are words correct per minute.

group be extended from 3 to 5 days a week? Should it be increased from 15 to 30 minutes of small-group instruction each day? Similar questions can also be asked when students are making strong gains: Would this student benefit from more challenging reading material? Is this student ready for fewer and shorter small-group sessions? Is this student ready to move on to the next level?

RTI is a model that becomes stronger when progress monitoring with fluency measures is used to make instructional decisions.

The average number of words per week students are expected to improve is reflected in Table 2.6. (For more information about how to use CBM for screening and progress monitoring, including how to determine the slope for expected rate of improvement, go to the National Center for Response to Intervention web site: http://www.rti4success.org)

Table 2.6.   Average number of words per week students are expected to improve, by grade

Grade	Growth rate per week (WRC)
1	1.80
2	1.66
3	1.18
4	1.01
5	0.58
6	0.66

Source: Deno, Fuchs, Marston, and Shinn (2001)

USING THE CORE READING PROGRAM WITH STRUGGLING READERS

No single core reading program provides the appropriate focus, teaching methods, materials, and pacing for all students, especially for struggling students. All core programs require some additional provision to help teachers meet the needs of all of their students. If teachers are aware of the strengths and weaknesses of core programs when making purchasing decisions and when planning their classroom instruction, then teachers will be more confident that the time they spend teaching at-risk readers uses the highest quality instructional material available.

Since the implementation of the No Child Left Behind Act of 2001 (PL 107-110) and the requirements of the Reading First initiative to use Scientifically Based Reading Research (SBRR) comprehensive core reading programs in schools across the nation, the major publishing companies have sought to incorporate scientifically based reading research in their reading programs. Historically known as *basal reading programs,* they are now referred to as *comprehensive core reading programs.* Many teachers have been implementing new comprehensive core reading programs during recent years and more will continue to do so in the next few years. These core programs will more closely meet the needs of struggling readers; however, currently, many teachers may have outdated basal series or no core reading programs. Other teachers may have the newer core programs, but even the new core programs will likely require some modifications to meet the needs of all of their students.

Teachers should become informed consumers. Ask the questions that will identify the foundation on which the reading program was developed. Find out if a program is right for your students. Was the program developed for a student population similar to your students' background and learning characteristics? Will you need to make modifications so that students can benefit from the structure and content of the core?

Common troublesome areas for struggling readers often found in core reading programs include the following:

1. *Too many learning activities to teach in daily lessons.* There is not enough time to teach all or even most of the activities. How do teachers determine which ones to teach? Select the activities that are most closely matched to a student's specific need as determined through assessment and careful monitoring during whole-group unison and individual oral responses. Identify the skills that are targeted on weekly unit assessments and teach those.

2. *Not enough direct, explicit instruction.* Struggling readers need a very clear, direct, precise, hands-on teaching approach with ample opportunities to practice the steps and strategies involved in learning a new skill. Provide lots of practice and chances for partner or small-group interaction and application.

3. *Not enough informal assessments.* Without informal assessments or progress monitoring assessments, it is difficult to design instruction based on students' critical needs. Teachers can create their own informal assessments in the five component areas (phonemic awareness, phonics, fluency, comprehension, vocabulary), use some informal assessments that are included in this book, or consider using the progress monitoring forms from DIBELS (Good & Kaminski, 2002), AIMSweb, or TPRI.

4. *Rate of presentation of new material is too fast.* Struggling readers often cannot keep up with the fast-paced introduction of new material. Teachers need to break down the new skills into smaller pieces, scaffold, teach the components, provide practice, and integrate the parts back into the whole concept. Students will benefit when their teachers model, demonstrate, and give students an opportunity to apply the new knowledge. Making connections between the old and new knowledge through retelling and demonstrating what they have learned will help ensure understanding and enhance retention of new concepts for struggling readers.

5. *Vocabulary and sentence structure used in instruction is too complex.* Carefully select the words used to describe new skills, concepts, or strategies. Keep sentence structure direct and simple. Remember, many students, especially English language learners, will not understand positional words (e.g., *first, last*) or words such as *same* and *different*. Demonstrate whenever possible. Ask for students to restate what they have just heard in their own words.

Students may have trouble with core reading programs separate from the design of the core. For example, students may not have the prerequisite background knowledge for comprehension or learning new vocabulary, which is a common problem. However, with fluency-based and other formative assessments, teachers can plan instruction based on where the student's skills fall in the stages of early reading development (e.g., phonemic awareness, blending, segmenting, alphabetic principle letter-sound correspondence, short vowels, blends) and realize the true meaning of assessment-informed instruction.

RESOURCES

Selecting Core Reading Programs

For those teachers and administrators who may be involved in helping to select a new core reading program for their district, several good resources are available.

Florida Center for Reading Research. (n.d.). *FCRR reports.* Retrieved on July 8, 2009, from http://www.fcrr.org/FCRRReports/reportslist.htm. (Includes information on programs for initial, supplemental and intervention instruction, as well as learning center activities)

Oregon Reading First Center. (2004). *Supplemental and intervention curriculum review.* Retrieved on July 8, 2009, from http://oregonreadingfirst.uoregon.edu/downloads/instruction/curriculum _review/si_review_6_23_04.pdf. (Provides a comprehensive review of supplemental and intervention programs)

Simmons, D., & Kame'enui, E. (2003). *A consumer's guide to evaluating a core reading program grades K–3: A critical elements analysis.* Retrieved from reading.uoregon.edu/cia/curricula/con_guide .php. (Identifies what to look for at each grade level and introduces a rating system that helps the user evaluate the suitability of the core program with the group of students the teacher has in mind)

Walpole, S., & McKenna, M.C. (2005). *The literacy coach's handbook: A guide to research based practice.* New York: The Guilford Press. (Provides a strong resource for those who are involved with adoption and selection of reading series with a complete start-to-finish step-by-step approach to the sometimes demanding and confusing process)

Program Resources

Dodson, J. (2007). *Fifty nifty activities: 5 components and 3 tiers of reading instruction.* Longmont, CO: Sopris West. (This popular resource is organized around the five components providing several activities for teachers to choose from for small-group instruction. Once teachers are familiar with the activities in *Next STEPS,* they may find additional instructional supports in this text.)

Kame'enui, K., Carnine, D., Dixon, R., Simmons, D., & Coyne, M. (2002). *Effective teaching strategies that accommodate diverse learners.* Upper Saddle River, NJ: Merrill Prentice Hall. (Provides teachers with the basics for designing effective curriculum and instruction for diverse, struggling learners in reading, science, social studies, and mathematics)

Moats, L.C. (2009). *Language essentials for teachers of reading and spelling (2nd ed.).* Longmont, CO: Sopris West. (This professional development series, LETRS, consists of 12 modules that cover a range of topics such as why reading is challenging for many, the five components of reading, and writing and assessment procedures. Supplemental modules include *LETRS foundations: An introduction to language and literacy* [Glaser, D., & Moats, L.C. (2008), and *ParaReading: A training guide for reading tutors* and Glaser, D. (2006). Longmont, CO: Sopris West.]

National Institute for Literacy. (2006). *What is scientifically based research? A guide for teachers using research and reason in education.* Retrieved July 8, 2009, from http://www.nifl.gov/partnership forreading/publications/science_research.pdf. (Answers many questions about the basics of scientifically based research and how it applies to classroom decision making)

National Reading Panel. (2000). *Teaching children to read: An evidence-based assessment of the scientific research literature on reading and its implications for reading instruction.* Bethesda, MD: National Institute of Child Health and Human Development, National Institutes of Health. (Critical document compiling recent research through meta-analysis summarizing critical areas of reading instruction: phonemic awareness, phonics, vocabulary, comprehension, and fluency)

Neuhaus Education Center. http://www.neuhaus.org (A full range of professional development options, both live and web based, are offered through this educational center. Training and materials published at Neuhaus are based in scientific research.)

Stern Center for Language and Learning. http://www.sterncenter.org (Stern Center Professional Development programs offer opportunities to learn best practices based in research. Live and web-based courses are available to share information about how to most effectively teach students from preschool through adulthood. Consultations are offered onsite in collaboration with school teams, parents, and medical professionals.)

Tanner-Smith, T., & Kosanovich, M. (2008). *Delivering scientifically based reading instruction: A participant's guide.* Portsmouth, NH: RMC Research Corporation, Center on Instruction. (Information for teachers, reading coaches, principals, school psychologists, and others who are looking for the fundamental, day-to-day specifics of using scientifically based reading instruction)

University of Texas Center for Reading and Language Arts. (2003). *Three-tier reading model: Reducing reading difficulties for kindergarten through third grade students.* Austin, TX: Author. (Provides a complete description, thorough background report, and research summary of the three-tier reading model.)

Vaughn, S., & Linan-Thompson, S. (2004). *Research-based methods of reading instruction grades K–3.* Alexandria, VA: Association for Supervision and Curriculum Development. (Systematic and explicit explanations for understanding the latest reading research and what it looks like in the early elementary classroom.)

Phoneme Awareness

● ● ● ● ●

PHONEME AWARENESS MEASURES

	DIBELS	AIMSweb	TPRI	FAIR
Kindergarten	Initial Sound Fluency* First Sound Fluency** Phoneme Segmentation Fluency	Phoneme Segmentation Fluency	Phonological/Phonemic Awareness: Blending Onset Rime & Phonemes (Screening); Rhyming (Inventory); Blending Word Parts; Blending Phonemes; Detecting Initial Sounds; Detecting Final Sounds	Phoneme Blending Phoneme Deletion Word Initial/Final
Grade 1	Phoneme Segmentation Fluency	Phoneme Segmentation Fluency	Blending Word Parts Blending Phonemes Detecting Initial Sounds Detecting Final Sounds	Phoneme Blending Phoneme Deletion Word Initial/Final
Grade 2			Spelling (phoneme segmentation)	

*DIBELS (Sixth Edition; Good & Kaminski, 2002)
**DIBELS NEXT (Seventh Edition; Dynamic Measurement Group, 2011)

● ● ● ● ● ●

INTRODUCTION

How do formative assessment measures evaluate phoneme awareness? Several different measures in DIBELS, AIMSweb, TPRI, and FAIR assess skills within the construct of phoneme awareness: First Sound Fluency (FSF; DIBELS Next, 7th Edition) and Phoneme Segmentation (PSF; DIBELS, 6th and 7th Editions, and AIMSweb) are timed measures. These assessments measure students' phoneme awareness through checking the student's ability to 1) respond with the beginning sound after the assessor says a word (FSF), and 2) segment sounds in words (PSF).

The TPRI tasks (rhyming, blending onset rimes and phonemes, and detecting initial and final sounds) all assess the early developmental stages of phonemic awareness to identify areas that may need more focused instruction, reteaching, or practice in small-group settings. FAIR phonemic awareness tasks include phoneme blending and phoneme deletion. Student performance on phoneme blending tasks helps to determine if a student is struggling at the word level or phoneme level. The phoneme deletion tasks provide information about how well a student manipulates sounds by either deleting an initial or final sound; for example, the teacher may instruct, "Say *boat* without saying the /t/."

In Figure 3.1, learning to read is compared with climbing a mountain (Good & Kaminski, 2002). As students move from the land of nonreaders to established

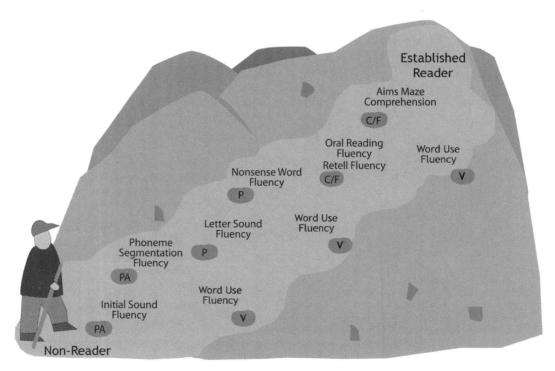

Figure 3.1. Steps to successful reading. (*Source:* Good and Kaminski, 2002.)

readers, they go through a progression of stages or steps. The first two stepping stones, or skills, that they encounter are phonemic awareness and vocabulary. While the students have one foot planted on the phonemic awareness stone, the other is planted on the vocabulary stone because students are also developing oral language, background knowledge, and language comprehension. Students progress up the mountain to the alphabetic principle (phonics) stone once phoneme awareness begins to develop. Students begin to learn about letters and letter–sound linkages, continuing to develop oral language and language comprehension as they climb. Finally, students arrive at the top of the mountain as established readers, with fluent reading skills that enable them to expand their exposure to new vocabulary and concepts through their reading and comprehending of connected text.

Figure 3.1 demonstrates the skill progression toward effective, competent, and fluent reading. Effective teachers understand this progression and the importance of assessment to plan appropriate instruction that will prepare students for each successive step along the way. For example, while students are establishing the ability to isolate initial sounds and segment sounds in words, teachers are teaching students to connect those sounds to letters to prepare them for the next step: decoding and the related Nonsense Word Fluency (NWF) assessment.

EXAMPLES OF PHONEME AWARENESS MEASURES

This section provides examples of phoneme awareness measures in DIBELS, AIMSweb, TPRI, and FAIR. As teachers begin intervention planning, they should consider the typical progression or sequence of phonological awareness development that their students will move through. Teachers can introduce instruction at the phoneme level with activities that teach students to segment the first sound or sounds in words. Many students, however, may need to go back a step, or even two steps, to the onset-rime or syllable level (see Figure 3.2 for developmental stages of phonological awareness) and engage in activities to improve those earlier skills (e.g., blending onsets and rimes, clapping syllables) while engaging in phoneme instruction at the same time.

DIBELS and AIMSweb: Phoneme Segmentation Fluency

Phoneme Segmentation Fluency (PSF) is measured in the winter and spring of kindergarten and fall and winter of first grade. In PSF, students hear a word and are asked to say all of the sounds in that word. The number of correct sound segments (phonemes) they produce in 1 minute comprises their score. A student's performance goal on PSF is 35 sound segments correct in 1 minute. Once students reach this level, teachers know that phoneme segmentation is established and that these students are prepared for successful experiences with decoding and spelling instruction.

Developmental Stages of Phonological Awareness

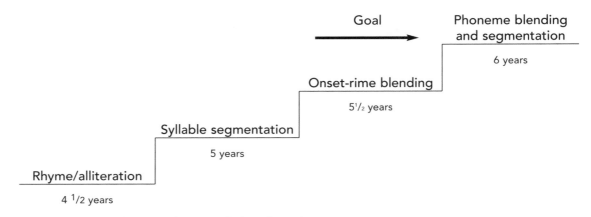

Figure 3.2.   Developmental stages of phonological awareness.

Texas Primary Reading Inventory

Rhyming is only measured when more information is needed to establish learning objectives after giving the screening task to kindergarten students. For the TPRI rhyming task, students listen to a set of rhyming words and respond with a rhyming word. For the blending task (part of the screening assessment), students blend word parts or phonemes to identify and say words. For the detecting initial and final sounds tasks (part of the screening assessment), students delete these initial or final sounds and say the new words.

Florida Assessments of Instruction in Reading

Similar to TPRI, FAIR asks students to blend word parts or phonemes and make a real word. For example, the teacher says, "/b/ /oa/ /t/," to which the students say, "boat." In addition, for the phoneme deletion tasks, students are asked to demonstrate their knowledge of sound manipulation by deleting either the initial phoneme or the final phoneme in a word. For example, the teacher may remark, "Say, *cat* without saying /c/."

Other Examples of Phonological and Phoneme Awareness Measures

Teachers can use other formal and informal measures of phonological awareness to identify how sensitive students are to the internal structure of language. Assessments that include measures of onset-rime, rhyming, and syllable detection abilities can provide important basic phonological information. In addition, measures such as the Comprehensive Test of Phonological Processing (CTOPP, see Resources) require students to repeat words and sentences or name pictures, numbers, colors, and letters quickly to measure aspects of phonological working memory and language retrieval abilities. All of these skills have their basis in language processing and contribute to becoming a skillful reader.

FUNDAMENTAL PRINCIPLES

Phoneme awareness is one of the five essential components of teaching reading identified by the National Reading Panel (NRP, 2000). Research has concluded that phonological awareness—an umbrella term that includes phonemic awareness—is the single best predictor of at-risk status for early reading difficulty. The developers of the four assessments described above—fluency-based measures and reading assessments for learning—all include phonemic awareness because it is one of the five "big ideas" of beginning reading. Phonemic awareness is a necessary component for learning to read and must be included in any comprehensive core reading program.

Phonemic Awareness

Phonemic awareness is the awareness that words are made up of individual sounds or phonemes. Before students can associate sounds with letters or benefit from phonics instruction, they need to have well-developed prerequisite phonemic awareness skills. For example, students must be able to segment and discriminate the /m/ in *mop, mat,* and *met* before they can understand that /m/ represents a sound in those words. This skill is called *sound isolation.* In Figure 3.3, notice that phoneme awareness is included under the phonological awareness umbrella and that isolation is an early developmental stage of phoneme awareness.

Phonemes are the basic building blocks of spoken language. The awareness that speech is composed of separate speech sounds that can be isolated one from the other, manipulated, and combined in multiple ways to form words has been proven to be one of the most fundamental skills for young readers to possess. Without the ability to identify sounds and to separate and blend speech sounds, children have serious difficulty with decoding and, consequently, with learning to read. Initially, young children learn to talk and associate meaning with words to converse and have their needs met. However, in order to learn to read, children must progress from listening and speaking to reading and writing by becoming aware that there is more to know about words than just meaning. Words are made up of groups of sounds or phonemes. By unlocking those sounds and connecting them with their corresponding letters, children learn to read and write. For example, if you say to a 4-year-old child, "Tell me the first sound in *dog,*" the child will likely reply, "Bow wow." It seems that some children catch on to the idea of individual sounds within words and can blend and segment almost naturally. Struggling readers, in general, cannot. Children who "catch on" effortlessly learn to read without difficulties. Children who do not "get it"—that is, they cannot isolate, blend, or segment sounds—have trouble with both learning the alphabetic principle and becoming successful readers.

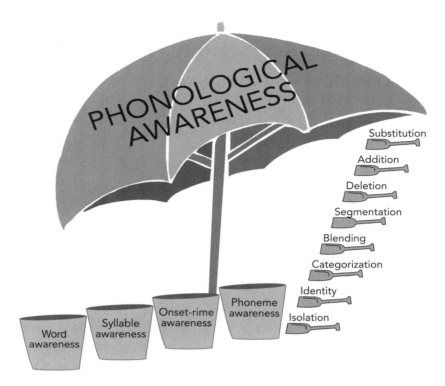

Figure 3.3. Phoneme awareness is included under the phonological awareness umbrella.

Fluency-based measures and other data-driven or formative assessments for reading instruction allow teachers to identify young students' current reading abilities and predict future reading success by providing information on how well the skill of phoneme segmentation is developing. When a student's PSF score is less than the benchmark level, attention to phoneme awareness through individualized and small-group instruction should be an immediate response. Such a student is at risk for reading failure. Research indicates that the earlier teachers provide multiple learning opportunities with effective practices for students to build phonemic awareness through segmenting and blending sounds in words, the more likely it is that students will be able to avoid reading difficulties.

What Is the Difference Between Phoneme Awareness and Phonological Awareness?

Phonological awareness and *phoneme awareness* can be confusing terms. Some educators think that these terms define the same skills, or even confuse them with *phonics,* when in fact there are clearly delineated distinctions between all of these terms. The terms are casually used when discussing early reading instruction. To many educators, they seem to share vague or nonexistent boundaries. Some teachers may use the terms to reference the same thing; however, all three terms have very distinct and separate definitions. Knowledgeable teachers who understand the differences between phonological awareness, phoneme awareness, and phonics—and the developmental sequences associated with acquiring these skills—are better prepared to assess, plan instruction, and appropriately teach their students.

Phonics is assessed through letter sound fluency (LSF) on AIMSweb, NWF on DIBELS, consonant and vowel substitution on TPRI, and word building on FAIR. Phonics will be discussed in Chapter 4.

Phonological Awareness

Phonological awareness refers to the explicit awareness of the sound structure or phonological structure of a spoken word (Gillon, 2004). This skill focuses on the sound structure of language, not letters. When we talk about awareness of the boundaries within our speech system (e.g., syllables, onset-rime), we are talking about phonological awareness. Researchers have suggested that there is a predictable sequence of development leading up to established phonological awareness. Figure 3.3 shows the concept of the overarching phonological awareness umbrella, with the individual phonological skills presented in order of typical development.

Children's phonological awareness develops from the larger level: syllables, onset-rimes, and then to the smaller, individual sound or phoneme level. When planning intervention, teachers need to be aware of this progression and follow this same sequence for instruction. Intervention that improves phonological awareness results in enhanced word recognition, spelling, and reading comprehension performance (Gillon, 2004). *Next STEPS* activities are ordered along this progression—from larger speech segments (i.e., syllables and onset-rimes) to smaller speech segments (phonemes)—to assist teachers with planning appropriate intervention.

If school-age students are not isolating phonemes, scaffolded instruction entails backing up and including instructional attention to the other lower level phonological skills under the umbrella, while at the same time attending to the development of phoneme awareness. For school-age children, most of the intervention time should be spent at the phoneme level.

Phoneme awareness is a subcategory of phonological awareness. It is the awareness of separate speech sounds in oral language—the ability to isolate, identify, and manipulate individual sounds in spoken language. Like phonological awareness, there is a step-by-step sequence from easier to more difficult skills in phoneme awareness (see the shovels in Figure 3.3).

What Are Key Guidelines for Phonological and Phoneme Awareness Intervention?

When students are below benchmark levels on phoneme awareness assessments, they may need instruction in basic phonological awareness skills. Teachers should use the following guidelines when making instructional decisions:

1. Begin with auditory phonemic awareness activities in the earliest stages to help direct young students' attention to language sounds, if necessary. Games, songs, nursery rhymes, and activities engage students in learning.

2. Use explicit and systematic instruction in small groups. Do not leave the learning to chance or discovery—tell, show, and model the skill.

3. Integrate phonological awareness instruction with letter-sound knowledge whenever possible, no later than the beginning of first grade. Remember, connecting speech to print improves phoneme awareness. Introduce a sound, isolate it, play with it using activities, and then introduce the letter for that sound.

4. Focus phonological awareness training at the phoneme level for school-age children whenever possible. Go back to a previous step, syllables, or onset-rime if needed for brief, focused, intensive intervention.

5. Provide individual or small-group instruction for at-risk students.

6. Monitor progress often, at least every 2 weeks. Change time, intensity (size of group), lesson content, or materials if adequate progress toward the goal or benchmark is not being made.

7. Provide direct instruction and modeling of phonological awareness activities and give focused attention to phoneme segmentation.

Teaching students to "deconstruct" words may take some time and patience because their only experience with words so far has been as whole meaningful units (e.g., *cup*). Teachers now expect them to take apart, or segment, the word into individual phonemes (e.g., /c/ /u/ /p/), which is not an easy task for many.

What Accomplishments Should We Expect of Kindergarten and First-Grade Students?

In *Preventing Reading Difficulties in Young Children,* the National Research Council (1998) recommended phonemic awareness accomplishments for kindergarten and first-grade students during the normal course of literacy development. The timing will vary among young children, but it is important for teachers to be prepared to teach these accomplishments.

For kindergarten students, accomplishments should include the following:

- When given spoken sets of similar syllables (e.g., *can, can, ken*), the student can identify the first two as being the same and the third as being different.

- The student can demonstrate understanding that spoken words consist of a sequence of phonemes (e.g., *sun* = /s/ /u/ /n/).

- When given spoken syllables (e.g., *pack, pat, sun*), the student can identify the first two as sharing the same middle sound.

- When given spoken speech sounds, the student can blend them into a meaningful target word (e.g., when the teacher says, "/m/ /a/ /n/," the student says, "man").

- When given a spoken word, the student can produce another word that rhymes with it (e.g., when the teacher says, "school," the student says, "pool").

For first-grade students, accomplishments should include the following:

- The student can do all of the tasks listed in the kindergarten accomplishments.
- The student can count the number of syllables in words.
- The student can blend and segment the phonemes in most one-syllable words.

Blending and segmenting phonemes is a major accomplishment toward becoming a reader. If students in second grade are below basic levels in reading, they may require further instruction to strengthen phoneme segmenting and blending. A PSF assessment will inform teachers of this requirement and assist with planning instruction.

HERE WE GO: READY TO TEACH!

Using the Weekly Small-Group Lesson Plan introduced in Chapter 2 as a framework, read through this vignette on the next page that describes what goes on inside a real classroom. "View" a Phoneme Awareness lesson being taught by Miss Garcia using the Weekly Small-Group Lesson Plan as her guide.

Watch for the five STEPS and think about which effective teaching behaviors you "observe."

1. **S**et-up
2. **T**each
3. **E**ngage
4. **P**ractice Activity
5. **Sh**ow You Know

Miss Garcia met with the other kindergarten teachers in her school to review their fall benchmark fluency reports. Following lively and engaging discussion wherein the teachers discussed their students' readiness skills, Miss Garcia decided to form a small group of students to work with during her core reading time. These students were below benchmark on phoneme segmentation. Miss Garcia knew that if phoneme awareness was not established, these students would have a difficult time mastering decoding skills.

Based on an additional quick phoneme awareness screener, these identified students were able to isolate some first sounds in words, but not consistently. Therefore, Miss Garcia decided on a goal of 18 phoneme sounds (low-risk level) by the winter benchmark period. She also decided to monitor the students' progress every 2 weeks to determine how well her instruction was working and to help her determine when changes in instruction needed to be made to help her students meet the established goal.

Here is what her first week of lessons looked like, along with a script of her explicit lessons. Note how frequently she asks students to repeat what she says. This is a critically

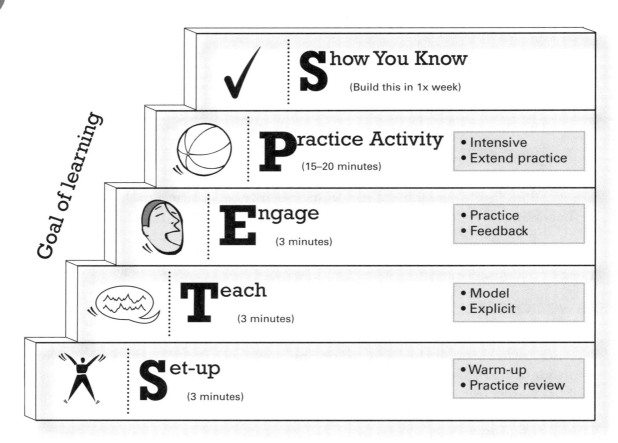

Figure 3.4. The five steps.

important feature of a phoneme awareness lesson, as students must be verbally engaged saying words and saying sounds.

Set-up

Students will explore the articulation of consonant and vowel sounds and learn sound associations.

Teacher: "Good morning, students! Let's get ready to learn about sounds in words today. Everybody stand up! Today's special sound is /mmmm/. Say it."

Students: "/mmmm/."

Teacher: "Good. When I say, '/mmmm/,' my mouth is closed and I feel the sound in my throat [holds hand on throat] and in my nose [lightly pinches nose while saying, '/mmmm/']. Do it with me."

Students: "/mmmm/" [exploring the articulation as directed].

Teacher: "/mmmm/ is a sound we say when something tastes really good [rubs stomach and says "/mmmm/"]. Everybody say, '/mmmm/' and rub your tummy."

Students: "/mmmm/" [rubbing stomachs].

Teacher: "Good! Let's listen for /mmmm/ in our words today. What sound?"

Students: "/mmmm/" [still rubbing stomachs].

During the next several lessons, the teacher and students will review all of the learned sounds and their associations, adding a new one each day. The teacher will make the motions and students will copy the teacher and say the associated sounds.

 Teach

The teacher will demonstrate, show, and model the segmentation and blending of sounds in two-sound words with large felt sound markers on a white board.

Teacher: "Watch me. I am going to say all of the sounds in some words. I will use these big circles to show the sounds in the words I say. My turn.
Me. Me [moving each of two felt circles down as each sound is voiced]: /m/ /ee/. Me. Watch and listen. Me [repeats the process, segmenting the sounds in *me*].
Watch me say the sounds in another word.
Shoe. Shoe [moving each of two felt circles down as each sound is voiced]: /sh/ /oo/. *Shoe*.
Watch and listen. Shoe" [repeats the process, segmenting the sounds in *shoe*].

The teacher then repeats the process with *she*.

 Engage

Students segment and say the sounds in two-sound words with the teacher.

Teacher: "Now it is your turn to say the sounds in words with me. I'll say the word, then you say the word. Then we will say the sounds in the word together. Ready? *Me*. Say it."

Students: "Me."

Teacher: "Say the sounds in *me*."

Teacher and students [as teacher touches and moves the felt circles]: "/m/ /ee/. Me!"

Teacher: "Nice job saying the sounds in *me!* /m/ /ee/. Let's do another one. Shoe."

Students: "Shoe."

Teacher: "Say the sounds in *shoe*."

Teacher and students [as teacher touches and moves the felt circles]: "/sh/ /oo/. Shoe."

Teacher: "Nice job saying the sounds in *shoe*."

The teacher then repeats the process with *she*.

 Practice Activity

Given two-sound words, students will segment the sounds through Touch and Say using colored discs. Students will also blend the sounds in two-sound words to say words through the activity, Robot Talk.

Teacher: "Now it is your turn to say the sounds in some words. Here are your sound markers [hands out two colored discs to each student]. Line up your sound markers like mine. Touch the first one. Touch the next one [leads students to touch the sound markers in left-to-right sequence]. I'll say a word, then you say the word, and then you'll say the sounds in the words. *Me*."

Students: "Me [then touching each sound marker]. /m/ /ee/. Me."

The teacher next repeats the process for the following words: *she, shoe, bee, do, may, see, go, dough*. Students say each word after the teacher says it. Then, students say the sounds in the words, sliding their sound markers to represent each sound, and always saying the word again after segmenting the sounds. The teacher then chooses students to perform the segmenting task independently to assess individual skills.

Teacher: "Sarah, your turn to say the sounds in a word. The word is *pay*."

Sarah: "Pay. /p/ /ae/. Pay."

Teacher: "Great job, Sarah! You said the sounds in pay!
            Now everybody, let's play Robot Talk. Listen to the sounds the robot says. Put the sounds together to figure out what the word is. Ready? Listen: /sh/ /oo/."

Students: "Shoe!"

Teacher: "Good listening! Here is another one: /m/ /ae/."

Students: "May!"

Teacher: "Yes, may! Here is another one: /d/ /oo/."

Students: "Do!"

The teacher then repeats Robot Talk with a few more two-sound words.

Show You Know

Each student will segment two-sound words at the close of the session. When students can segment three of these words with no errors, Miss Garcia will move to three-sound words, then words with consonant blends. Every 2 weeks, she will monitor student progress with phoneme segmentation fluency probes.

ACTIVITIES

Activities are organized into two stages of phonological awareness development:

1. Basic phonological awareness: syllable awareness and onset-rime awareness
2. Phoneme awareness: initial sound, segmenting, and blending

These specific activities can be used during the Practice Activity step of the *STEPS* small-group lesson (see Figure 3.4). Refer to the Resources page at the end of this chapter for additional ideas.

Activities

BASIC PHONOLOGICAL AWARENESS ACTIVITIES

Syllable Awareness

The purpose of syllable awareness is to help children learn that whole words are made up of smaller units called *syllables*. It is difficult for very young children and some older school-age struggling readers to distinguish individual syllables in words. When this is the case, start out by having the children place the back of their hands under their chins, then say the word. Point out to them that their chin will drop for each syllable. Practice with several words while the students count the number of chin drops.

Helpful hints: Prepare lists of words ahead of time to use with the syllable activities. Use teacher-prepared books of lists, vocabulary from books you read to them, and books they are reading for word-list sources.

• • • • •

Block It

Explain that syllables are parts of words. Demonstrate by pushing out a block for each word part as you say a word. Return the blocks to a pile before trying the next word. Give each child small paper squares instead of blocks to use at their desk for a group activity. Have a prepared list of words to dictate for the practice. You may want to use vocabulary from one of your areas of study.

• • • • •

Syllable Your Name

Use the students' names as a source for practicing syllabication. Have the class clap each student's name all together. Add the students' last names the next time you do it. Whose name has the most syllables? Whose name is the shortest? Ask student volunteers to segment and clap their own names.

Extension: When creating background familiarity prior to reading a story, use the names of characters from the story to discover the number of syllables. Consider writing them on the board. This provides practice with seeing, hearing, and clapping the names to help the students read the names in the story.

● ● ● ● ● ●

Syllable the Room

Choose objects from the room as a source of words to break into syllables. Have the children take turns choosing items for the class to clap the syllables. Watch them study the room for things that will give them the big words.

● ● ● ● ● ●

Syllable the Picture

Use pictures as a source of words for the children to practice identifying syllables. Say the word, then have the children repeat the word as they clap the syllables. Many learning kits contain collections of pictures that work well for this. Coloring books and story books also provide good sources of pictures for this activity.

Variation: Use pictures that present a wide variety of language use for syllable work. Make sure the picture is big enough for all of the children to see when you have them seated in a circle, or use a picture from the students' book if every child has a book at their desk. The tendency will be to name the nouns. For a change, have the students identify words for the action (verbs) in the picture. Then have them identify words to describe (adjectives) the nouns in the picture.

Onset-Rime Awareness

Most every syllable has an onset and a rime. The term *onset* refers to the first written or spoken single consonant or consonant cluster in a word, such as /s/ in sit or /str/ in *strip. Rime* refers to the rest of the word, the vowel and the final consonant(s) in a syllable. For example, the *at* in *cat* and the *itch* in *switch* are both rimes. From a developmental perspective, young children first start becoming aware of the whole words in language, then progress to syllable awareness, and often quickly move to onset-rime awareness.

Once students are comfortable blending onsets with rimes, reverse the activity (change it into a segmentation activity) by saying words and asking the students to segment the onset from the rime. For example, the teacher says, "Back," to which the student replies, "/b/ /ack/."

Rhyming Picture Sort

Copy sets of rhyming pictures from commercial materials (see Resources) or download clip art from the Internet. Provide a set for each student and one for the teacher. Instruct students to name each picture before the game begins. Hold up a picture and ask students to name the picture and select a rhyming picture from their set. Direct students to say each word, compare it with the picture selected, and emphasize the final rime.

Sound Categorization by Rhyme

To play the game, the students need 3–5 sets of rhyming and nonrhyming cards. This works best if you keep them in baggies or clipped together in their individual sets of four (3 rhyming and 1 nonrhyming) cards. The players must decide which one of the four pictures on the table does not belong in the set. They can say or sing the familiar song (sung to the tune of "This Is the Way We Wash Our Clothes"):

Which little picture shall I pick?
One of them does not fit.
Which little picture shall I pick?
[Say each picture word.]
This is the picture I will pick! [Say the picture name.]

After the song has been sung, ask the students to name each picture. Then ask, "Which one does not belong?" Have the student tell which card does not belong and why. They might say, "They all end the same" or "They all rhyme except this one."

You Can Make a Rhyme

Read phrases to students and have them fill in the missing word that rhymes. Students will frequently fill in nonsense words, but acknowledge this as a positive sign because they now are listening for phonological cues and producing a match. Try to gently move them toward a logical, contextually accurate response. Examples include the following sentences, with the desired student response in parentheses:

- A bug crawled under the (rug).
- A bat was wearing a (hat).
- Airplanes fly up in the (sky).
- A duck is driving a (truck).
- Smell the rose with your (nose).
- We drove far in our (car).
- An owl dries off with a (towel).
- The fox fell in a (box).
- A goat is sailing a (boat).
- A cat is wearing a (hat).

On My Way to the Store

Have the students sit in a circle and provide something to toss, such as a small ball or beanbag. To begin the game, say, "I was on my way to the store to buy some cheese," then toss the ball to a student. The student must repeat the phrase and add a rhyming word at the end, such as "I was on my way to the store to buy some peas (or *trees, fleas, bees, knees,* and so forth)." The student should then toss the ball back to the teacher, who repeats the original phrase with a new rhyming word (e.g., "I was on my way to the store to buy some jam (or *ham, Sam, Pam, ram*"). Keep the pace moving quickly so children do not lose interest.

● ● ● ● ●

Guess My Word

Add onsets (consonant sounds and consonant blends) to the following list of rimes to create words for this listening activity. Provide words for students to blend by saying the onset separated from the rime. Instruct students to give you the secret word. For example, the teacher says: "/b/ /ack/." Students then reply, "Back!" The teacher says, "/br/ /ight/." Students reply, "Bright!"

Figure 3.5 includes a list of rimes; you can provide the onsets to play *Guess My Word* with your students.

ack	ank	eat	ill	ock	ump	ail
ap	ell	in	oke	unk	ain	ask
est	ine	op	ake	at	ice	ing
ore	ale	ate	ick	ink	ot	ame
aw	ide	ip	uck	an	ay	ight
it	ug					

Figure 3.5. List of rimes.

PHONEME AWARENESS ACTIVITIES

First Sound Awareness

Phoneme Isolation and Identity

The following activities are designed for teachers to use in intervention groups for improving initial sound isolation. Repetition and practice are essential when working with struggling readers and will help ensure learning. Teachers can work to develop fluency with emphasis on quick, accurate responses in all activities once the basic concepts have been mastered.

● ● ● ● ●

Building First Sound Fluency with Pictures

If you have students with low oral language skills and you are concerned they may have trouble following directions on phonemic awareness assessments,

(continued)

(continued)

try this activity. Ask students identification questions: "What picture starts with /s/? And ask production questions: "What sound does *moon* begin with?" Place the pictures and directions in a large envelope in a learning center or use it for a take-home activity.

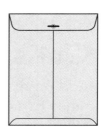

• • • • •

Articulation Features

Some sounds in English are difficult for non–English-speaking students to isolate and identify. For example, Spanish speakers have a difficult time reproducing /ch/. These students—and all young students—benefit from instruction that includes investigation of the articulatory features of sounds. Use mirrors to observe what the lips, tongue, and teeth do while producing the sound. Assist students in describing how the sounds are made. Feel the throat while saying the sound. Do you feel a vibration in the vocal chords? Apply this technique to help students determine if the sound is voiced or unvoiced.

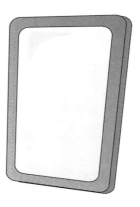

Note: It is critically important that teachers correctly pronounce the sounds of English for their students. Professional development is available through Language Essentials for Teachers of Reading and Spelling (http://www.letrs.com) and the Neuhaus Education Center in Texas (http://www.neuhaus.org), which are both strong sources for learning this information.

• • • • •

First Sound Sorts with Pictures

Picture sorts (see Figure 3.6) are particularly good for students who do not have extensive vocabularies or for English Language Learner (ELL) students who are

(continued)

(continued)
struggling with unfamiliar sounds or vocabulary (Bear, Invernizzi, Templeton, & Johnston, 2008). This activity also helps to increase vocabulary by providing multiple exposures and opportunities to use the vocabulary words. Throughout the activity, the student is required to compare and contrast what is heard when the student names the picture on the word card. The student sorts the words into groups that begin with the same sound as the target sound. Here are the steps:

1. The teacher models with a group of picture cards, sorting those that go together and those that do not.
2. The teacher holds up a picture, names the picture, names the initial sound of the picture, and then repeats the word and sound.
3. Students do this activity in small groups as the teacher observes and provides feedback-guided practice. The activity may sound like this:
   Teacher: "Good job finding the pictures that begin with /mmm/. What is this picture?"
   Student: "Boat."
   Teacher: "Tell me the first sound."
   Student: "/b/"
   Teacher: "Does *boat* go with *man* or *bear*?"
   All phonological practice activities are more successful when students are using language, repeating the words and phonemes often!
4. After students demonstrate to the teacher that they can complete the task through guided practice, students continue to sort pictures through independent practice in center and workstation time.

   Note: This same sorting activity can be used with rhyming words and later with letters as the category headings once the sound symbols have been introduced.

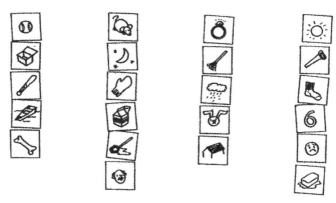

Figure 3.6. Examples of picture sorts.

Identifying First Sounds

Make use of this simple activity to help students increase first sound identification. Use the list of words in Figure 3.7 or use words that are included in the core reading series. In this activity, the teacher says a word (e.g., "moon"), then the students repeat the word and say the first sound ("moon, /mmm/"). When students do not respond appropriately, the teacher should model the correct word and initial sound, and then instruct students to repeat the word and sound again with the teacher. Apply hand gestures to initiate choral responses from students. This is a good "sponge" time activity. Use it when you're waiting in line for lunch or for the physical education teacher to come to your class.

can	bridge	charm	bat	ant	beet	fall
dirt	cold	even	fear	garden	gas	fry
gum	happy	date	end	dime	duck	music
kick	home	high	nose	land	off	miss
leaf	horn	nest	pat	night	pea	odd
menu	ladder	party	mouse	pink	race	seal
rat	soft	table	shade	tall	pin	tent
thin	under	top	valley	wait	tiger	walk
yard	zoo	yellow	vase	wire	zebra	two
turn	wax	cold	down	ever	door	wave
ham	girl	harm	puzzle	seed	point	tag
vote	wig	born	check	shell	throw	wool

Figure 3.7. Words to help students increase first sound identification.

Sound Associations

Young children who are not yet aware of the separate sounds in their oral language benefit from attention to those sounds through sound associations. Introduce sounds with accompanying hand motions and lead students to follow along. For example, the teacher may say, "When we eat something really good, we say, '/mmmmm/,' while rubbing our tummy for /mmmmmm/ good!"

(continued)

(continued)

Use these activities to strengthen attention to individual sounds in words:

/m/   humming or "/mmmm/ /mmmm/ good" sound from the Campbell's soup song

/p/   quiet motor boat or motor scooter sound

/b/   babbling brook, blowing bubbles, or "baa, baa" sheep sound

/w/   ceiling fan

/wh/   blowing sound (e.g., blowing out birthday candles)

/h/   laughing or big sigh sound (remember, this is unvoiced)

/t/   ticking clock or metronome sound

/d/   pecking woodpecker or noisy tugboat engine sound

/n/   neighing horse or maddening mosquito sound

/ng/   ringing bell sound (ding-dong)

/k/   coughing or cawing sound

/g/   emptying water jug or gurgling baby sound

/y/   yipping puppy or yipping coyote sound

/f/   mad cat sound (unvoiced)

/v/   big black fly sound

/sh/   "be quiet" sound

/zh/   electric razor, hair clipper, or vacuum sound

/l/   singing or humming telephone ring

/th/   "tickles my tongue" sound (for voiced /th/ as in *them*)

/th/   spitting mad goose sound (for unvoiced /th/ as in *thumb*)

/r/   crowing rooster, fire engine, or roaring lion

/s/   hissing snake or flat tire sound (e.g., air hissing out of tire)

/z/   buzzing bee sound

/ch/   chugging "choo choo" train

/j/   large diesel train or "Jack and Jill" sound

● ● ● ● ●

Associate Sound with Letter

Combine lessons on letter naming with sound by providing explicit requests for letter or sound (e.g., "Tell me the letter. Tell me the sound."). Teach students to use sound sentences, as in the following example:

(continued)

(continued)

Teacher:	"What is the first sound in *mop?*"
Student:	"/m/."
Teacher:	"Tell me the letter."
Student:	"*M.*"
Teacher:	Say the sound sentence.
Student:	"/m/. Mop. *M.*"

Animal Names

The teacher can use pictures cut from magazines or the picture cards similar to the Webber Animal Photo Cards (see Resources). The teacher should give students pictures and ask them to name the animals. The teacher may ask, "What sound do you hear at the beginning of that animal's name?" If students have also worked on final sounds, the teacher may ask, "What sound do you hear at the end of that animal's name?" This idea could be expanded with more pictures and could be "played" in centers with pairs of students.

Variation: Assign pairs of students to a sorting task. For example, all of the animals whose names begin with /m/ could be placed in one stack and all of those that begin with /t/ could be placed in another.

Play with Student Names

Student names are a wonderful resource for initial sound word play. The teacher may say, "I am thinking of someone in our class whose name starts with /sh/. Say the sound and the name: /sh/, Shane."

• • • • •

Simon Says

The teacher should prepare a list of words in advance, many of which share the same initial sounds. Have students stand in a line in the back of the class. Give a series of three words to students with the instructions, "I will say three words. The three words may or may *not* all begin with the same first sound. You say, '*yes*' or '*no*' depending on whether or not they all begin with the same first sound." Then add the tricky part: They must also listen for "Simon says." If they answer correctly—only when the teacher says, "Simon says"—they get to take a step forward, as in the following examples:

Simon says the following words all have the same beginning sound: *cat, coat,* and *cot.*

Simon says the following words all have the same beginning sound: *tom, top,* and *sun.*

The following words all have the same beginning sound: *boat, bed,* and *ball.*

• • • • •

Stand, Sit, and Clap

The teacher should select a sound such as /m/. Ask all students whose names begin with /m/ to stand, say the sound, sit, and clap.

Variation: Give each student a picture card. Make sure students know the names of their pictures. Say a sound and have the student stand, say the sound, sit, and clap when their sound is called. Remember to ask students to repeat the speech sounds for a stronger learning opportunity.

Segmenting and Blending Phonemes

Through testing and analysis, teachers are able to identify which step or stage of instruction is appropriate for their students. Activities for phoneme isolation, identity, blending, and segmentation are included in this section. Deletion, addition, and substitution skills are higher level phoneme awareness skills generally included in second- and third-grade curricula. See Resources at the end of this chapter for higher level phoneme manipulation teaching ideas. See Table 3.1 for a phoneme awareness progression.

Table 3.1.   Phoneme awareness progression

Skill	Definition	Example
Phoneme isolation	Students isolate and say individual sounds in words.	"What is the first sound in *sun?*" "/s/"
Phoneme identity	Students identify the same sound in several words.	"What sound is in *man, monkey,* and *mix?*" "/m/"
Phoneme categorization	Students identify a word that does not share the same sound as others in a group of words.	*"Book, baby, mother.* What word doesn't belong?" "Mother."
Phoneme blending	Students hear the separate sounds in a word and blend the sounds together to say the whole word.	"What word: /l/ /ee/ /f/?" "Leaf!"
Phoneme segmentation	Given a word, students segment and say all the sounds in that word.	"Say the sounds in *house."* "/h/ /ou/ s/"
Phoneme deletion	Students manipulate sounds in a word, deleting a sound and saying the remaining word.	"What is drip without the /d/?" "Rip!"
Phoneme substitution	Students substitute a sound in a word with another sound and say the new word.	"The word is *cop.* Change the /o/ to /u/." "Cup."

Phoneme Isolation and Identity

Use these activities to strengthen attention to individual sounds in words.

● ● ● ● ●

Silly Words

Give the children a sound and have them replace the sound at the beginning of their names or any other desired words. The teacher may say, "The silly sound is /b/. Change the first sound in your name to /b/," such that *Mary* becomes *Barry* and *Sam* becomes *Bam.*

● ● ● ● ●

Stand Up, Sit Down

Students are asked to stand up when they hear a given sound in a word the teacher says. The teacher may say, "Listen for the sound /oo/ like in *moon,"* then say several words, some with /oo/ (e.g., *spoon, loon, boom, coop*) and others without. Students stand up when they hear words with the /oo/ sound. Say the word and the sound together as a class after they stand up (e.g., "spoon, /oo/").

Let's Go Shopping

Begin this game by telling the students that they are going shopping. The only things they can buy are things that start with, end with, or have a middle sound that you provide. (Use just one of the criteria.) The teacher may say, "Let's go shopping! We are going to buy things that have a middle (vowel) sound /a/." Examples include *cats*, *mats*, *fans*, *rats*, and *banners*. The teacher then models the first sentence: "Today I am going shopping and I am going to buy some [middle vowel /a/ word]." The teacher continues until each child has a chance to "go shopping." Pictures may be provided to help less verbal children "think" of words.

Phoneme Blending

Use these activities to build students' awareness of blended sounds.

Kid Sounds

Bring two or three students to the front of the room. (The number of students needs to correspond to the number of sounds in the word to be blended.) Whisper the sounds of a word (one sound per child) in their ears. When you touch a student's head (touching left to right), he or she says the sound. The class blends the sounds to make the secret word. Whisper new consonant sounds and use the same vowel, or change the vowel to continue the practice.

Robot Talk (Secret Code)

Say a word stretched out with every phoneme separated by about a second of time. The students then repeat the word back to you as a whole unit. For example, when the teacher says, "/b/… /l/…/a/…/ck/," the students respond, "Black!"

● ● ● ● ●

I'm Thinking

The teacher can create riddles with a focus on students' experiences. The teacher may say, "I'm thinking of something we eat every day: /l/ /u/ /n/ /ch/." This activity can also be used to practice other phoneme awareness skills, as in the following examples:

"I'm thinking of something good to eat. It starts with /p/." (e.g., *pizza, pickles, pineapple*)

"I'm thinking of something in the room that ends with /r/. It is in your desk." (e.g., *eraser, marker, sticker*)

"I'm thinking of someone's name that has the /o/ sound in it." (e.g., *Tom*)

Phoneme Segmentation

Even though DIBELS and AIMSweb assess only segmentation, both segmentation and blending are important to teach. Include attention to both, regularly throughout each day. Use one-syllable words that present opportunities to practice with sounds and combinations of sounds that result from the individual fluency measure or formative assessment performance analysis.

● ● ● ● ●

Eat Your Sounds

Use small edible items, such as goldfish crackers or popcorn pieces, to segment sounds. Give students a small pile of edible items. Instruct students to show the sounds in a given word, then identify and "eat" a given sound. Model the process for students who are just beginning to segment sounds with manipulatives:

Teacher: Show me the sounds in snow.

Teacher and student together: /s/ /n/ /o/.

Teacher: Point to /n/. Eat the /n/.

Note: Providing Elkonin Boxes on a card or piece of paper makes it easier for the students to capture their sounds.

Head-Waist-Toes

This is a great activity to help students identify internal sounds. The teacher should say a three-sound word, such as *mitt*. Students then stand and touch their heads while saying the first sound (/m/), waists while saying the second sound (/i/), and toes while saying the final sound (/t/). The teacher can then touch the waist again while saying, "What sound?" The teacher can continue to elicit the sounds in positions that students need help identifying.

Touch and Say

In this activity, students use paper squares, tiles, or cubes as sound markers to count out the sounds in words. Students should line up sound markers left to right and pull one down for every sound in a word, saying the sounds as they touch the markers.

Step and Say

Students should stand and, while segmenting a given word, take one step for each sound in a word. Students can be told that they are snails or turtles, which move very slowly, while they are saying each sound in a word.

· · · · ·

Elkonin Boxes

The teacher can provide blocks or tokens to the students. Ask the students to represent each sound of a word by a token or block inside of a grid of squares. Instruct students to move tokens into small boxes on a piece of paper (or laminated cardstock) as they say the sounds of words (e.g., *cat* = /c/ /a/ /t/). Use the same number of squares as sounds in the word for young students.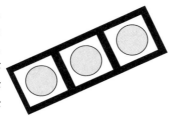

Note: For most students, phoneme blending comes easier than segmenting. However, there are some young readers who have special difficulties with auditory blending. When this is the case, blending and reading activities that include practice with onset-rime may be included in daily lessons. According to Adams (1990), research has shown that students who have persistent difficulty with auditory blending often experience success when instructed with phonograms (onset-rimes and word families). If needed, return to the previous onset-rime activity section to practice auditory blending, then move back into phoneme blending and segmentation again for repeated instruction and practice.

RESOURCES

Basic Phonological Awareness

Adams, M.J., Foorman, B.R., Lundberg, I., & Beeler, T. (1998). *Phonemic awareness in young children: A classroom curriculum.* Baltimore: Paul H. Brookes Publishing Co.

Blachman, B.A., Ball, E.W., Black, R., & Tangel, D.M. (2000). *Road to the code: A phonological awareness program for young children.* Baltimore: Paul H. Brookes Publishing Co.

Catts, H., & Olsen, T. (1993). *Sounds abound: Listening, rhyming, and reading.* East Moline, IL: LinguiSystems. (1-800-776-4332, http://www.linguisystems.com)

O'Connor, R.E., Notari-Syverson, A., & Vadasy, P.F. (2005). *Ladders to literacy: A kindergarten activity book* (2nd ed.). Baltimore: Paul H. Brookes Publishing Co.

Wagner, R., Torgesen, J., & Rashotte, C. (1999). *CTOPP–Comprehensive Test of Phonological Processing.* Austin, TX: PRO-ED. (Standardized phonological assessment with norms for ages 5–24, with several subtests provide a thorough picture of an individual's phonological processing; 1-800-897-3202, http://www.proedinc.com)

Webber, S.G. Webber photo cards. Greenville, SC: Super Duper Publications. (1-800-322-8737, http://www.superduperinc.com)

First Sound Fluency

Bear, D.R., Invernizzi, M., Templeton, S.R., & Johnston, F. (2007). *Words their way.* Upper Saddle River, NJ: Prentice Hall. (A "must have" for teachers of literacy of all ages, with ideas for sorting activities and other games to teach phoneme awareness, spelling, vocabulary, and phonics)

Birsh, J. (2005). *Multisensory teaching of basic language skills.* Baltimore: Paul H. Brookes Publishing Co. (The chapter by Joanna K. Uhry titled, "Phonological Awareness and Reading: Research, Activities, and Instructional Materials," is highly recommended for those who are looking for a better understanding of phonological awareness and for more ideas for how to improve phonological awareness in struggling readers.)

Neuhaus Education Center. (2002). *Reading readiness.* Bellaire, TX: Author. (This manual provides several activities for building phonological awareness skills that develop prior to being able to identify the initial sounds required in FSF, such as understanding *same* and *different,* identifying rhyming words, producing rhyming words, segmenting words in sentences, and segmenting syllables in words. The manual also provides activities for identifying initial and final sounds; http://www.neuhaus.org)

O'Connor, R.E. (2007). *Teaching word recognition: Effective strategies for students with learning difficulties.* New York: The Guilford Press. (This book contains informative, up-to-date chapters on 37 scientifically validated reading strategies in a well-organized and easy-to-read format. The phonemic awareness chapter includes topics on linking phonemic awareness, reading words, and activities to develop phonemic awareness. Information about children learning English as a second language is included along with assessing phonemic awareness.)

Robertson, C., & Salter, W. (1998). *Take home: Phonological awareness.* East Moline, IL: LinguiSystems. (1-800-776-4332, http://www.linguisystems.com)

Phoneme Segmentation Fluency

Blevins, W. (1999). *Phonemic awareness activities: For early reading success.* New York: Scholastic Publishing.

Blevins, W. (2006). *Phonics from A to Z: A practical guide* (2nd ed.). New York: Scholastic Publishing. (Even though the title suggests this is a book for teaching phonics, there is a section titled "35 Quick and Easy Activities for Developing Phonemic Awareness" with many appropriate games and activities for teaching phoneme segmentation and blending.)

Fitzpatrick, J. (1997). *Phonemic awareness: Playing with sounds to strengthen beginning reading skills.* Huntington Beach, CA: Creative Teaching Press. (This entire book is full of ideas for teaching phonemic awareness. It is conveniently divided into five levels of phonemic awareness so teachers can select activities in the level or stage most needed by their students. There are many reproducible resources for making games and activities for use as manipulatives and hands-on activities for students to enjoy. Caution is suggested in selecting activities. Sequence may differ from that traditionally accepted for teaching phonological awareness.)

Fredericks, A.D. (2001). *The complete phonemic awareness handbook.* Greenville, SC: Super Duper Publications. (This easy-to-use resource guide, with playful activities for Grades K–2, includes letters to parents for activities at home, reproducible phonograms, rhyming picture cards, animal picture cards, and word family lists.)

Honig, B., Diamond, L., & Gutlon, L. (2008). *CORE: Teaching reading sourcebook for kindergarten through eighth grade.* Novato, CA: Academic Therapy Publications. (This oversized book is a true encyclopedia of teaching reading, with a strong commitment to research-based practices. It contains many descriptions of phonological and phonemic awareness strategies and activities for use in the classroom. There is a particularly helpful chart on phonological awareness skills by level, in which the scope and sequence of phonological awareness is provided along with a description and example of each skill given. This chart helps emphasize the developmental nature of phonological awareness and phonemic awareness and the need to plan instruction accordingly.)

Hults, A. (2003). *Reading first: Unlock the secrets to reading success with research-based strategies.* New York: Scholastic Publishing. (This book provides a concise summary of the National Literacy Council's Put Reading First report with instructional activities in all five critical components of reading instruction—phonemic awareness, phonics, fluency, vocabulary, and comprehension—with many hands-on games and phonemic awareness activities for small groups.)

Phonics

EARLY PHONICS MEASURES: LETTER-NAMING KNOWLEDGE

	DIBELS	AIMSweb	TPRI	FAIR
Kindergarten	Letter Naming Fluency	Letter Naming Fluency	Letter Name Identification Inventory	Print Awareness Letter Name Knowledge (targeted direct assessment)
Grade 1	Letter Naming Fluency	Letter Naming Fluency		

Phonics is the lynchpin, embracing elements of print to represent oral language within a highly dependable, systematic structure. This chapter identifies multiple fluency measures and other formative assessments used to evaluate the alphabetic principle and phonics knowledge of students during various phases of reading skill development. Letter naming is addressed first, followed by instructional activities. Letter sound, word decoding assessments, and instructional tools follow.

INTRODUCTION

What Is Letter Naming Fluency?

Researchers have documented the importance of letter naming fluency (LNF) and accuracy as strong predictors of success in early and later reading. Some researchers claim that LNF is the single best predictor of reading failure (Elliott, Lee, & Tollefson, 2001; Hintze, Ryan, & Stoner, 2003). The purpose of the DIBELS/AIMSweb measure of LNF is to assess whether students can name letters accurately and fluently. This measure requires students to name randomly presented uppercase and lowercase letters for 1 minute. On TPRI and FAIR, accuracy of letter name knowledge is measured without a timed component. After saying the name of the letter, the student is asked to tell the sound the letter makes for a separate measure of letter-sound knowledge.

Letter recognition is an important beginning step in learning to read. Although most parents may not understand how to help their preschool or kindergarten child develop phonological awareness at home, parents often do teach their young children the *ABCs* and how to sing the alphabet song. According to Marilyn Adams (1990), knowing the letter names helps young readers associate the letter sounds because many of the sounds are embedded in the letter names. For example, when students say the letter name for *m,* they can hold onto and isolate the sound /m/. Letter and sound naming skills, along with phonemic awareness, for the beginning and middle of kindergarten predict grade-level performance on norm-referenced tests, according to the developers of FAIR (Foorman, 2008).

What Is the Relationship Between Letter Recognition and the Alphabetic Principle?

Letter recognition is a critical building block in the basic foundation of reading. It prepares the student for learning the alphabetic principle (i.e., letter-sound correspondences and blending; phonics)—one of the five essential components of early reading. Mature reading is accomplished not only through overall oral language development but also by a logical, ordered phonological progression that begins with the most basic phonological language concepts (e.g., onset-rimes, syllables) and builds to more demanding advanced linguistic expectations (e.g., sounds or phonemes). Mastery of early phonological awareness and instant letter recognition builds a strong foundation for learning letter-sound correspondence through systematic instruction.

Rather than devoting extended amounts of time working on isolated letter recognition skills, a more integrated approach is recommended. For example, within the context of developing phonemic awareness, knowledgeable teachers begin teaching the alphabetic principle. They may elect to teach letter recognition for short, 7- to 10-minute chunks of time and during additional "sponge" times interspersed throughout the school day (see Activities).

What Are the Steps for Teaching Letter Recognition?

1. Administer AIMSweb, DIBELS, TPRI, or FAIR benchmark assessments.

2. Analyze data. Identify letter names the student does not know. If between benchmark assessment periods, use the teacher-made Letter Naming Fluency Assessment Form (Figure 4.1) to identify the letters a student has not mastered.

3. Teach the unknown letters through multisensory approaches (visual, auditory, and kinesthetic).

4. Sequence steps of instruction from easiest to more difficult, matching letters, naming letters, and then sequencing letters.

5. Direct students to practice saying letter names while being timed to increase fluency.

6. Monitor progress to evaluate the effectiveness of classroom instruction.

Sample activities are provided in this section for teaching and practicing letter recognition and improving letter-naming fluency. For some of these learning activities, students will need a set of three-dimensional plastic letters, an alphabet matching mat, and/or an alphabet strip. See the Resource section at the end of this chapter for ordering information.

Letter-Naming Fluency
Assessment Form

k	J	B	O	W	h	q
a	V	f	T	X	d	u
M	s	P	c	E	n	Y
i	R	A	g	L	w	b
F	H	z	S	D	k	l

Figure 4.1. Letter-Naming Fluency Assessment Form.

Early Phonics Activities

TEACHING LETTER RECOGNITION

Two questions are helpful in determining where students should begin in this first letter recognition teaching activity:

1. Can the student name and place plastic 3-D letters on top of the printed letters on the alphabet mat within 5 minutes? If no, start with Step 1. If yes, proceed to the next question.

2. Can the student name and sequence the letters of the alphabet? If no, start with Step 2.

• • • • •

Step 1: Matching and Naming ABCs

Give each student an alphabet mat and a set of 3-D plastic uppercase letters. Instruct students to turn the letters right side up, oriented correctly inside the mat. Tell the students that these are letters we use to read and write. Next, point to the letters across the top of the mat. Lead the students to discover that the alphabet contains the 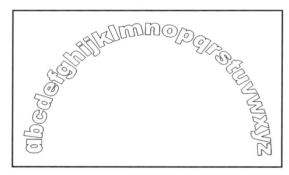 same letters in a certain, fixed order. Ask students to name each letter *before* they place the plastic letter on top of the printed letter on their mats. Instruct students to check their work by touching and naming their letters after each letter is placed. For example, a student says, "T" and touches the plastic letter sitting on top of the printed letter.

Goal: To be able to match all letters within 5 minutes. If students do not reach the goal the first day, the same activity is continued the following day, starting with the letters that were matched correctly the previous day and continuing with the remaining letters.

Once the student is successful with placing letters on top of printed forms, instruct students to place plastic letters beneath the printed letters at the top of the alphabet mat. Once students can place letters beneath letters at the top of the alphabet mat within 5 minutes, give them an arc without the printed letters. Direct students to place letters in the arc on the mat to begin learning the *ABC* sequence.

Step 2: Sequencing ABCs

On a chalkboard arc, write *A, M, N,* and *Z,* with *M* and *N* at the top of the arc, and *A* and *Z* at the beginning and end. Ask students to name and place the initial letter of the alphabet on their mats. Ask them to say, "*A* is the initial letter of the alphabet." Follow the same procedure with *Z,* saying, "*Z* is the final letter of the alphabet."

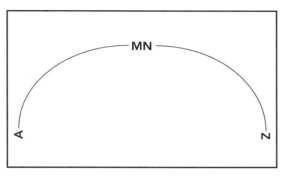

Then say, "Name it, find it, place it." Students should fill in the arc with missing letters until the arc is complete. Students may check their work by touching and naming each letter from *A* to *Z* with their index finger or writing hand. After students have had an opportunity to practice this activity, the teacher begins to time them.

Goal: Initially, the goal is accurate naming and placement of all letters in less than 5 minutes; however, the ultimate goal is 2 minutes or less.

Random Naming: Uppercase/Lowercase

Once students have learned to recognize and sequence letters it is time to work on improving accuracy and fluency. One way to do this is for a teacher to point to letters randomly on an alphabet strip and ask the student to name them, indentifying them as uppercase or lowercase. The teacher then notes both accuracy and relative speed. Plastic letters can be arranged randomly and the teacher and students can take turns pointing to and naming a letter. Alphabet letters can be written on the board with two students taking turns, one being the "teacher" and one being the student. One student can point to the letter while the other names it.

• • • • •

Match It

Give each student in the group a card with an alphabet letter written on it. Write a letter on the board and ask the student with that letter to come to the front and say the name of the letter. Request the sound, if previous instruction has included sounds. Divide the class of students in half. Write uppercase letters on half and lowercase letters on the other half of a set of cards. Give each child in one group the uppercase letter cards, while giving the children in the other group the lowercase letter cards. Ask students to find their uppercase or lowercase match and be ready to say the letter names.

• • • • •

Alphabet Bingo

For this game, each student will need an individual alphabet strip and a set of 3-D letters. To begin, students select any seven (or other teacher-determined number) letters from their container and place them on their desk in a vertical column on the left side of the desk. The unused letters are put away. The teacher selects

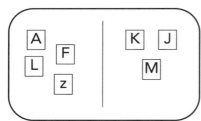

one letter from another container, shows it to the students, and names it. The students repeat the name. If the students have the letter on their desk, they move it to the right side of their desk, while saying the letter name. The first person to move all seven letters to the right side of his desk is the winner.

Note: This activity can also help improve directionality. You may want to consider having a dividing line down the middle of the desk.

• • • • •

Flashcards

Flashcards lend themselves to many activities for letter naming. Use a letter deck (deck of cards with the letters written or printed on them). Pairs of stu-

(continued)

(continued)

dents play, with one student showing the cards and the other naming the letters. Students can also pretend that they are the teacher and "play" this activity with the teacher, volunteer, or assistant.

Students may try to improve their speed recognizing and naming the letters. A timer can be used and individual student times can be recorded. Initially, students are instructed to make two piles, letters they know and ones they need to work on. This is an effective daily activity and also works well in learning centers.

Sponge Activities

Sponge activities are space fillers. When teachers have a few minutes between activities (e.g., waiting for announcements), they can fill these minutes with productive learning activities, such as the following:

- Write a letter on the board. Have all of the students whose names begin with that letter come to the front of the room, raise their hand, or stand up. They must repeat the letter and say their name. Repeat with other letters.
- Write a letter on the board. Ask for a volunteer to read the letter and then line up.
- Write a letter on the board. Ask for a volunteer to read the letter and find something in the room that begins with that letter. Make sure the room is labeled so that the students have words to choose from.
- Write a letter on the board. Ask for a volunteer to name that letter, as well as the letters that come before and after the target letter.

Tactile Practice

Provide lots of tactile involvement through sand trays, salt trays, instant pudding, shaving cream, hair gel, finger paints, clay and playdough, magnetic letters, edible alphabet, pretzels, and other edibles. Instruct students to say letter names as they trace and write letters (multisensory). Instruct students to glue macaroni onto letter forms and say letter names.

IMPROVING LETTER-NAMING FLUENCY

There are many ways that teachers can help students improve their fluency and auto-maticity of letter recognition once students have mastered overall letter recognition.

● ● ● ● ● ●

Teacher-Made Letter-Naming Fluency Practice

Teachers can type or write a random list of uppercase and lowercase letters on a grid form. Next, ask the student to say the names of as many letters as possible. The teacher gives the student 1 minute and then makes a note of how many letters were named cor-rectly and which letters were named incor-rectly or omitted. Giving the directions that are the same as those on the DIBELS or

Letter-Naming Fluency Assessment Form						
k	J	B	O	W	h	q
a	V	f	T	X	d	u
M	s	P	c	E	n	Y
i	R	A	g	L	w	b
F	H	z	S	D	k	l

AIMSweb measures will help your students become familiar with what is expected of them. The teacher may say, "Here are some letters [points to the student probe]. Tell me the names of as many letters as you can. Ready, begin." Say stop after about 1 minute. This practice can be done with or with-out being timed. It can also be adapted by asking the student to say the sound the letter makes after the student gives the letter name or in place of the let-ter name, which is more compatible with TPRI and FAIR tasks.

Note: This works best when the letters are printed in landscape format (horizontally). If handwritten, they should be printed with a marker so the stu-dent has no trouble recognizing the letter formation.

● ● ● ● ● ●

Developing Letter-Naming Fluency Skills

This activity is adapted from the Neuhaus Education Center (see Resources) and can be used with individuals, small groups, or the entire class. The follow-ing activity is designed for a whole class or small-group instruction. The teacher should follow the following steps:

(continued)

(continued)

1. Make a transparency of Figure 4.1 and place the transparency on the overhead projector.
2. Ask students to listen. Review and warm up by pointing to and saying the letters in the top row.
3. Repeat, with students naming the letters in the top row together with the teacher.
4. After the warm-up procedure, point to letters on the chart, starting with the top row and working across each successive row.
5. Ask students to name the letters in the squares.
6. Complete the activity by reviewing any troublesome letters. Randomly point to them on the chart by saying, "When I touch it, you name it." Students name the letters.
7. Continue this activity daily with subsequent charts. Identify only about six letters that the students have trouble with and use those six repeatedly in the chart so that there will be abundant practice and repetition for the students.

A blank form (Figure 4.2) is provided for teachers to create their own Letter-Naming Fluency Practice Forms.

Variation: Use this same form with individual students. Time each student's performance to see how many letters the student can name correctly in 1 minute. Chart each student's performance daily or at least three times a week. Bar graphs work well for charting. Students are highly motivated by seeing their progress documented in a tangible way. Be sure to identify which specific letters need to be taught. A sample chart is shown in Figure 4.3. A blank chart for graphing results is shown in Figure 4.4.

Alphabet Books

Teach letter names through literature. There are many delightful ABC books to choose from at local libraries and book stores. The Hennepin County Library in Minnetonka, Minnesota, has compiled a list of 40 alphabet books for young readers, including colorful book covers and annotated descriptions, at http://www.hclib.org/BirthTo6/booklistaction.cfm?list_num=597.

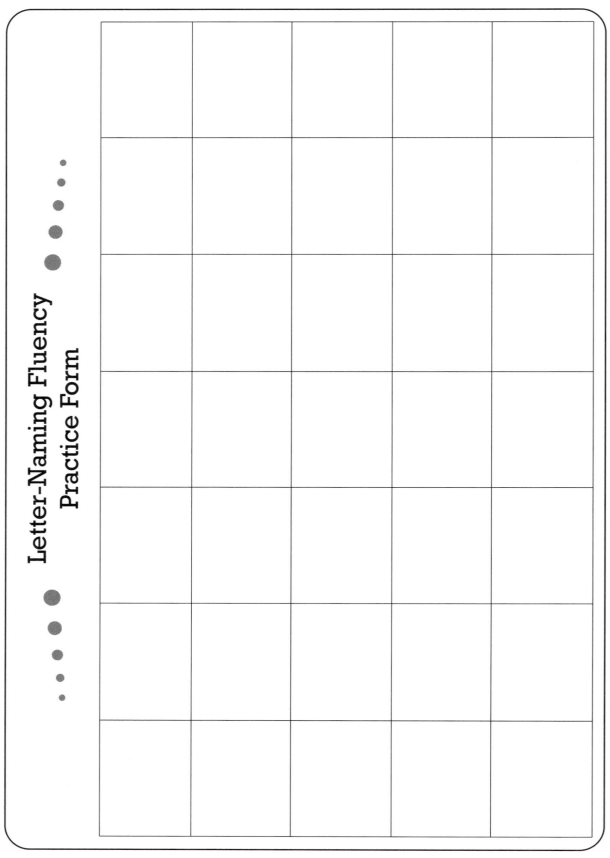

Figure 4.2. Blank Letter-Naming Fluency Practice Form.

Used with permission from Neuhaus Education Center, Bellaire, Texas. © Neuhaus Education Center. Permission to duplicate the forms for classroom use is granted.

In *Next STEPS in Literacy Instruction: Connecting Assessments to Effective Interventions* by Susan M. Smartt and Deborah R. Glaser. (2010, Paul H. Brookes Publishing Co., Inc.)

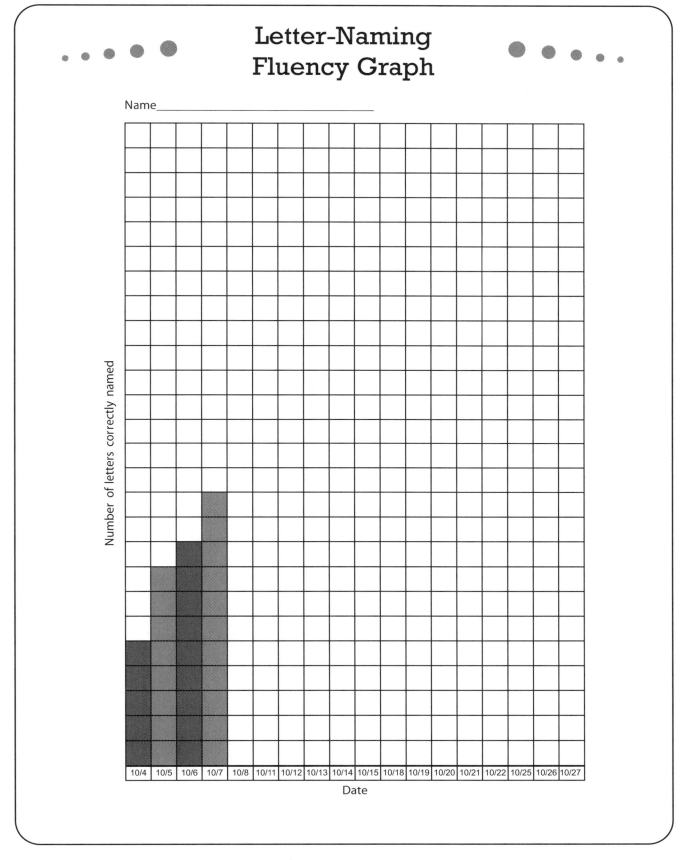

Figure 4.3. Sample Letter-Naming Practice Graph.

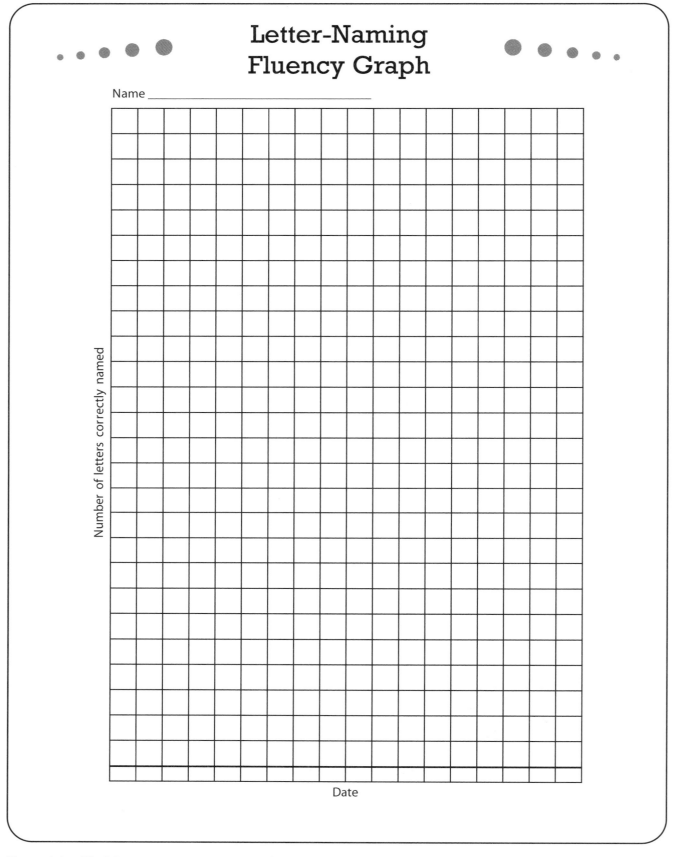

Letter-Naming Fluency Graph

Name _____

Number of letters correctly named

Date

Figure 4.4. Blank Letter-Naming Practice Graph.

THE DECODING MEASURES

	DIBELS	AIMSweb	TPRI	FAIR
Kindergarten	Nonsense Word Fluency (mid-year)	Letter Sound Fluency Nonsense Word Fluency (mid-year)	Letter Sound Identification (screening) Letter to Sound Linking (inventory) Word Reading	Letter Name and Sound Knowledge Letter Sound Connection Initial & Final Consonants Word Building: Initial & Final Consonants Word Building: Medial Vowels
Grade 1	Nonsense Word Fluency	Letter Sound Fluency Nonsense Word Fluency	Letter Sound Identification (screening) Graphophonemic Knowledge (inventory) Substitution: Initial, Final Consonant, Medial Vowel Blending in Final Position Word Reading	Letter Sound Knowledge Word Building: Consonants, Vowels, CVC /CVCe, Blends
Grade 2	Nonsense Word Fluency (beginning of year)		Graphophonemic Knowledge (inventory) Spelling of CVC, CVCe, long vowel words Orthographic patterns, conventions and past tense Orthographic patterns, conventions, and inflectional endings Word Reading	Word Building: Blends & Vowels Multisyllabic Word Reading
Grade 3			Word Reading	Word Analysis (targeted diagnostic inventory)

Formative assessments evaluate phonics knowledge in different ways. First, two fluency measures can be used to assess phonics skills: Letter Sound Fluency (LSF: AIMSweb) and Nonsense Word Fluency (NWF: DIBELS and AIMSweb). These assessments measure students' decoding abilities by how automatically they are able to say letter sounds and also how well they are able to recode or blend sounds to decode unfamiliar words within a 1 minute time frame.

Untimed measures such as Letter Sound Knowledge (LSK) and Letter Sound Connection (LSC) on the FAIR and Letter-to-Sound Linking (LSL) on the TPRI all measure a student's early decoding ability by calling on the student to recognize individual letters and companion sounds. At a more advanced level, they measure the student's recognition of sounds and their corresponding letters within words. This knowledge of phoneme–grapheme correspondence is a critical step in mastering the alphabetic principle. Expectations are increased on the FAIR Letter Sounds Connection task in which students are expected to begin to manipulate letters and word parts within words to form new words. At this point, students can demonstrate their knowledge of word structure and reflect expanded expertise in word recognition skills. These measures, in general, have equal or higher predictive ability to later general reading skills (Elliott et al., 2001; Hintze et al., 2003).

NWF measures the ability to decode (say the letter sound) and recode (blend the sounds together to say a word). Students are asked to read short, one-syllable nonsense words. Early literacy formative measures use a variety of letter sound tasks and nonsense word measures—some timed and some untimed—to assess how well students can apply decoding skills to reading words they do not know or recognize. LSF, LSL, LSC, and NWF help teachers to know whether young students' phonics skills are progressing at levels that will ensure fluent reading later. Performance on these tasks also helps to guide instructional decision making, identify specific instructional needs for planning differentiated instruction, and develop instructional goals. LSF and LSL assess letter sound and NWF assesses CVC patterns called closed syllables, which are the most common pattern in early phonics instruction. All vowel sounds are short on the LSF, LSL, and NWF measures.

More Advanced Decoding Measures

The Word Reading tasks (TPRI) assess students' proficiency with a wider range of phonics components, including consonant sounds, consonant blends, digraphs and trigraphs, short vowels, long vowels, vowel teams, vowel diphthongs, and irregular vowel patterns. Word Reading is comprised of 20 words grouped into four sets of five items; each set contains words with similar phonic elements or syllable patterns. Students are not timed during this task. Teachers may use the information from Word Reading in a variety of ways. For many students, teachers might gauge ability or progress by noting how many sets those students mastered (e.g., correctly read 4 of 5 words). However, for struggling readers, teachers may dig down to analyze knowledge of particular phonic elements or syllable types for targeted instruction.

The Word Building task (FAIR) is conducted with initial and final sounds, medial vowel sounds, blends, and even different syllable patterns, such as consonant–vowel–consonant (CVC) and consonant–vowel–consonant–silent *E* patterns. This measure provides clues into how well students can hear (distinguish) sounds, associate sounds with letters, and manipulate individual letters within words.

The Multisyllabic Word task (FAIR) is only administered to Grade 2 students who are given the Targeted Diagnostic Inventory (TDI) when there is a need to provide more in-depth study into the students' reading difficulties.

Why Is Learning to Decode Important?

A young or struggling reader faces tasks similar to ones that detectives confront. Detectives decode mysteries and readers decode words. Fortunately for readers, there is a consistent set of sounds that can be applied to letters and groups of letters (graphemes) to solve the mysteries. This application of sounds to letters to decode words is called *phonics.*

Studies have shown that the first strategy proficient readers apply when coming across an unfamiliar word is to sound it out. Studies that compare the brain activity of struggling readers with accomplished readers demonstrate how difficult this decoding process is for the struggling reader (Shaywitz, 2003). We also know that when students spend time analyzing words or decoding them, they are more likely to automatically recall that word the next time they come across it, thus enabling a more fluent reading process.

Decoding, or phonics, is the application of analysis that originates from the basic sound–symbol relationship of our written language. In other words, decoding can be thought of as converting the written or printed word into its spoken form. To solve the mystery or break the code, students use their knowledge of letter-sound relationships and/or word parts, which are critical elements in the reading process.

How Can Letter Sound Knowledge (AIMSweb, TPRI, and FAIR) Help with Planning Instruction?

When students score below benchmark on any of the letter-sound measures, a close analysis of responses will reveal some known and unknown letter sounds. By using this information, along with additional informal assessment, lessons can be designed to teach the unknown letter sounds and strengthen automatic letter-sound decoding. Several activities to improve letter-sound recognition and fluency are included in this chapter.

How Can Nonsense Word Fluency (DIBELS and AIMSweb) Help with Planning Instruction?

When students score below benchmark on a measure of reading nonsense words, a close analysis of responses, information gained from informal assessment with a phonics survey, and classroom performance will help determine the letter sounds and processes that need instruction. Inspect students' NWF responses, using the following questions as a guide.

1. Is the student at the sound-by-sound, whole word, or transition (some of both) decoding stage?
2. Is the student reading initial sounds only?
3. Is the student reading final sounds?
4. Is the student reading long vowels instead of short vowels?
5. Which short vowel sounds do you need to teach?
6. Which beginning or final consonants do you need to teach?
7. Was the student slow and accurate (i.e., single sounds mostly, but accurate)?
8. Was the student fast and inaccurate (i.e., blending well, but making errors on letter sounds)?
9. Are there any other observations to note?

After answering these questions, select from the phonics surveys described later in this chapter to help plan instruction that addresses the identified weak decoding areas.

How Can Word Building Tasks (FAIR) Help Guide Instructional Planning?

During the word-building tasks, students have a concrete way to demonstrate what and how they are thinking about phonemes and graphemes. As tasks are being administered and scored, close observation will yield specific information regarding whether or not students know initial or final sounds, medial vowels, blends, or even more complex syllable patterns.

How Can Word Reading Tasks (TPRI) Help Guide Instructional Planning?

The extensive phonics sequence included in the TPRI Word Reading tasks provides feedback on students' decoding skills mastery levels. The skills are presented in a reasonable instructional sequence that covers individual sounds up through complex units (e.g., irregular vowels, L-controlled, multisyllable). Teachers are asked to refer to their instructional reading programs for the sequencing of which phonics to teach and when. It is especially important to note whether a particular set of individual phonics patterns have not been taught and thus, are not expected to be mastered.

What's Next to Ensure Accelerated Reading Progress?

1. Collect and analyze errors for planning instructional routines.
2. Differentiate instruction.
3. Provide small-group instruction.
4. Use the *STEPS* lesson plan, incorporating the elements of teaching with abundant practice.
5. Include contextual practice (reading sentences and stories that provide abundant opportunities to read words that students are learning).

Additional Diagnostic Assessments

Quite often, additional assessment is required to gain more information about a student's decoding skills before planning lessons. For example, when students do not reach benchmark levels in oral reading fluency (ORF, R-CBM), rather than focusing intervention time on reading rate or fluency, it is usually more appropriate to determine which underlying alphabetic principle or decoding skill(s) may be weak or unknown. Informal decoding measures often accompany comprehensive reading programs; they can also be found within informal reading inventories. These assessments will provide more information about decoding strengths and weaknesses to assist with planning appropriate instruction. This section describes two informal surveys that can be used if further assessment is desired: Phonics Survey and Six Syllable Types—Plus!

Phonics Survey

Before administering the Phonics Survey, some teachers prepare the test by printing the words on 5" x 8" blank index cards (enlarging the font size) or cutting the page into strips so that only the words they want to present can be shown to the child. Teachers who choose to give the test on a full page can use a blank piece of paper to cover the items not being read.

When giving the Phonics Survey, the student is asked to read the words going across the row (see Figure 4.5) while the teacher circles the incorrect words on a separate scoring sheet (see Figure 4.6). The teacher reads the directions as given on the Teacher Form. Because this is an informal assessment, there are no standardized scores; however, teachers should consult the scope and sequence of their comprehensive reading program and their state standards to determine when mastery of each skill (e.g., initial and final consonants, short vowels, long vowels, blends, digraphs, *r*-controlled vowels) is expected and use that information as a guideline for planning the intensity and focus of instruction.

It is recommended that teachers record the decoding errors that students make in order to address sound symbol confusion. For example, if a student reads the nonsense word *maf* as *muv*, teachers would note a short *u* sound above the *a* in *maf* and a *v* above the *f*. This confusion indicates that the student may not be discriminating between similar vowel and consonant sounds; direct instruction to address these confusion errors is important.

Note: Current research findings are helping reading teachers understand that accuracy deserves critical attention when interpreting fluency measure outcomes (R-CBM, ORF). Fluency measure scores are reported as words correct per minute (WCPM), which reflects the errors made. Errors are subtracted from the total number of words read; therefore, the errors become a hidden piece of information unless teachers look at the percent accuracy score. Early studies indicate that teachers need to pay attention to accuracy levels, not just speed, when interpreting results. A goal of 95%–97% accuracy will lead to higher levels of reading comprehension.

Phonics Survey: Blending (Student Form)

lip	bat	get	nut	dog
bem	fap	hun	mot	sim
dag	jun	rit	neb	lom

thin	sham	when	chop	latch
split	glob	brim	block	clap
thut	thrum	glick	blem	brop
sath	splen	blesh	chod	clep

late	bone	cute	dime	Pete
dute	cede	drime	plove	pake
sone	trobe	mide	lete	mune

park	burn	fern	core	stir
turp	mir	vor	herp	har
tark	lerd	garn	bort	fler

day	round	paid	coin	boat
doud	woaf	faul	taw	fleach
zoin	dail	spound	prew	glay

cactus	compute	locate	cable	barber
pitten	zombat	sublish	motate	excrode
duppet	brinish	monfuse	aboke	dateful

Figure 4.5. Phonics Survey: Blending (Student Form).

Phonics Survey: Blending (Teacher Form)

Instructions: "I want you to read some words for me. Some of them will be real words and others will be nonsense words. I will tell you when the rows are real or nonsense." First rows in each section are real. Use a line marker to cover up lower rows as the student reads. Record student responses. This assessment can be given in parts at separate times.

Name: _____ Date: _____

lip	bat	get	nut	dog
bem	fap	hun	mot	sim
dag	jun	rit	neb	lom

CVC Score: ____ /15

thin	sham	when	chop	latch
split	glob	brim	block	clap
thut	thrum	glick	blem	brop
sath	splen	blesh	chod	clep

Blends and Digraphs Score: ____ /20

late	bone	cute	dime	Pete
dute	cede	drime	plove	pake
sone	trobe	mide	lete	mune

CVCe Score: ____ /15

park	burn	fern	core	stir
turp	mir	vor	herp	har
tark	lerd	garn	bort	fler

R-Controlled Score: ____ /15

day	round	paid	coin	boat
doud	woaf	faul	taw	fleach
zoin	dail	spound	prew	glay

Vowel Combinations Score: ____ /15

cactus	compute	locate	cable	barber
pitten	zombat	sublish	motate	excrode
duppet	brinish	monfuse	aboke	dateful

Two Syllable/Syllable Types Score: ____ /15

Comments:

Figure 4.6.   Phonics Survey: Blending (Teacher Form).

Six Syllable Types—Plus!

Six Syllable Types—Plus! is another phonics screener that can be used for assessment and informal progress monitoring. All students should be familiar with the six syllable types by the end of second grade. Teachers can develop targeted intervention programs around their students' phonics knowledge (or lack of knowledge) gleaned from this assessment. Students are asked to read the following items:

- Real and nonsense syllables representing the six syllable patterns
- Words and syllables with soft *c* and *g*
- Words and syllables with /z/ spelled *s*
- Words and syllables with the trigraphs *-tch* and *-dge*
- Multisyllable words
- Words with the common endings *-s, -ed, -ing, -er, -est,* and *-y*
- A sampling of phonetically irregular sight words

The summary sheet, student version, and teacher form for Six Syllable Types—Plus! are provided in Figures 4.7–4.9. Instructions recommend that the teacher circle words read incorrectly or omitted by the student and write the substituted word in the adjacent empty space. Within each test section, there are 15 small boxes provided for adding progress monitoring scores when Six Syllable Types—Plus! is used as a progress monitoring tool. Some may elect to use this instrument only for pre- and posttest measures and others will determine that it may serve a progress monitor function in their classrooms. Graphing the progress as students learn fundamental phonic elements will prove to be a rewarding activity for many.

Other phonics surveys are readily available; some examples are provided in the Resources section at the end of the chapter.

Why Is a Phonics Skills Sequence Important?

There are many different phonics skills sequences, but the most effective ones share a common characteristic: the order in which sound spellings are introduced. Consonants are introduced first because they are easier than vowels. Consonants with high utility, that are easy to discriminate (both auditorially and visually), and that have the highest frequency of use are typically presented first (e.g., *s, m, t, f, b, r*). These consonants are called *continuant sounds,* which means they make a prolonged or stretched-out sound. It is easier for beginning readers to hear their sounds separate from other sounds. After a few consonants are learned, a vowel will be taught to allow for blending and making real words to read. The short vowels *a* and *o* may be introduced as the first short vowels because of their ease in discrimination. Gradually, more consonant and vowel spellings are introduced, with ample opportunities to master each set of sounds before adding new ones. Digraphs follow the gradual introduction of a few single-letter sound spellings and blends are introduced next. Jeanne Chall (1996, p. 105) described phonics instruction as being designed to go from easy to hard. It should be "just right" in difficulty—not too hard and not too easy.

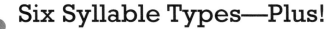

Six Syllable Types—Plus!

Phonics Screener for Progress
Monitoring: Summary Sheet

Teacher: _____ Student: _____ Date: _____

Single Syllables	Real words	Nonsense words	Initial testing		Percent correct	
			Date	Total score	Pre	Post
1. **Closed Syllable** a. **Single Consonant** Short vowel: cvc	__/10	__/10				
b. **Consonant Combinations** Short vowel; digraphs, blends: ccvc, cvcc, ccvcc	__/10	__/10				
2. **Open Syllable** One vowel at the end of the syllable; vowel "says its name"	__/10	__/10				
3. **Vowel-Consonant-*E* Syllable** One vowel, followed by one consonant, followed by *e*. Vowel says long sound; *e* is silent: cvce	__/10	__/10				
4. **Vowel + *R* Syllable** One vowel, followed by *r*. The *r* controls the vowel. Together they form one sound.	__/10	__/10				
5. **Vowel Team Syllable** More than one letter spells the vowel sound.	__/10	__/10				
6. **Consonant + *le* Syllable** One consonant followed by *le*; makes its own syllable at the end of a word	__/10	__/10				
Plus:	__/10	__/10				
7. **Soft *c, g*; *s* /z/; *tch, dge***	__/10	__/10				
8. **Multisyllable Words**	__/10	__/10				
9. **Words with Common Endings** (*s, ed, ing, er, est, y*)	__/10	__/10				
10. **Phonetically Irregular (Sight) Words**	__/20					

Figure 4.7. Six Syllable Types—Plus! Phonics Screener for Progress Monitoring—Summary Sheet (blank).

Next STEPS in Literacy Instruction: Connecting Assessments to Effective Interventions by Susan M. Smartt and Deborah R. Glaser
Copyright © 2010 by Paul H. Brookes Publishing Co. All rights reserved.

Six Syllable Types—Plus!

Phonics Screener for Progress Monitoring: Student Version

Instructions: Enlarge and display one set per card (1a. words on index card, 1b. words on separate index card, and so forth). Number each card on back.

Instructions for student: "I want you to read each line of words out loud. Some of the words are real and some are nonsense words. You aren't expected to know all of the words. Just do the best you can." (Discontinue testing on each card if a student cannot read two or more real words in each line.)

1a.

top	fed	mom	lid	hug
lip	bat	get	nut	dog
bem	fap	gub	sot	lim
dag	cun	rit	neb	hom

1b.

thin	sham	when	chop	bath
split	glob	brim	block	clap
thut	trum	glick	blem	brop
sath	splen	blesh	chod	clep

2.

she	no	we	fly	hi
me	spy	I	go	my
wo	ki	che	mo	fe
ru	de	fo	ri	lu

3.

side	tube	robe	made	hope
late	bone	cute	dime	Pete
fute	cede	drime	plove	pake
sone	trobe	mide	lete	mune

(continued)

Figure 4.8. Six Syllable Types—Plus! Phonics Screener for Progress Monitoring: Student Version.

(continued)

4.

curb	her	bird	part	fort
park	burn	fern	core	fir
turp	mir	chor	herp	har
tark	lerd	marn	bort	curp

5.

day	joy	paid	coin	boat
round	loaf	haul	paw	bleach
zoin	dail	spound	prew	glay
woon	neek	fie	dight	slue

6.

tumble	candle	bottle	circle	purple
cable	riddle	miracle	able	bugle
starble	sigle	tizle	robcle	somple
nogle	zoble	moodle	makle	critle

7.

edge	cell	hose	itch	patch
catch	bridge	rice	fence	cent
gen	cif	ratch	podge	facy
mence	detch	motch	cim	gid

8.

cactus	compute	locate	cable	barber
instrument	fantastic	photograph	sacrifice	envelope
tumpest	motate	zombat	danby	sublish
supertant	manotop	tillophen	tumpastic	binderly

9.

better	puppies	animals	bigger	handed
jumping	kitten	cupful	dropped	finest
voys	rinning	mipped	rappy	meps
hoding	smorty	sloces	drepped	tillest

10.

was	have	what	one	mother
where	said	does	pull	could
nothing	many	today	shall	laugh
above	thought	whose	toward	honest

Six Syllable Types—Plus!

Phonics Screener for Progress Monitoring: Teacher Scoring Sheet

Instructions: Use this form to record individual students' responses. Scoring boxes are provided for only pre- and posttesting *or* progress monitoring over 17 intervals.

Teacher: _____   Student: _____

1a. Closed syllable:
cvc

top	fed	mom	lid	hug
lip	bat	get	nut	dog
bem	fap	gub	sot	lim
dag	cun	rit	neb	hom

	PRE						PROGRESS MONITORING									POST	
Date																	
Score	__/20																__/20

1b. Consonant combinations:
ccvc, cvcc, ccvcc

thin	sham	when	chop	bath
split	glob	brim	block	clap
thut	trum	glick	blem	brop
sath	splen	blesh	chod	clep

	PRE						PROGRESS MONITORING									POST	
Date																	
Score	__/20																__/20

2. Open syllable:
cv, ccv

she	no	we	fly	hi
me	spy	I	go	my
wo	ki	che	mo	fe
ru	de	fo	ri	lu

	PRE						PROGRESS MONITORING									POST	
Date																	
Score	__/20																__/20

(continued)

Figure 4.9. Six Syllable Types—Plus! Phonics Screener for Progress Monitoring: Teacher Scoring Sheet.

(continued)

3. Vowel–consonant-*E* syllable: cvc-e

side	tube	robe	made	hope
late	bone	cute	dime	Pete
fute	cede	drime	plove	pake
sone	trobe	mide	lete	mune

	PRE						PROGRESS MONITORING												POST
Date																			
Score	__/20																		__/20

4. Vowel + *R* syllable

curb	her	bird	part	fort
park	burn	fern	core	fir
turp	mir	chor	herp	har
tark	lerd	marn	bort	curp

	PRE						PROGRESS MONITORING												POST
Date																			
Score	__/20																		__/20

5. Vowel team syllable

day	joy	paid	coin	boat
round	loaf	haul	paw	bleach
zoin	dail	spound	prew	glay
woon	neek	fie	dight	slue

	PRE						PROGRESS MONITORING												POST
Date																			
Score	__/20																		__/20

6. Consonant + *le* syllable

tumble	candle	bottle	circle	purple
cable	riddle	miracle	able	bugle
starble	sigle	tizle	robcle	somple
nogle	zoble	moodle	makle	critle

	PRE						PROGRESS MONITORING												POST
Date																			
Score	__/20																		__/20

(continued)

7. Soft *c*, *g*; *s* /z/; *tch*, *dge*

edge	cell	hose	itch	patch
catch	bridge	rice	fence	cent
gen	cif	ratch	podge	facy
mence	detch	motch	cim	gid

	PRE						PROGRESS MONITORING											POST
Date																		
Score	__/20																	__/20

8. Multisyllable words

cactus	compute	locate	cable	barber
instrument	fantastic	photograph	sacrifice	envelope
tumpest	motate	zombat	danby	sublish
supertant	manotop	tillophen	tumpastic	binderly

	PRE						PROGRESS MONITORING											POST
Date																		
Score	__/20																	__/20

9. Words with common endings

better	puppies	animals	bigger	handed
jumping	kitten	cupful	dropped	finest
voys	rinning	mipped	rappy	meps
hoding	smorty	sloces	drepped	tillest

	PRE						PROGRESS MONITORING											POST
Date																		
Score	__/20																	__/20

10. Phonetically irregular (sight) words

was	have	what	one	mother
where	said	does	pull	could
nothing	many	today	shall	laugh
above	thought	whose	toward	honest

	PRE						PROGRESS MONITORING											POST
Date																		
Score	__/20																	__/20

Research has not endorsed one sequence for phonics instruction over another as being more effective. Most important, a sequence should be followed and applied. Planning and following lessons based on a phonics skill sequence ensures that learning is systematic and progressive, with one skill building on the next and with each step supporting the previous in a cumulative process.

Figure 4.10 provides an example of a skills sequence by Traub and Bloom (2003). It is a classic systematic phonics program effective for teaching phonics intervention groups. (It should be read in list form starting with the first column on the left side, then the middle list, then the final list on the right). This sequence can be referenced to guide instruction if no other skills sequence is available. Use a good word source book (*see* Resources) to find word items for teaching the phonic elements when designing individual and small-group lessons.

How Does One Develop Target Word Lists for Instruction?

This manual provides practice activities to be used for strengthening decoding skills; the teacher must prepare the target word lists that will be used during the practice activity instruction of *STEPS*. Teachers are advised to use words provided in their reading programs and, if desired, to add additional word items for practice. To prepare an extended target word list (one that includes additional word items for students to practice decoding), teachers need 1) a list of phonic elements with which students are not fluent, and 2) a word source book that categorizes words by phonic element (e.g., words that contain *ow* are grouped together). Several word source books are listed in the Resources section at the end of this chapter.

What Is the Role of Decodable Text?

When students are developing decoding skills, it is important that they have many opportunities to practice these skills in context. This practice can be accomplished by reading decodable books. Decodable texts are books made up primarily of the phonetic elements that have already been taught to the students. By having students read decodable texts, their new phonics skills are reinforced in an integrated format. Students are more readily assured of immediate successful reading experiences, and the chances for increasing their reading fluency and reading comprehension for the long term are increased. Decodable text sources are listed in the Resources section of this chapter.

What Should We Expect Elementary Students to Accomplish in Phonics?

The National Research Council (1998) listed accomplishments in phonics for children in K–3 on the normal course of literacy development. Although the timing will vary among young children, teachers should be prepared to teach these accomplishments so that all students can achieve them. Teachers can use these lists of accomplishments, along with their state standards and core reading program scope and sequence guides, to make sure that they are teaching the necessary components of reading at each grade level and that each child achieves their benchmarks.

Recipe for Reading Sequence Chart

First group
(c-o-a-d-g-m-l-h-t)
i (as in igloo)
j
k
p
ch (as in chin)
u (as in up)
b
r
f
n
e (as in egg)
s (as in sit)
sh
th (hard-as in that)
w
wh
y (as in yes)
v
x
z
th (soft-as in thin)
qu (as in queen)
Review tests: CVC words
Two-syllable compound words
Spelling rule: ff-ll-ss
Detached syllables
Review tests: CVC detached syllables
Two-syllable words
Consonant blends
Review tests: Consonant blends
Detached syllables: Consonant blends
Review tests: Detached syllable-consonant blends

Two-syllable words using consonant blends
Endings: ing-ang-ong-ung-ink-ank-onk-unk
"Magic e"
Review tests using "Magic e" words
Detached syllable "Magic e"
Two-syllable words containing "Magic e"
ph (as in phone)
ea (as in eat)
oa (as in soap)
ai (as in mail)
ee (as in tree)
ay (as in play)
oe (as in toe)
Syllable division
Review tests: Two-syllable words
er (as in her)
ir (as in bird)
ur (as in burn)
ow (as in clown)
ou (as in ouch)
igh (as in light)
Endings: ble-fle-tle-dle-gle-kle-ple-zle
ild-old-ind-ost-olt
ar (as in star)
or (as in horn)
oo (as in zoo)
Endings: ly-vy-by-dy-ty-fy-ny-py-sy
ck (as in black)
Hard-soft c
Hard-soft g
ge – dge

Review: Hard-soft c and g
"y" as a vowel
Long vowel in syllable division
aw (as in straw)
au (as in August)
a (as in ball)
oi (as in oil)
oy (as in boy)
"ing" as an *Ending*
VCV spelling rule
Suffix: "ed"
ew (as in grew)
tch (as in catch)
eigh (as in eight)
ie (as in chief)
eu (as in Europe)
ei (as in ceiling)
tion (as in action)
ue (as in rescue)
sion (as in division)
ow (as in snow)
ch (as in school)
ea (as in head)
oo (as in good)
ew (as in few)
ei (as in vein)
ue (as in true)
ou (as in group)
sion (as in mansion)
ea (as in great)
ch (as in machine)
s (as in is)
Affixes and root words
Spelling with affixes

Figure 4.10. Recipe for reading sequence chart. (From Traub & Bloom, 2003. Used by permission of Educators Publishing Service, Cambridge, MA, 1-800-225-5750, www.epsbooks.com)

For kindergarten students, accomplishments should include the following:

- The student can recognize and name all uppercase and lowercase letters.
- The student understands that the sequence of letters in a written word represents the sequence of sounds (phonemes) in a spoken word (alphabetic principle).

- The student has learned many—although not all—one-to-one letter-sound correspondences.
- The student can recognize some sight words immediately, including a few very common ones (e.g., *a, the, I, my, you, is, are*).

For first-grade students, accomplishments should include the following:

- The student has made the transition from emergent to "real" reading.
- The student can accurately decode orthographically regular, one-syllable words and nonsense words (e.g., *sit, zot*) using print-sound mappings to sound out unknown words.
- The student can use letter-to-sound correspondence knowledge to sound out unknown words when reading text.
- The student can recognize common, irregularly spelled words by sight (e.g., *have, said, where, two*).
- The student monitors his or her own reading and self-corrects when an incorrectly identified word does not fit with cues provided by the letters in the word or the context surrounding the word.
- The student can count the number of syllables in a spoken word.

For second- and third-grade students, accomplishments should include the following:

- The student can accurately decode orthographically regular, multisyllable words and nonsense words (e.g., *capital, Kalamazoo*).
- The student uses knowledge of print-sound mappings to sound out unknown words.
- The student can accurately read many irregularly spelled words and such spelling patterns as diphthongs, special vowel spellings, and common word endings.
- The student uses letter-to-sound correspondence knowledge and structural analysis to decode words.

Teaching Morphology Is Phonics Instruction, Too: Advanced Phonics

Historically, phonics instruction was perceived as the traditional beginning process of learning sound (phoneme) and symbol (grapheme) correspondences. Indeed, this is the basic decoding assessed by fluency measures (letter sound, nonsense word, and word identification) and is necessary for novice readers to learn and apply automatically while they read. Educators typically believe that phonics instruction should end once students have learned the basic decoding skills. Although the content of basic phonics ends usually around third grade (or is reviewed occasionally as needed) once students have mastered the basic set of grapheme spellings, we strongly advise that advanced phonics then becomes the target of word analysis instruction, continuing through the intermediate grades and into high school.

Advanced phonics embraces word study beyond the correspondences of phoneme and grapheme to include meaningful chunks of words—morphemes. For example, the word *restrain* has two morphemes: *re* (meaning "again") and *strain* (meaning "to bind tight"). *Restrained* has three morphemes, with *-ed* adding a third meaningful part, indicating past tense. These three morphemes compose visual and meaningful units that, when recognized as whole units for reading and oral language, assist with fluent decoding. In fact, researchers have found a relationship between morphology skills and single-word decoding and reading fluency in both beginning readers and struggling older readers (Norton & Wolf, 2008). Knowledge of morphology affects phonological awareness, orthographic skills, and vocabulary skills (Berninger & Wolf, 2009). Thus, teachers should not *restrain* themselves from teaching morphology!

Even though early phonics instruction is justifiably focused on the basics of sound–symbol relationships, it has become clear that young readers also benefit from instruction focused on understanding of meaningful parts of words—morphology (Berninger & Wolf, 2009). Moats (2004) found that young students are limited in the knowledge they bring to writing words with inflectional endings, such as past tense (*-ed*), and urged educators to begin teaching the morphemes that even young children encounter in their reading, writing, and speech early with continued explicit instruction over time.

What are the restraints to teaching morphology? Many teachers do not understand the term or concept of *morpheme*. To acquaint teachers with morphemes and the teaching of morphemes, here are a few suggestions for teachers that will benefit all students:

1. This text contains the most frequently used affixes and roots. They are listed in Chapter 5 because automatic recognition of word parts assists students with developing increased reading fluency. However, creating morpheme awareness through instruction can happen during any reading or content area lesson.

2. Teachers should prepare lessons with an eye for the vocabulary with common morpheme units such as the affixes and roots listed in Chapter 5.
    - Preteach the vocabulary through the phonological channels (e.g., "I say the word and then you say the word").
    - Provide a student-friendly definition based on the context in which students will be reading the word and within contexts that are familiar to students.
    - Ask students to read the word, then show and tell them the meanings of the parts of the word.
    - Ask students to repeat what they have learned, then to write the word and its meaning.

3. Teachers may need to hone their morphology skills, too. Use a good dictionary to research the morphemes and their meanings for the words students will encounter in their reading or in read-alouds provided by the teacher.

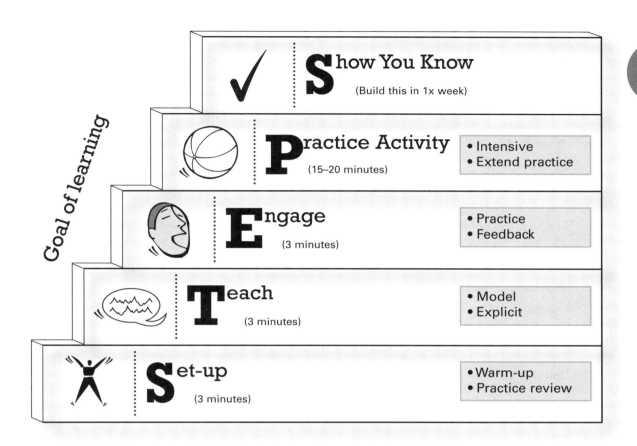

HERE WE GO: READY TO TEACH!

Follow along as we take a glimpse into a real second-grade classroom to observe Mr. Chapman using the STEPS Small-Group Reading Lesson format to teach his students who are struggling with early decoding skills.

Inside A Real Classroom: A Phonics Lesson Snapshot

Mr. Chapman has identified a group of his second-grade students whose scores on an NWF assessment were below benchmark levels. These students have not acquired basic decoding and recoding (blending sounds to say a word) skills with simple CVC pattern words. Two out of five of the students are well established in phoneme awareness, but the others are not and will also need additional instruction to develop phoneme segmentation skills. Mr. Chapman knows that phoneme awareness is essential to the development of decoding ability.

Mr. Chapman developed a phonics lesson to cover a week's worth of small-group instruction. None of the students are solid on short vowel sounds and blending to read words, so the lesson is focused on teaching those skills. He will also include review of the phonic elements that are taught during the core whole-group reading lesson. He knows he will need to generate word lists for each day's lesson. The words he chooses will reflect the letter sounds students need work on.

Progress monitoring using nonsense word reading will begin in 2 weeks and will continue every 2 weeks thereafter as RTI is measured. The two students with low phoneme seg-

mentation scores are also scheduled for progress monitoring of that skill. Here is what his lessons looked like, along with a script.

Set-up

Students will segment sounds in three sound words using Head-Waist-Toes (see Chapter 3 Activities).

Teacher: "Let's get ready to read some words today by first saying all of the sounds in some words. Everybody stand up! Let's play Head-Waist-Toes. First word: *sun.* Say it."

Students: "Sun."

Teacher: "Watch me. [Teacher segments sounds while touching head, waist, and toes.] /s/ /u/ /n/. Do it with me."

Students: [while touching head, waist, and toes] "/s/ /u/ /n/."

Teacher: "Touch your waist. What sound?"

Students and teacher: "/u/."

Teacher: "Good! Here is another word: *map.* Say it."

Students: "Map!"

Teacher: "Head, waist, toes together."

Students and teacher: "/m/ /a/ /p/."

Teacher: "Touch your waist. What sound?"

Students: "/a/."

The teacher repeats the process with several more words: *job, met,* and *chip.*

Teach

The teacher will demonstrate, show, and model the decoding and blending of letter sounds to read cvc words. The teacher says, "Watch me. I am going to read this word. I will touch each letter and say its sound. Then I will say the sounds together to read the word. My turn."

The teacher writes the word *sun* on the white board. He touches each letter and says each sound. He then runs his finger under the letters, blending the sounds together. "*Sun.* Watch me sound out another word. First, I say the sounds, then I blend them together to read the word."

The teacher then repeats the process with two more words, *man* and *sit.*

Engage

Students segment and blend the sounds to read words with the teacher.

Teacher: "Now it is your turn to read some words with me. Let's say the letter sounds and then blend the sounds together to read the word." [Teacher writes words one at a time and proceeds with the process, doing it with the students. Mr. Chapman closely observes (monitors) student performance, noting any difficulties or ease with the task.]

Teacher and students: [Touch each sound and read a series of words that reflect all of the short vowels: *not, mud, did, fat, fed.*]

Teacher: "Nice job saying the sounds and blending the sounds together to read these words. Let's read some words using the letter sounds we learned this morning."

The teacher then reteaches the sound–symbol relationship students learned earlier. He presents words that students read during whole-group lesson for review and additional practice. He models touching the letters and blending the sounds to read, just like the students have been doing with CVC words. Then the students do it with him.

Practice Activity

Mr. Chapman has decided to use Letter Flip (*see* Activities) as a practice activity this week. He carefully chooses beginning and ending consonants and consonant digraphs that the students have learned, and places each of the five vowel letters *a, e, i, o,* and *u* in the middle.

Teacher: "Now it is your turn to sound out and read some words. We'll make words with this flip chart and read them. Some of the words will be real words and some of the words will be nonsense words. You will use your white boards and markers to write the real words you read. Here is the first one. All together, say each sound and then blend the sounds to read the word."

Students: [Say each sound as the teacher points to it. Then when the teacher runs his finger under the letters, students say the word.]

Teacher: [Repeats the word.] "Is _____ a real word or a pretend (nonsense) word?"

Students: [Respond with "real word" or "pretend word."]

Teacher: [Uses the word in a sentence if it is real] "Write the word on your boards."

The teacher then asks one student, "Which letter shall we change?" The student points to the first, middle, or last letter and the teacher flips it to reveal a new letter underneath. The teacher calls on one student to read it. All students respond "yes" or "no" (thumbs up or thumb down) indicating whether it is a real word and all write it on their boards if it is a real word. The teacher repeats the process until all students have read two or three words.

 ## Show You Know

Each student will read the words that they have collected on their white boards as an individual check on how well they can read cvc words independently. The teacher notes any errors or hesitations and will include these "hot spots" in the lesson tomorrow. Before the students leave the small group, Mr. Chapman asks them to read words from the whole-group reading lesson. He chooses to use flashcards for this practice. Students pair up and read them to each other as Mr. Chapman monitors their reading.

Individual & Small-Group Activities

INDIVIDUAL AND SMALL-GROUP ACTIVITIES

Intense, Systematic, and Explicit Instruction Are Key Elements

The activities listed in this section are appropriate for individualized and small-group instruction. However, for these (or any other) activities in this curriculum to be effective, they must be delivered with these proven teaching elements that will ensure success:

- *Intense:* Instruction is frequent, provided in small groups with multiple student responses. Students are held to high levels of performance, are given numerous opportunities to practice, and have their progress monitored.
- *Systematic:* Lessons follow a skills sequence. Students are given multiple opportunities to practice the skills they are taught, and the lessons provide word items that gradually progress from simple to complex. Learning is planned in a step-by-step process.
- *Explicit:* Students are provided with explanations, direct teaching, and modeling of the process with the purpose of helping students make connections and activating background knowledge. Multiple examples (and even nonexamples) are given. Pacing and content may be adapted to meet the needs of individuals and small groups.

Decoding

Explicit, systematic phonics instruction is best accomplished with a reading program that applies a well-designed skills sequence and supplies decodable and controlled text for students to practice the decoding skills they learn (Foorman et al., 1998). Teachers can use data from the formative assessments listed above (DIBELS, AIMSweb, TPRI, FAIR), from core reading program assessments, and from phonics screeners or surveys such as those found in this book to isolate the letter-sound combinations with which students are not yet fluent, then focus instruction on these areas using any of the practice activities below. These activities are meant to supplement core reading program lessons and to plan practice activities in the *STEPS* lesson for necessary reinforcement and acceleration of reading growth.

● ● ● ● ●

Flashcard Fun! Letter-Sound Practice

Letter Sound Fluency (LSF), Letter Sound Knowledge (LSK), Letter-to-Sound Linking (LSL), Letter Sound Connections (LSC)

Flashcards have high utility for practicing many reading skills. All it takes is a little time to create the flashcards and lots of creativity to think of different

(continued)

(continued)

ways to use them. (For teachers who would rather purchase flashcards, ordering information is provided in the Resource section). Here are a few ideas for using flashcards to teach and practice letter sounds.

Making the Flashcards

Use the core reading program skills sequence as a source for letter sounds, practicing the letter sounds that have been introduced and adding others as lessons progress. Letter sounds that students did not know on the assessment may also be included. Write lowercase letters on 3" x 5" cards for small-group use and 5" x 7" cards for whole-group or circle-time use. Include several letter cards for the letter sounds that are not mastered to provide multiple opportunities for practice with the more difficult letter sounds.

Preparing the Flashcard Pack

Order the letter cards so that for every five cards, students will know three or four of the letter sounds well. This way, students will experience greater success with the task and there will be less chance for overload when learning new letter sounds.

Core Reading Materials

Many programs include two or three sizes of letter-sound cards that come with the reading program materials: one size for whole class display, one for small group, and one for individual students to handle. Take advantage of these letter-sound cards to use as daily reminders for individuals to practice associations of sound, picture and letter name. Teach students to associate the picture on the letter card with the sound and letter and be able to repeat in a drill-like fashion, "*A, apple, /a/; B, ball, /b/; C, cat, /c/*"; and so forth.

• • • • •

Oh, Oh!

This game is played with a small group. Place two or three cards that say *Oh, Oh!* in the deck of sound cards. Students sit at a reading table with the teacher. Students take turns saying the sounds for letters as the teacher flips through the deck of letter-sound cards. Each student takes their card when they say the sound correctly. The student whose turn  gets an *Oh, Oh!* card must place all of his or her cards back into the deck, and play then resumes around the table.

• • • • •

What a Deal

Deal each student five cards. Students place the cards face up left to right on the table in front of them and practice saying the letter sounds, with the teacher's help if needed. Each student then says his or her sounds while pointing to them. All cards are collected and the process is repeated as many times as desired.

• • • • •

Quick Flash

This activity has several variations:

1. *Choral response:* All students respond when teacher flashes the cards.
2. *"Be ready" response:* The teacher randomly calls on students to say the letter sound on the flashcard. Students do not know who will be next, so they are always ready.
3. *Timed response:* The teacher times a student to see how long it takes to say all letter sounds in the deck. Incorrect answers or hesitations are placed in a separate pile during the timing for review.
4. *Back in the deck:* Students get the cards that they say correctly. When a student hesitates or does not know a letter sound, the teacher tells the student the correct response, then slides the card back into the deck for another practice try.

• • • • •

Concentration

Create a set of cards with two cards for each sound. Sounds can be repeated to speed up the game and provide multiple exposures to difficult sounds. Limit the total sounds to no more than 10 (for a total of 20 cards). Lay the cards face down in two separate groups, with each group having one set of sounds so that the pairs can be made with one from each group. Students take turns turning over one card from one group, saying the letter sound, and then turn-

(continued)

(continued)

ing over a card from the second group, saying the sound, and taking the pair if the sounds match. If they do not match, the cards are returned to their face-down position.

Note: Many of the flashcard activities for learning sounds can be modified for learning letter names as well.

Letter-Sound Correspondence

The following activities are helpful for practicing letter-sound correspondence.

● ● ● ● ● ●

Letter Flip

Create three stacks of letters on cards: 1) consonants, 2) vowels, and 3) consonants. Have students decode and blend the sounds, change one of the sounds, then decode and blend again. Repeat the process several times to provide decoding practice. Move toward fluent and instant decoding of the words. If this is used as a center activity, ask students to write or make a list of the words they created to turn in to the teacher.

● ● ● ● ● ●

Word Chains

Students use moveable magnetic or other letter tiles to spell words dictated by the teacher. Each word differs from the previous by one sound only. It is important for the letter tiles to represent one phoneme with the grapheme that spells that sound, even if the sound is spelled with more than one letter. For example, the phoneme /sh/ should be written on one tile as *SH* together, not as separate *S* and *H*  tiles. A word chain uses words that differ from each other by one sound. This chain would be appropriate for students who are having difficulty discriminating between /i/ and /e/: *big, beg, bet, set, sit, pit, pet.* Strengthen the practice by asking students to write each word they build and then to read the collected words at the close of the lesson.

Word Sorts

Choose words that represent the phonic elements that students have difficulty decoding. Provide these words on slips of paper, or dictate the words and instruct students to write the words on slips of paper. Practice reading the words, then direct students to group the words according to your rules for sound and spelling. The teacher may say, "Find all words that have the /o/ sound. Read them. Find all words that have /e/ spelled *ea*." Always instruct students to read the words after they complete their sort. Increase practice by initiating a rule: Every time you touch a word, READ IT!

Phonics Book

Assist students in maintaining an individual phonics book. Students write the target phonic element at the top of the page. Provide words that contain the identified phonic element for students to spell on the same page. Let them draw a picture of a target word of their choice to help them remember the sound and spelling. Students finish each page by writing sentences using the listed words, or the teacher dictates a sentence.

Sound Spelling Boxes

Students segment sounds in words using small manipulatives. Each sound is represented within one square on graph paper. The sounds are then replaced with the spelling of the graphemes. Here is an overview of a simplified process:

1. Provide students with graph paper that has at least 1-inch squares and sound manipulatives (squares of paper or small plastic discs).

(continued)

(continued)

2. Dictate a word, such as *west,* and ask students to segment the sounds orally. Students segment the sounds again as they push a sound marker into each square.

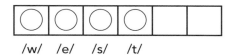

/w/   /e/   /s/   /t/

4. Ask students to show you the target sound /e/. Students point to the /e/ square and say the sound.

5. Students then say each sound as they push up the sound tile and write the letter or letters that represent that sound in the square.

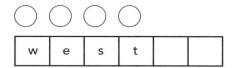

Note: A similar process was developed by Grace (2005) called *Phoneme-Grapheme Mapping.* She developed a manual complete with word lists and mapping processes for phonics and spelling through Phoneme-Grapheme Mapping, available through Sopris West Educational Services (http://www. sopriswest.com).

Take this concept to Syllable Spelling for older students. Say a multisyllable word. Students dot the box as they say each syllable and then go back and spell each syllable. Cut apart the syllables and reassemble the words. Read them again!

RESOURCES

Materials

Alphabet cards and games, including pocket flashcards, alphabet bingo, and sentence strips. Trend Enterprises; http://www.trendenterprises.com.

Alphabet plastic mats. Nixon Education Services; http://www.alphabetmats.com.

Alphabet strips and three-dimensional alphabet letters. Abecedarian; http://www.alphabetletter.com.

Letter tile kit for spelling and reading. Really Great Reading; http://rgrco.com/lettertiles.html.

Plastic alphabet letters and flashcards (letter decks). Educators Publishing Service; http://www.epsbooks.com.

Letter Naming

Beck. R., Anderson, P., & Conrad, D. (2009). *Practicing basic skills in reading: One-minute fluency builders series.* Longmont, CO: Sopris West Educational Services. (This is a skills-building, drill activity book that contains practice activities for letters, words, and syllables, in almost any combination you may need. These practices increase students' ability to process words accurately and automatically while helping to improve phonemic awareness, phonics, letter knowledge, vocabulary, and comprehension.)

Allen, K.A. (with Neuhaus, G.F., & Beckwith, M.C.) (2005). Alphabet knowledge: Letter recognition, naming, and sequencing. In J.R. Birsch (Ed.), *Multisensory teaching of basic language skills* (2nd ed.). Baltimore: Paul H. Brookes Publishing Co. (This chapter is highly recommend for those who are looking for more ideas of how to improve letter recognition in struggling readers.)

Blevins, W. (2006). *Phonics from A to Z: A practical guide* (2nd ed.). New York: Scholastic Press. (This popular book from the Teaching Strategies series has many practical ready-to-use activities, specifically a section titled "35 Quick-and-Easy Activities for Developing Alphabet Recognition" that teachers will welcome).

Neuhaus Education Center. (2002). *Reading readiness.* Bellaire, TX: Author. (This manual provides an entire chapter on teaching letter recognition. It includes the masters for the cards, alphabet matching mat, and alphabet arc that are enlarged to 155% and printed on card stock for individual students.)

Interactive Electronic Resources

Earobics

Earobics is a research-based interactive, multisensory software program with emphasis on all five of the critical components of reading (phonemic awareness, phonics, fluency, vocabulary, and comprehension). Earobics is primarily designed for preschool through Grade 3. The software responds to student input and adjusts instruction accordingly. Earobics is truly a multimedia product with big books, little books, leveled readers, alphabet mats, manipulatives, word cards, letter-sound review decks, cassettes, videos, music, CD-ROM talking tapes, and much more to keep even the most reluctant reader engaged.

Alphabet Books

Hennepin County Library. Letter sounds book list. Retrieved July 20, 2009, from http://www.hclib.org/BirthTo6/booklistaction.cfm?list_num=597. (Provides a list of 40 alphabet books for young readers, including colorful book covers and annotated descriptions.)

Hopkins, B.L., & Arenstein, M. (1971). From apple pie to zooplankton: A selected list of alphabet books for use in the elementary grades. *Elementary English, 48,* 788–792. (Provides a list of 26 books used with children throughout the elementary grades to engage them in numerous ABC activities)

Phonics Supplementary Programs

The following web sites offer reviews of many supplemental programs:

http://www.fcrr.org/reports.htm

http://www.fcrr.org/FCRRReports/tier3interventions.htm

http://www.fcrr.org/FCRRReports/CReportsCS.aspx?rep=supp

http://oregonreadingfirst.uoregon.edu/inst_curr_review_si.html

http://reading.uoregon.edu/au/au_benchmarks.php

Blachman, B.A., & Tangel, D.M. (2008). *Road to reading: A program for preventing and remediating reading difficulties.* Baltimore: Paul H. Brookes Publishing Co. (For Grades 1–3, this well-validated decoding instruction can be implemented with any core reading program when additional systematic and explicit instruction is needed in word identification, oral reading, and spelling. It also can be used as a stand-alone core reading program. The book includes a CD-ROM with handy classroom-ready teaching materials such as lesson plan forms, high-frequency word cards, syllable patterns, and much more. It is a strong, research-based book that is practical for classroom and small-group instruction.)

Clark-Edmonds, S. (2005). *S.P.I.R.E. and sounds sensible.* Cambridge, MA: Educators Publishing Service. (The complete teacher set forms a comprehensive reading intervention program for students in K–8. The instructional design and content are compatible with the National Reading Panel (2000), and each of the five essential components of reading are taught: phonological awareness, phonics, fluency, comprehension, and vocabulary. The author is an Orton-Gillingham (OG) Fellow so the programs align with typical OG teaching with clear scope and sequence, abundant practice and review, progress monitoring, lots of hands-on activities with manipulatives, and scaffolded instruction. The programs can be used by teachers, tutors, or specialists in one-to-one or small-group settings.

Grace, K. (2005). *Phonics and spelling through phoneme–grapheme mapping.* Longmont, CO: Sopris West. (This teaching resource helps students understand the relationship between phonemes and graphemes, and helps students transfer their phonological awareness to print by mapping words and diagramming sound–letter relationships.)

Lacey, K., & Baird, W. (2007). *Watch word.* Longmont, CO: Sopris West. (This research-based multisensory reading and writing program for K–1 develops phonological, letter recognition, and phonics skills students need to become fluent readers. It is used with whole classes, small groups, or individual students.)

Mathes, P.G., Allor, J.H., Torgesen, J.K., & Allen, S.H. (2001). *PALS: First-grade peer-assisted literacy strategies*. Longmont, CO: Sopris West. (This 16-week peer-assisted reading curriculum with a strong research base includes fun phonemic awareness and reading fluency tasks. It uses three 35-minute sessions per week to motivate students to become better readers and double or triple their reading practice.)

McGuinness, C., & McGuinness, G. (1999). *Phono-Graphix*. (This research-based structured, systematic, multisensory reading and spelling program teaches phonemic awareness and alphabetic code knowledge for students ranging in age from preschool through Grade 5. The program can be used for individual remediation, small-group, or even larger group intervention. Students learn to "map" sounds to corresponding letters as they write. There are simple assessments that can be given before and after starting instruction to measure growth. Phonics instruction is direct, explicit, and taught within the context of a word so that meaning can be maintained. A multisyllabic level is available for older or more advanced students in which students break two- to five-syllable words into chunks and analyze them; http://www.readamerica.net.)

Morris, D., & Bloodgood, J. (2004). *Elements of reading, phonics and phonemic awareness*. Cumming, GA: Steck-Vaughn. (This book is designed for students in grades K–2 who need additional small-group support in early reading skills, phonemic awareness, and phonics. Teachers are instructed to use elements for 10 minutes a day to supplement their core reading programs. Along with fundamental phonological awareness skills, students are provided with vocabulary development in each of the early lessons through the use of big books and large, colorful posters. The program is well designed with ample teacher modeling, teacher-friendly daily lesson plans, and a detailed, well-organized scope and sequence; http://steck-vaughn.harcourtachieve.com/en-US/eor_home.)

Nelson, J.R., Cooper, P., & Gonzalez, G.E. (2004). *Stepping stones to literacy*. Longmont, CO: Sopris West (http://www.sopriswest.com). Focuses on small group or individual instruction for 15-minute sessions, early literacy (pre-k), identifying letter names, phonological awareness, phonemic awareness, listening, etc.

Orton, J. (2005). *A guide to teaching phonics*. Cambridge, MA: Educators Publishing Services.

Traub, N., & Bloom, F. (2000). *Recipe for reading* (3rd ed.). Cambridge, MA: Educators Publishing Services. (This is a simple yet comprehensive, research-based, multisensory, phonics-based reading program that is designed for at-risk struggling readers in Grades K–6 or beginning readers. The teacher's manual can be used alone with structured lessons beginning with initial consonants; however, there are student materials that include workbooks, writing paper, alphabet series readers, sound cards, and affix and root cards.)

Vadasy, P., Wayne, S., O'Connor, R., Jenkins, J., Firebaugh, M., & Peyton, J. (2005). *Sound partners*. Longmont, CO: Sopris West. (This evidence-based phonics program is designed to improve word attack, word identification, and spelling skills in grades K–2 in a one-to-one tutorial setting using decodable readers.)

Wilson, B. (2002). *Fundations.* Oxford, MA: Wilson Language Training Corporation. (This book provides a K–2 early literacy multisensory, research-based program; www.fundations.com.)

Word List Sources

Bear, D., Invernizzi, M., Templeton, S., & Johnston, F. (2008). *Words Their Way: Word study for phonics, vocabulary, and spelling instruction.* Upper Saddle River, NJ: Prentice Hall. (Ample word lists are located at the end of the book, organized starting with word families and then vowel sounds and patterns for each vowel. Under some features, words are grouped by frequency and complexity.)

Jones, T.B. (1997). *Decoding and encoding English words: A handbook for language tutors.* Timonium, MD: York Press. (A great source of words for vocabulary, spelling and reading practice. It explains phonics regular and irregular patterns, roots, prefixes and suffixes along with Greek, Latin, and other language origins.)

Minsky, M. (2003). *Greenwood word lists, one-syllable words.* Longmont, CO: Sopris West. (Word lists organized by six syllable types)

Slingerland, B. *Teacher's word lists for reference.* Cambridge, MA: Educators Publishing Services.

Phonics Activity Resources

Bear, D., Invernizzi, M., Templeton, S., & Johnston, F. (2008). *Words Their Way: Word study for phonics, vocabulary, and spelling instruction.* Upper Saddle River, NJ: Prentice Hall. (This book contains a developmental spelling assessment that assists teachers in identifying the stage of spelling development that parallels reading development, making it easy to match instructional activities to student needs. This book does a nice job of helping teachers integrate spelling, reading, writing, and listening through countless word sort activities, learning games, and other hands-on activities. The accompanying CD-ROM provides practical classroom materials for teachers in the way of lessons, games, pictures, and much more.)

Blevins, W. (2006). *Phonics from A to Z: A practical guide* (2nd ed.). New York: Scholastic Press. (This is an excellent, comprehensive guide for teaching phonics, high-frequency words, phonograms, and structural analysis, with 35 "Quick and Easy Activities for Developing Phonemic Awareness.")

Enfield, M., & Green, V. (1969). *Project Read.* Bloomington, MN: Language Circle Series. (This is a comprehensive language arts program, with systematic direct instruction in the five essential components of reading plus written expression. It can be used for whole class, small group, and intervention. The program weaves decoding instruction with comprehension and vocabulary development, with a clear scope and sequence with direct teaching elements laid out such as pacing, modeling, guided practice with feedback, as well as visual, auditory, kinesthetic, and tactile strategies to extend and support instruction. It has a particularly strong phonics component with body language supports and gestures to strengthen each lesson. The research history of Project Read is promising and its instructional strategies align with current research; however, future research should include random assignments to strengthen the validity of Project Read; http://www.projectread.com.)

Ganske, K. (2000). *Word journeys: Assessment-guided phonics, spelling, and vocabulary instruction.* New York: Guilford Press. (This is a strong supplementary resource for teachers looking for a method for strengthening phonics, spelling, writing, and listening skills. It provides a straightforward introduction to developmental word knowledge and assessment, and is an excellent source of word lists and word-sorting activities in reproducible forms. Some teachers find this resource easier to understand than Words their Way when first getting into word study and sorting activities.

Ganske, K. (2006). *Word sorts and more: Sound, pattern, and meaning explorations K–3 (solving problems in the teaching of literacy).* New York: Guilford Press. (This resource is designed to be used for pre-K through Grade 3, but has also been used successfully with older struggling readers to help them understand how words work through categorization activities. It saves teachers valuable preparation time by providing extensive word lists, pictures, and practical classroom suggestions for engaging students in word study of various features of the English language system.)

Controlled and Decodable Text

Bonnie Kline Stories (Language Circle, 1-800-450-0343)

Building Blocks to Reading (PS Publications, 425-401-6482)

Phonics Readers (Steck-Vaughn, 1-800-531-5015)

Power Readers (Sopris West, http://www.sopriswest.com, 1-800-547-6747)

Primary Phonics (Educators Publishing Services, http://www.epsbooks.com, 1-800-225-5750)

Success Stories 1 and 2 (Educators Publishing Services, http://www.epsbooks.com, 1-800-225-5750)

Supercharged Readers: Decodable Chapter Books (Sopris West, http://www.sopriswest.com, 800-547-6747)

The Alphabet Series (Educators Publishing Services, http://www.epsbooks.com, 1-800-225-5750)

The Wright Skills (PreK–3) Decodable Books (https://www.wrightgroup.com/family.html?&gid=156)

Core Reading Programs with Decodable Books

Macmillan/McGraw-Hill

Pearson

Imagine It!

Intervention Programs

Corrective Reading
Reading Mastery

Phonics for Teachers

Balmuth, M. (2009). *The roots of phonics: A historical introduction* (rev. ed.). Baltimore: Paul H. Brookes Publishing Co. (This comprehensive handbook provides a global overview of the history of our English language, specifically how modern English phonics developed, along with answers to some more specific questions such as why our alphabet has 26 letters. Phonics terms are defined, competing philosophies of reading instruction are discussed, and many questions about why the English language works the way it does are answered.

Henry, M. (2004). *Unlocking literacy: Effective decoding and spelling instruction.* Baltimore: Paul H. Brookes Publishing Co. (This comprehensive handbook for teachers presents why and how to teach phonics and spelling.)

Moats, L. (2000). *Speech to print: Language essentials for teachers.* Baltimore: Paul H. Brookes Publishing Co. (This book is a fundamental roadmap for how the English language system works, including the basics of phonetics, phonology, morphology, and orthography. Before teachers can teach phonics, they must understand the underpinnings. This book gets them well on their way to that primary understanding. An accompanying workbook is also available.)

O'Connor, R. (2007). *Teaching word recognition: Effective strategies for students with learning difficulties.* New York: Guilford Press. (This book presents research to validate strategies and activities that cover the broad range of skills from beginning reading to more advanced, skilled reading. For example, the first chapter opens with oral language; the second and third chapters move readily into phonemic awareness, the alphabetic principle, and beginning to decode. Chapters on sight words, multisyllabic words, and improving fluency are also included. Of particular interest is Table 1.1 on scientifically validated reading strategies, which reflects the progression of skills that contribute to reading words along with the specific location in the book where the reader can find the instructional strategy to teach.)

Instructional Software

Note: All students who struggle to read need a teacher who provides explicit instruction and immediate corrective feedback. If technology is used for intervention, provide a balance of teacher-directed instruction.

Lexia Reading

Lexia Reading, version 5, is a software program designed for students ages 4 through adult to help build basic reading skills. It is considered a supplementary program and is designed to complement a research-based core curriculum. Lexia provides independent practice and is often used in Tier II and Tier III intervention programs. The early reading level includes focus on phonological awareness activities such as rhyming, recognition of initial and final sounds, segmenting, and blending sounds. Level 2 moves into activities designed to reinforce letter-to-sound correspondence, short vowels, and consonants. Lexia has a web interface that allows students to transfer their work from school to home and back. Not only is the Lexia instruction intensive, structured, and systematic, but the students are given quick, immediate feedback, which serves to keep them highly motivated as well. (800-435-3942, http://www.lexialearning.com/about)

iStation Reading

iStation Reading is a data-driven reading intervention program for students in pre-K through Grade 5. iStation Reading promotes reading acceleration and progresses through a high-interest online interactive curriculum. ISIP assessment results automatically place students in the appropriate reading intervention level. The curriculum systematically teaches students as they learn developmentally appropriate skills in the essential reading areas of phonological and phonemic awareness, phonics, vocabulary, fluency, and comprehension. This program is currently being evaluated to determine its effectiveness. (http://www1.istation.com)

Additional Phonics Surveys

Besides those discussed in this chapter, some other phonics surveys have recently gained high utility in classrooms in which teachers want to plan targeted phonics lessons.

Diamond, L., & Thorsnes, B.J. (2008). *CORE phonics survey. Assessing reading: Multiple measures*. Novato, CA: Arena Press. (www.corelearn.com)

Farrell, L., & Hunter, M. (2008). *Diagnostic reading surveys*. Cabin John, MD: Really Great Reading. (http://rgrco.com/pending/decodingsurveys.html)

Hasbrouck, J. (2006). *Quick phonics screener*. St. Paul, MN: Read Naturally. (http://www.readnaturally.com/products/qps.htm)

5

Fluency

ORAL READING FLUENCY MEASURES

	DIBELS	AIMSweb	TPRI	FAIR
Kindergarten	NA	NA	NA	NA
Grade 1 (mid-year)	DIBELS Oral Reading Fluency (DORF)	Reading Curriculum-Based Measure (R-CBM)	Reading Fluency	Oral Reading Fluency
Grade 2	DIBELS Oral Reading Fluency (DORF)	Reading Curriculum-Based Measure (R-CBM)	Reading Fluency	Oral Reading Fluency
Grade 3	DIBELS Oral Reading Fluency (DORF)	Reading Curriculum-Based Measure (R-CBM)	Reading Fluency	Oral Reading Fluency
Grade 4	DIBELS Oral Reading Fluency (DORF)	Reading Curriculum-Based Measure (R-CBM)		Oral Reading Fluency
Grade 5	DIBELS Oral Reading Fluency (DORF)	Reading Curriculum-Based Measure (R-CBM)		Oral Reading Fluency
Grade 6	DIBELS Oral Reading Fluency (DORF)	Reading Curriculum-Based Measure (R-CBM; through grade 8)		Oral Reading Fluency (through Grade 12)

INTRODUCTION

What Is Oral Reading Fluency?

Reading fluency is described as complex and multifaceted, not simply defined as reading fast. Hudson, Lane and Pullen (2005) asserted that there are three elements involved in reading fluency: accuracy, rate, and appropriate prosody or reading with expression. Although prosodic reading reflects understanding of meaningful phrases and syntax, the research between the relationship of prosody and reading comprehension is not well established (Breznitz, 2006; Rasinski, 2004). There is a broad research base (Deno, Marston, Shinn, & Tindall, 1983; Fuchs & Fuchs, 1992; Fuchs, Fuchs, Hosp & Jenkins, 2001; Hosp, Hosp, & Howell, 2007), however, to support the measurement of reading rate and accuracy of oral reading fluency through curriculum-based measures (CBM) providing valid and reliable measures that are useful in determining:

> • • • • •
>
> **Student-Friendly Fluency Definition**
>
> Not too fast,
> not too slow
> Make few mistakes
> as you go,
> Read as if talking
> to a friend—
> It is what you know
> in the end!
>
> Christianne Lane
> Director of Professional
>   Development
> Lee Pesky Learning Center
> Boise, Idaho
>
> • • • • •

1. Which students might be at risk for future reading failure
2. Which students are not making sufficient progress to meet end-of-year goals
3. Specific student instructional levels
4. Which students may need additional diagnostic assessment

The oral reading fluency measure on DIBELS, AIMSweb, and FAIR, and the reading accuracy task on the TPRI all measure reading accuracy and fluency by having students read connected text. This generic measure is strongly correlated with reading comprehension. It also provides an indication of decoding accuracy and fluency. Students are asked to read three separate passages for 1 minute each. Fluency scores are determined by calculating the number of words read correctly in 1 minute.

The ultimate goal of reading is for students to become fluent readers, gain meaning from the written word, apply higher order thinking skills to infer meaning, expand their knowledge, and experience pleasure from reading.

What Does Research Say About Improving Reading Fluency?

To become fluent readers, students must reach a level of automaticity with phonemic awareness, decoding, word recognition, and accessing word meaning.

Once a student is a fluent reader and the demanding task of decoding is automatic, *then* the energy, effort, and focus of reading can be directed toward comprehension of the material being read.

Reading fluency is a well-proven way to distinguish good readers from poor readers. Good readers tend to read accurately in a fluid, smooth, expressive manner. Poor readers read in a very slow, labored, word-by-word, disconnected manner, or too slowly to maintain appropriate levels of comprehension. Poor readers focus at the word level and have limited capacity or attention left to focus on comprehension. Reading fluency is also a strong predictor of reading comprehension (Hintze, Callahan, Matthews, Williams, & Tobin, 2002; Stanovich, 1991). In fact, Torgesen and Hudson (2006) summarized the research with the following statement: "For students at all levels—but particularly for students at the beginning stages of learning to read—oral reading rate is strongly correlated with students' ability to comprehend both simple and complex text."

Some teachers prematurely and incorrectly conclude that when a student performs below benchmark on oral reading fluency, fluency alone should be the focus of instruction. Mistakenly, they provide an abundance of repeated reading as the sole instructional response. Although researchers have agreed that fluency is critical to solid, proficient reading success, fluency is not the *only* reading skill of instructional focus. Decoding and recognizing words automatically, background knowledge, and vocabulary all play important roles in fluency and ultimately in comprehension. Pikulski and Chard stressed the critical connection between fluency and comprehension: "While fluency in and of itself is not sufficient to ensure high levels of reading achievement, fluency is absolutely necessary for that achievement because it depends upon and typically reflects comprehension" (2005, p. 517).

How Do Students Develop Fluency?

Students become fluent by reading and rereading and rereading—thus, by accumulating "miles on the page," as some might say. We know from research and from common sense that good readers read more than poor readers. As Stanovich (1986) helped us to understand, "The rich get richer and the poor get poorer"—meaning that we must find ways to get our struggling readers to read more, to do something that is not easy for them, and that, in many cases, is even unpleasant for them. Reading voraciously will provide, for struggling readers, an avenue to catch up with their peers who are average achieving in vocabulary, sentence structure, and word structure, especially as they move into the intermediate and middle grades.

Research has shown that repeated reading of the same passage at least twice increases both fluency and recall for storytelling (O'Shea, Sindelar, & O'Shea, 1987; Sindelar, Monda, & O'Shea, 1990). Dowhower (1987) found that reading rate, accuracy, comprehension, and prosodic reading (i.e., reading with expression) were significantly improved by repeated reading practice, regardless of the training procedure used.

How Do We Get Struggling Readers to Read More?

Enticing struggling readers to read can present a real challenge for the classroom teacher. Reading is not a task that this group of students willingly chooses to do; therefore, the amount of text that they encounter decreases and, subsequently, the opportunities to improve decline. Reading practice that builds fluency must be oral, planned, and monitored. Several proven interventions, including many opportunities for repeated reading, are described in this chapter. But first, consider these 10 basic guidelines for providing planned and monitored oral reading fluency practice:

1. Use passages that are on the students' instructional level but are a little bit challenging (i.e., can be read with approximately 90% to 95% accuracy).

2. Practice several times each day for only a few minutes, increasing to longer periods of time. As students get older, third grade and above, increase length of practice period.

3. If a student is just beginning to learn letter names, letter sounds, or how to decode or blend words, practice building automaticity through timed readings at these subskill levels, too.

4. When measuring rate and accuracy of connected text, it is important to include a measure of comprehension. This can be done with a quick request such as, "Tell me about what you just read."

5. Use decodable texts with struggling readers. *Decodable texts* are connected texts in which a high percentage of words are decodable, the text is connected to a sound/spelling scope-and-sequence program or text, the students have been taught the letter-sound correspondences and can sound out the words, and the remaining high-frequency words and story words are previously taught.

6. Frequent, brief distributed practice spread out over a number of days is more effective than concentrated practice (i.e., a long period of time over 1 or 2 days).

7. Model fluent oral reading using teacher read-alouds as part of repeated reading interventions (Chard, Vaughn, & Tyler, 2002).

8. Provide immediate feedback on words missed (Chard et al., 2002).

9. Emphasize instruction designed to develop oral reading fluency as soon as students can read at least 60 words (Hasbrouck & Denton, 2005).

10. Let students chart their own progress. Charting is a strong motivator.

Why Does Charting Progress Work?

Charting progress works for the following reasons:

- Students can see their gains.
- Students are competing only against themselves.

- The teacher can tell easily if improvement is occurring and when to change something in the instructional plan.
- The benchmark is clearly visible and obtainable to the student and to the teacher.

How Does the Oral Reading Fluency Decision Tree Work?

The ORF decision tree (see Figure 5.1) was designed to help teachers analyze their students' performance on an ORF measure. The analysis will assist with the process of identifying and planning the most appropriate instructional responses to improve reading fluency. Two aspects of oral reading fluency are identified: *rate* and *accuracy*. Follow these steps with several students' ORF benchmark or progress monitoring assessments to become acquainted with the process. The analysis process will become automatic with time and experience.

1. *Begin.* Look at the student's performance on his or her reading fluency assessment and ask the following: Is the student's score at benchmark level with accuracy above 95%?

   If the score is at benchmark and above, with accuracy 95% and higher: Celebrate! The student is on track for reading success! The student does not require fluency training through timed repeated readings, but will continue to benefit from multiple opportunities to read a variety of materials.

   If the score is near benchmark, slightly below or slightly above: The student will benefit from focused reading and rereading practice. These students should be placed in whole-group lessons and may benefit from the reading program's extensions. Remember, all students benefit from practice, so read, read, read!

   If the score is at benchmark, with accuracy below 95%: Listen to the student read a selection from the reading program, then consider the following points.

   - Were the errors on the assessment a result of reading fast, without attention to reading carefully? If so, talk with the student about what good reading is: "When we read, we read to learn something. We read to find out what the author wants us to learn. That means that we need to read every word carefully. Keep up your pace while reading to help you remember what you read, but read carefully."
   - Does the student have difficulty decoding? If so, include the student in word fluency practice drills, reading words from phonics lessons. Dictate words from reading lessons for spelling and administer a Phonics Survey.
   - Monitor the progress of reading accuracy using passages in the reading program.

   If the score is below benchmark: Look more closely at the performance and type of errors: Is the student slow, with 95% or better accuracy? This indicates that rate will be the focus for intervention, but phonics diagnostics may also be required to ensure that proper instruction is identified.

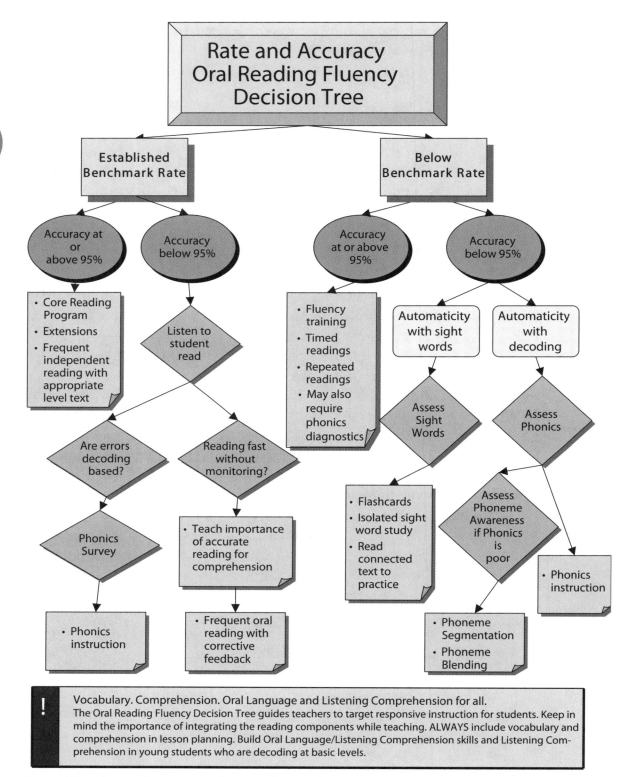

Figure 5.1.   Rate and accuracy oral reading fluency decision tree.

2. *Instruct:* The student needs fluency training through repeated readings and oral timed readings with charting. Include frequent comprehension checks. Is the student slow and inaccurate, with less than 95% accuracy? This indicates that there is a word identification issue that may originate with decoding, possibly phoneme awareness, and/or perhaps lack of quick accurate sight word recognition. Additional assessment is required before focused, more precise, or differentiated instruction can take place. Look for tests that provide diagnostic or individual skill information: "What do I need to know about this student's strengths and weaknesses in specific skills in order to teach him with a focused, effective, research-based approach on Monday morning?"

3. *Assess phonics:* Consider performance on DIBELS Nonsense Word Fluency, TPRI Graphophonemic tasks, Word Reading, and FAIR Word-Building tasks. Conduct a phonics survey (see Chapter 4), give a core reading program phonics inventory, and use the CORE Phonics Survey (Diamond & Thorsnes, 2008) or other phonics screening measures mentioned in Chapter 4.

4. *Assess phoneme awareness:* Consider performance on DIBELS Phoneme Segmentation Fluency and phoneme blending on Nonsense Word Fluency, AIMSweb Phoneme Segmentation Fluency, TPRI Phonemic Awareness tasks, and FAIR Phoneme Blending and Deletion. Use a reading program assessment. Conduct informal inventories for phoneme awareness from instructional manuals such as *Phonemic Awareness in Young Children* (Adams et al., 1998) and *Ladders to Literacy, A Kindergarten Activity Book, Second Edition* (O'Connor, Notari-Syverson, & Vadasy, 2005) or activity books such as *Phonics from A to Z* (Blevins, 2006). The CORE Reading Phonemic Awareness Assessment Measures (Diamond & Thorsnes, 2008) or another phoneme awareness assessment can be administered to gather and clarify information needed for teaching.

5. *Assess sight word recognition:* Any sight word list will help teachers identify the sight words that students may need to practice to build instant recognition. Two graded lists for consideration are the Smartt Sight Word Assessment (see next section) and the CORE Graded High-Frequency Word Survey (Diamond & Thorsnes, 2008).

6. *Instruction:* Use the student's performance on the additional assessments to plan instruction specific to the identified needs. For example, if the student does not decode short vowels correctly, then plan instruction to teach the short vowels. If the student does not segment phonemes in three sound words, then teach phoneme segmentation with words that the student will be asked to read. If the student does not read sight words quickly, then provide sight word fluency drills and multiple opportunities to read sight words in phrases, sentences, and connected text.

7. *Test:* Use progress monitoring passages to measure amount of growth during intervention through progress monitoring and determine what additional instruction, if any, may be needed if a student is not making progress.

Sight Word Screening and Progress Monitoring Tool

The Smartt Sight Word Screening Test is composed of high-frequency words, subdivided into two groups:

*   *Sight words:* Words commonly found in children's text that are phonetically irregular and therefore must be memorized (e.g., *said, what, one*).

*   *High-frequency words:* Words that appear most often in children's texts, many of which are phonetic and can be sounded out. However, they may be presented in texts long before the phonetically based series or the Core program teaches the concept; therefore, they must be taught directly (e.g., *away, big, play*).

Directions

1. Make flashcards (3" x 5" or 5" x 7" index cards will do) from words on the Sight Word Checklist in Figure 5.2. Write the card number on the back of each card.

2. Ask the student to make two stacks as he or she reads the words aloud: words the student knows in one stack and words the student does not know in the other. For older students, print the sight word assessment lists in a comfortable font size on card stock, with one set of words on each card. Number each card on the back. Ask the student to read as many words as he or she can.

3. Use Figure 5.2 to record each student's responses. Circle misread words or unknown words, and tally percent correct. (See Table 5.1 for Percentage Conversion Chart.)

4. Transfer the scores (both percentage correct and raw number correct out of total possible, such as 38/43) to the Sight Word Assessment Progress Monitoring Summary (see Figure 5.3). List the words that have then been identified for targeted, focused, explicit instruction. Remember, the words in boldface in Figure 5.2 are **phonetically irregular** (i.e., sight words) and must be memorized. A multisensory approach is recommended to ensure mastery.

5. To assist with progress monitoring see Figure 5.4, a tool used for record keeping. List words missed on the screening evaluation, form a small group that needs practice on the same few words, teach students missed words (generally three to five words are chosen for intervention; see Activities), then test again for progress monitoring. The progress monitoring "test" can be made up of words the student reads successfully on the card as well as the targeted, instructional words. Give the student only 3 seconds to read the word.

Sight Word Screening Test

Name: _____ Grade: _____ Date: _____

Examiner: _____ Pretest: ____ Posttest: ____ % correct: ____

Note: Words have been alphabetized for the teacher's convenience. Words that must be taught as memorized words are **bold**. Circle misread or unknown words. Use different colored ink for posttest.

CARD 1 (43 words)	# correct:	% correct:

a, and, **away**, big, **blue**, can, **color, come, down, find, for, funny**, go, help, **here**, I, in, **is**, it, jump, **little, look**, make, me, **my, name**, not, **one, play, print**, red, run, **said**, see, **the, three, to, two**, up, we, **where, yellow, you**.

CARD 2 (54 words)	# correct:	% correct:

all, am, **are**, at, ate, be, **black, brown**, but, came, cat, did, **do**, eat, **four, get, good, have**, he, **into**, like, must, **new**, no, **now**, on, **our, out, please, pretty**, ran, ride, **saw, say**, she, so, **soon**, that, **there, they, this, too, under, want, was**, well, went, **what**, white, **who**, will, wish, with, yes

CARD 3 (42 words)	# correct:	% correct:

after, again, an, **any, as**, ask, **by, could, every, fly, from, give, going, has**, had, **her**, him, his, **how**, just, **know**, let, **live, may, of, old, once, open**, over, **put, round, some**, stop, take, thank, them, then, think, **walk, were**, when, why

CARD 4 (44 words)	# correct:	% correct:

always, around, because, been, before, best, **both, buy**, call, **cold, does, don't**, fast, **first**, five, **found**, gave, **goes**, green, its, made, **many, off**, or, **pull, read, right**, sing, sit, sleep, tell, **their, these, those, upon**, us, **use, very, wash, which, work, would**, write, **your**

CARD 5 (41 words)	# correct:	% correct:

about, better, bring, **carry, clean**, cut, **done, draw**, drink, **eight**, fall, **far, full**, got, **grow, hold**, hot, **hurt**, if, keep, **kind, laugh, light**, long, **much, myself, never, only, own**, pick, seven, **shall, show**, six, small, **start**, ten, **today, together, try, warm**

Begin testing with Cards 1, 2, and 3 for elementary students. If the student misses more than one third of the words, stop testing. Do *not* ask the student to read Cards 4 and 5 until the student has mastered the words on Cards 1, 2, and 3. For middle and high school students, begin testing on Cards 4 and 5 and test back down on Cards 3, 2, and 1. It is essential that these sight words be mastered at the 100% level by the end of second grade.

Figure 5.2. Sight Word Screening Test.

From Anderson, C.W., Jr. (2003). *Dolch words and sight words: Differences explained.*
Prior Lake, MN: Education Consultants of the Midwest, © 2003 by Education Consultants of the Midwest; reprinted by permission.
In *Next STEPS in Literacy Instruction: Connecting Assessments to Effective Interventions* by Susan M. Smartt and Deborah R. Glaser. (2010, Paul H. Brookes Publishing Co., Inc.)

Table 5.1. Sight Word Screening Test percentage conversion chart

Number wrong	Card 1	Card 2	Card 3	Card 4	Card 5
0	100	100	100	100	100
1	98	98	98	98	97
2	95	96	95	93	95
3	93	94	93	91	93
4	90	92	90	89	90
5	88	91	88	86	88
6	86	89	86	84	85
7	84	87	83	81	83
8	81	85	81	79	80
9	79	83	78	77	78
10	77	81	76	75	76
11	74	79	74	73	73
12	72	78	71	70	71
13	68	76	69	68	68
14	67	74	67	66	66
15	65	72	64	63	63
16	63	70	62	61	61
17	60	68	59	58	58
18	58	67	57	56	56
19	56	65	55	54	54
20	53	63	52	54	51
21	51	61	50	50	49
22	49	59	48	48	46
23	46	57	45	45	44
24	44	55	43	43	41
25	41	54	40	41	39
26	39	51	38	37	36
27	37	50	36	36	34
28	35	48	34	34	31

From Anderson, C.W. Jr. (2003). *High frequency words, Dolch words, and sight words: Differences explained* (Rev. ed.). Prior Lake, MN: Education Consultants of the Midwest; Inc.; reprinted by permission.

Monitor progress every 2 weeks or more frequently. Change intervention as needed based on the student's level of response to instruction.

Goals

- By end of kindergarten, student will read words on Cards 1 and 2 with 100% mastery.
- By end of Grade 1, student will read words on Cards 1, 2, and 3 with 100% mastery.
- By end of Grade 2, student will read words on Cards 1, 2, 3, and 4 with 100% mastery.

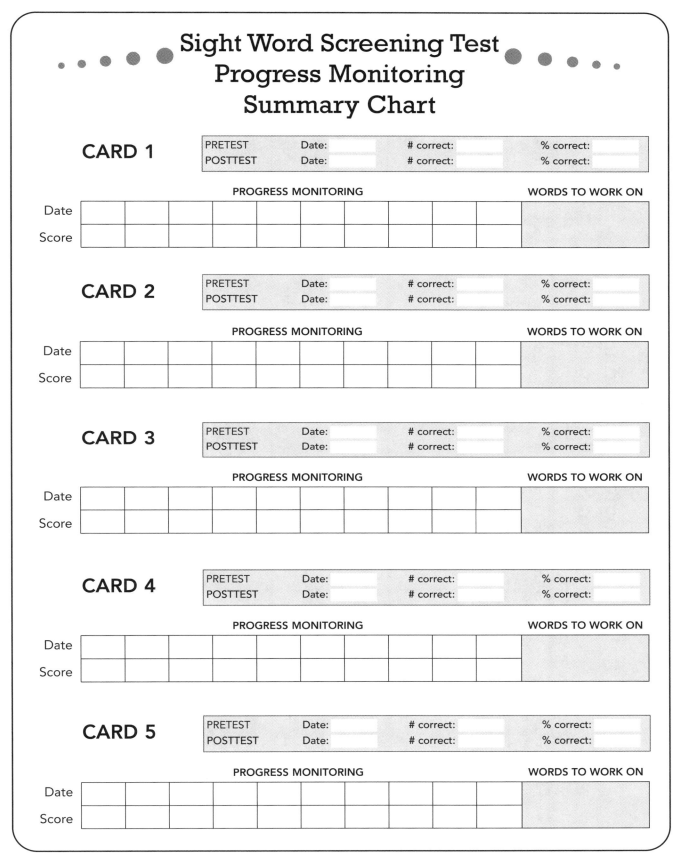

Figure 5.3. Sight Word Screening Test Progress Monitoring Summary Chart. (*Source:* Blachman & Tangel, 2008.)

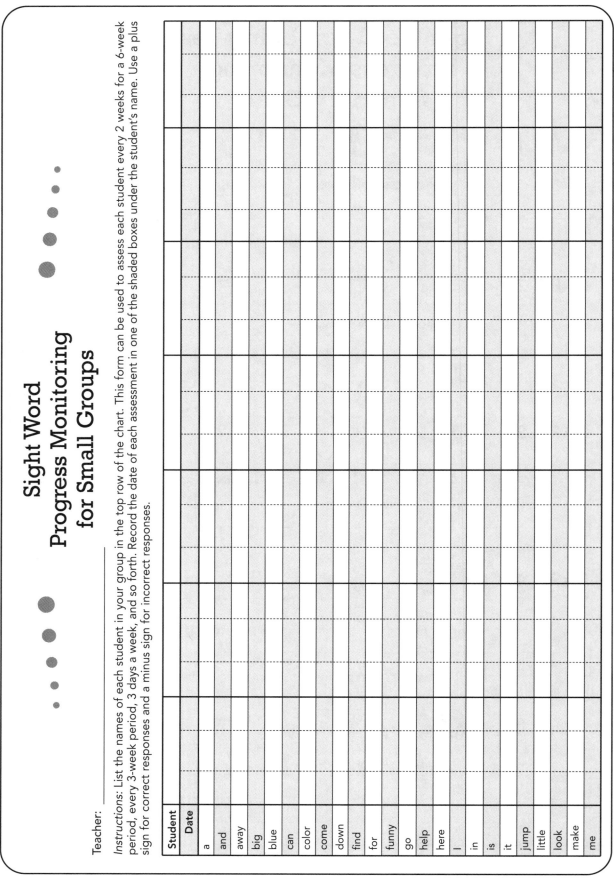

Sight Word
Progress Monitoring
for Small Groups

Teacher: _____

Instructions: List the names of each student in your group in the top row of the chart. This form can be used to assess each student every 2 weeks for a 6-week period, every 3-week period, 3 days a week, and so forth. Record the date of each assessment in one of the shaded boxes under the student's name. Use a plus sign for correct responses and a minus sign for incorrect responses.

Student						
Date						
a						
and						
away						
big						
blue						
can						
color						
come						
down						
find						
for						
funny						
go						
help						
here						
I						
in						
is						
it						
jump						
little						
look						
make						
me						

Figure 5.4. Sight Word Progress Monitoring for Small Groups form.

- By end of Grade 3, student will read words on Cards 1, 2, 3, 4, and 5 with 100% mastery.

Note: Teachers working with early readers may find the Letter Name and Sound Progress Monitoring Summary (Figure 5.5) a useful tool as they closely monitor students' growth in letter and sound identification.

Improving Fluency Through Instant Sight Word Recognition

Efforts to increase automaticity with sight vocabulary can be beneficial to students' oral reading fluency growth. When a student expends less effort to retrieve or remember a word, the student will have more attention and focus for comprehension—the ultimate goal. But are sight words, high-frequency words, irregular words, regular words, and trick words all the same?

The term *sight words* has traditionally referred to words commonly found in children's text that are phonetically irregular and therefore must be sounded out. *High-frequency words,* on the other hand, may be a mixture of both phonetically regular and irregular words. According to Fry, Fountoukidis, and Polk (1985), only approximately 100 of these high-frequency words make up 50% of the words in English print. Although these words are essential for comprehension, many of them are abstract and have very little meaning on their own (e.g., *was, at, if, the, will*). Teachers want students to be able to recognize them instantaneously or upon sight; hence, they are often referred to as *sight words,* so the terms may end up being used interchangeably. It is important for teachers to know which words are considered regular in their spelling or letter-sound pattern and which ones are irregular. Nothing is more confusing to a novice reader than when a teacher asks him to sound out the word *said.*

Regular words are spelled with letters that represent their common sounds, such as *at, that, can,* and *she.* Many words, however, are *irregular,* which means they do not fit any predictable spelling pattern (e.g., *was, do, some*). Sometimes irregular words are referred to as *trick words,* because they try to trick you!

Regular sight words can be taught early to readers, even before they have learned all of the letter-sound correspondences. Students can then practice reading decodable texts containing words for which they have been taught all of the letter-sound correspondences (CVC) and a select few sight words they have also been taught. Teachers should wait a bit longer to teach irregular sight words—but not too long. The word *the* is irregular, and it is the most common word in print! Some researchers suggest initiating irregular sight word instruction after students can read CVC words at a rate of 1 word every 3 seconds. If teachers wait too long, students will be dependent on sounding-out each word rather than trying to recognize the word as a whole (Carnine, Silbert, Kame'enui, Tarver, & Jungjohann, 2006).

The most effective way to learn irregular sight words is through contextual exposure (Carreker, 2005). Ideally, teachers should introduce the new word at

Letter Name and Sound Assessment
Progress Monitoring

Teacher: _____

Instructions: List the names of each student in your group in the top row of the chart. This form can be used to assess each student every 2 weeks for a 6-week period. Record the date of each assessment in one of the shaded boxes under the student's name. Use a plus sign for correct responses. Record incorrect responses for the name (n) or the sound (s). A 1-minute timed component should be included in this assessment after first determining which letters and/or sounds the student knows.

Student																																		
Date																																		
Name/Sound	n	s	n	s	n	s	n	s	n	s	n	s	n	s	n	s	n	s	n	s	n	s	n	s	n	s	n	s	n	s	n	s	n	s
s																																		
m																																		
h																																		
l																																		
o																																		
a																																		
f																																		
v																																		
k																																		
n																																		
p																																		
c																																		
w																																		
b																																		
e																																		
q																																		
t																																		
y																																		
j																																		
r																																		
u																																		
i																																		
g																																		
x																																		

Figure 5.5. Letter Name and Sound Assessment Progress Monitoring Chart.

From Blachman, B.A., & Tangel, D.M. (2008). *Road to reading: A program for preventing and remediating reading difficulties.* Baltimore: Paul H. Brookes Publishing Co.; © 2008 by Paul H. Brookes Publishing Co.; reprinted by permission.

In *Next STEPS in Literacy Instruction: Connecting Assessments to Effective Interventions* by Susan M. Smartt and Deborah R. Glaser. (2010, Paul H. Brookes Publishing Co., Inc.)

least one lesson before it is read in connected text (Simmons & Kame'enui, 2000) and then provide numerous opportunities for practice reading the words through controlled vocabulary texts and decodable readers. When teaching irregular sight words, teachers should be sure to focus on all of the letters that make up the word (Shefelbine & Newman, 2004):

1. Display the word card for *the* and say, "This word is *the*. Say the letter names in *the: T–H–E*." This will keep the student in the habit of visually scanning the word.

2. Use the word in a sentence: "The cat is in the box."

3. Point to the left of the word and ask, "What is this word?" Quickly sweep your finger under the whole word to cue the student to respond.

4. Ask, "How do you spell the word *the?*" Point to each letter as the student spells.

5. Point to the left of the card and ask, "What is this word?" Quickly sweep your finger under the whole word to cue the student to respond.

6. Ask, "How do you spell *the?*" Quickly point to each letter as the student spells the word.

7. Repeat the *read-and-spell* steps three times. Ask the student to write the word from memory. Direct the student to compare his or her spelling with the spelling on the flash card. Collect words in a card file for everyday review and practice.

The two most common word lists that teachers use are the *Dolch Basic Sight Vocabulary* (Dolch, 1948) and the *1000 Instant Word List* (Fry, 1994). The Instant Words are ranked in order of frequency, with the first 25 words making up about one-third of all elementary reading material. The first 100 instant words make up about 50% and the first 300 make up about 65% of all printed elementary reading text.

Teachers should compare the *Instant Word List* with the most frequently used words in the core reading program used in their classroom, then develop a list based on the two sources. The following guidelines will help teachers to identify the most appropriate words for placement on that list (Honig, Diamond, & Gutlon, 2000, 2008).

1. Select the words that are the most useful: those that will appear in upcoming passages.

2. Limit the numbers of words that are introduced at one time. In kindergarten, introduce 1–2 words per week; in first grade, 3 words; and in second grade, 5–7 words. Gradually add more as students are successful. Use teacher judgment.

3. Do not introduce similar words at the same time (e.g., *was/saw, where/were*). Be sure to separate the introduction of similar words by several weeks, giving

the students plenty of time to master the original word before introducing the potentially confusing word.

4. Introduce related words together (e.g., *other, mother, brother*).

5. Provide a 2- to 3-minute cumulative review of high-frequency words as part of daily reading instruction.

6. Frequently monitor your students' success in learning both regular and irregular sight words separately to find out if students are in fact learning what is being taught. Carnine et al. (2006) recommended progress monitoring at the following intervals:

- *On or above grade level:* every 4–6 weeks
- *Slightly below grade level:* every 2 weeks
- *Significantly below grade level:* weekly

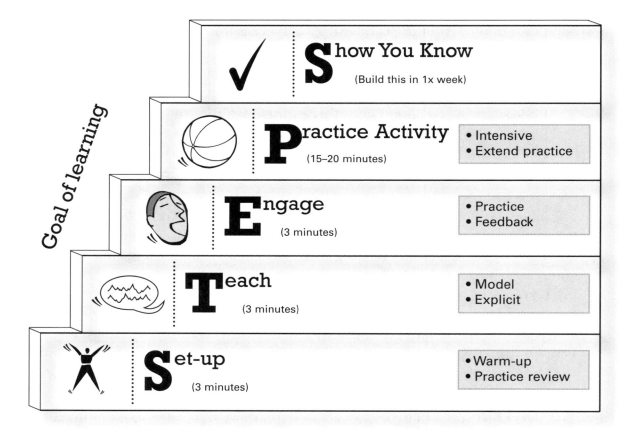

HERE WE GO: READY TO TEACH!

Now that we've looked at fluency and methods for assessing different components of fluency, let's visit a real classroom and observe how a fluency lesson is taught using the STEPS Small-group Lesson Planning format.

Inside A Real Classroom: A Fluency Lesson Snapshot

Mr. Young has a goal: 95% of his students will be at benchmark levels on an ORF measure by the end of the year. He knows that systematic, explicit instruction in all five reading components within the setting of his language-rich classroom where students are motivated will help him reach his goal. Teaching reading is complex. Mr. Young used to have all of his students do timed repeated readings to improve their fluency and WCPM scores. Now he knows that individualizing his approaches in whole group and small group goes a long way toward ensuring mastery levels of reading ability.

Mr. Young provides strong decoding and vocabulary instruction, and lots of engaged reading time to practice the skills he teaches. He has a group of students for which repeated readings are the recommendation. These students are accurate decoders and sight word readers. However, they are slow in their reading, so they spend a portion of small-group time doing timed repeated reading with instructional-level material at 90%–95% correct.

Mr. Young conducted a small-group lesson, during which the practice time was spent building fluency. Here is what his lesson looked like, along with a script.

Set-up

Students engage in free-choice oral reading to peers and Mr. Young monitors their reading. A basket of books holds the decodable texts and leveled readers that the students have read before and can choose from. The students log the book titles they choose in their reading folders.

Teach

Teacher: "Let's get ready to read the story from this morning. Here are the words you need to be able to recognize right away while you are reading the story." [Teacher presents several words from the phonics lesson and vocabulary words written on strips of tag paper. They are displayed in the pocket chart.]

Teacher: "Listen. My turn to read." [Teacher decodes and reads the words, pointing to the phonic elements that were taught while saying the sounds.]

Teacher: "Listen. I will say our vocabulary words and their meanings." [Teacher reads each word, asking students to repeat the word, and gives a brief definition within the context of the story.]

Engage

Students decode and read the story words with the teacher.

Teacher: [Sounds out word, touching each grapheme.]
Students: [Read each word after sounding them out with teacher direction.]
Teacher: "Nice job sounding out these words. Now I will touch each word, you think about what it says, and then when I give the signal, you say the word. You will sound them out in your heads. Ready?"
Students: [Say the words as whole units automatically.]
Teacher: "Now let's read our vocabulary words. Read the words to your partner. Take turns. Then choose one to use in a sentence to tell about the story."

 Practice Activity

Students read and reread passages from the story, practicing the skills they have been learning. They time each other and record their performance on a chart. The teacher says, "Please get ready to practice reading. Partner up with your stopwatches. I'll monitor and help out. Let me know when you reach your goal and I will listen to your last reading."

Students know the routine of getting into pairs and doing repeated readings. Each student has a goal of a 10% increase in words per minute based on their last repeated reading score. Before students are finished reading, Mr. Young does the final check out on the text. If students make their goals, they can check the story off on their list. If the goal is not reached, the student will reread the selection during the next lesson.

 Show You Know

Mr. Young finishes these repeated reading lessons with a focus on comprehension and asks students to show they know by answering questions about the story content. He asks a variety of recall and higher level inferential questions and prompts students to use the vocabulary words they have learned in their answers.

Activities

Repeated Readings

Here are some ideas for activities using repeated readings.

• • • • •

Repeated Reading: Fluency Process

The teacher should instruct the student: "Please read this passage for your fluency training today. Begin reading here [point] and read until I tell you to stop. If you come to a word you don't know, I will tell you the word." Time the student for 1 minute and note the number of words the student reads. Subtract the errors for a total WCPM. This process takes place in one sitting.

1. Chart the WCPM on Figure 5.6. Show the student how to graph his or her own performance using different colors for a bar graph.
2. Review the errors with the student. Show and tell the words you helped with, words the student omitted or substituted, and hesitations.
3. Instruct the student to read the passage again, following the same procedure.
4. Repeat for a total of three times. Instruct the student to graph his or her performance after each reading. Work with the student to set goals between readings. The teacher may say, "How many words can you read next time? Can you beat your time?"

When you do repeated readings you will also need to know what to count as a reading error. The following guidelines tell you what to count as a reading error:

• *Unknown word:* The student hesitates or attempts to read a word but does not produce the correct word in 3 seconds. Provide the correct word for the student and mark it as an error on your sheet.

• *Substitution:* The student misreads a word, substituting a different word for the actual word in the text.

• *Omission:* The student leaves a word out while reading.

• Do *not* count the following as errors: rereading words or phrases, self-corrections made within 3 seconds, or skipping a line (i.e., do not count the words in the omitted line as errors).

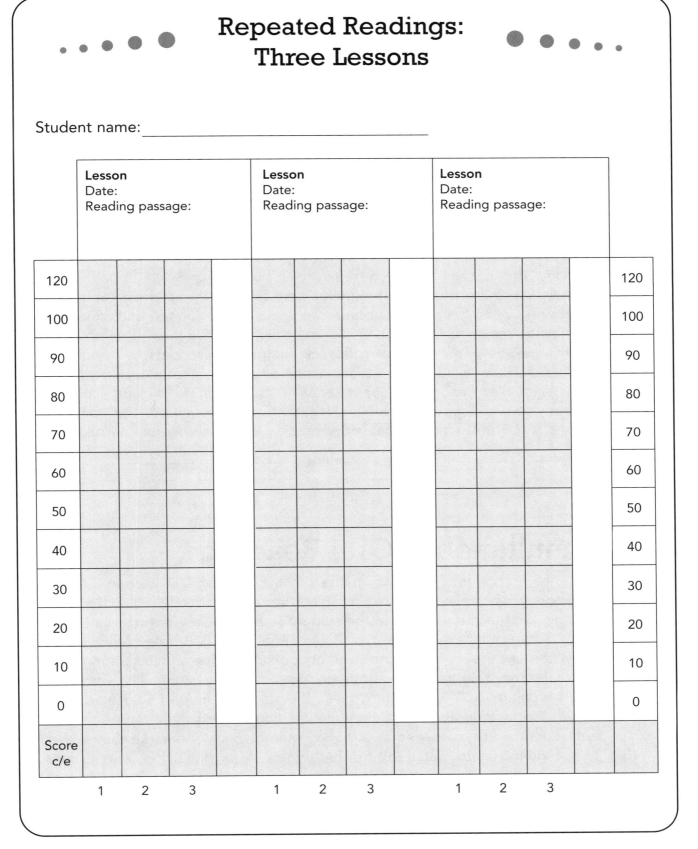

Figure 5.6. Repeated Readings chart: Three Lessons.

• • • • •

Repeated Reading with Recorded Models

When comparing students who used audiotape with those who used unassisted repeated readings, studies have shown that both gained in higher word reading accuracy, comprehension, fluency, and prosody. However, those students who used the audiotape seemed to have improved levels of prosody. That is, they appeared to read with better expression.  Teachers are urged to be careful when setting up listening centers for improving fluency because many times the tapes will be too fast and difficult for struggling readers to follow along. Several programs have been developed just for this purpose (i.e., developing fluency in struggling readers by listening to models) and are listed in the Resource section of this chapter, including *Read Naturally, Quick Reads*, and *Great Leaps*. These programs provide a process whereby several steps of listening and following along are followed by independent reading. The student finishes with a reading to the teacher for final approval.

• • • • •

Simultaneous Oral Reading

This intervention was first documented in the reading literature in 1969 by Heckelman, who called it the Neurological Impress Method (NIM). In this intervention, the teacher sits next to the student so the teacher (or tutor) can direct his or her voice into the student's left ear ("imprinting"). Before beginning the story, preview the story with the student, look at the title and illustrations, discuss what the story might be about, and introduce any vocabulary words that may be unfamiliar. The teacher moves the student's index finger across the text line simultaneously while they are reading aloud together. The teacher reads aloud with expression at a slightly quicker pace and somewhat louder. The student tries to match the teacher's voice. After practicing this step several times, the student is ready to read the parts of the passage independently and then the entire passage. This is a very demanding task for students; therefore, only a couple of minutes are recommended, with a maximum of 15-minute intervention blocks over time.

• • • • •
"Take Turns" Oral Reading

The leader (a parent, peer, tutor, or teacher) and the student take turns reading part of a passage (a paragraph or a page) that is familiar. Reader 1 is the stronger reader; this person should read first, while Reader 2 follows along by pointing to the text. Then they swap, with Reader 2 taking over where Reader 1 left off. The teacher monitors reading for accuracy and a smooth, fluid pace. After the students have completed the passages, they are asked to go back and take turns asking questions (e.g., "Tell me what happened here"). It is a good idea to have the students keep a list of the books they read and to give them points for being good listeners and following directions. Ask the readers to share with others what their stories were about. This activity is adapted from the peer-assisted literacy strategies (PALS; Mathes, Torgesen, & Allor, 2001).

• • • • •
Echo Reading

With this training method, the teacher (or a stronger reader) reads a brief section of material aloud. The other students follow along and then immediately reread the same material. The material is parsed into a page, a paragraph, or even a sentence. As the name implies, the leader (stronger reader) reads first and the students read the
same material in an echo fashion in immediate succession. The critical feature is that the students need to follow along using their fingers to point to the phrase or line of text to make sure they are not just mimicking the leader. This method's use is recommended when the reading material is new to the reader and at a challenging level. This intervention is a critical component of the PALS program, and its fidelity has been well supported in research (Mathes et al., 2001).

● ● ● ● ●

Paired Whisper Reading

This repeated reading process works well in small or whole groups. It is a real timesaver because it allows more students to be reading at one time than traditional one-on-one repeated reading methods. Monitor the students' reading during the process.

1. Copy two different sets of reading prompts (e.g., short stories, paragraphs) at appropriate reading levels for your reading groups.
2. Pair children up, 1s with 2s, linking a stronger reader with a weaker reader, typically.
3. Pass out reading prompts. (Keep face down.) Each team has two different reading prompts (labeled *1* and *2*, carefully chosen to match student reading levels).
4. The teacher then times reading for 1 minute. All children turn over papers and immediately start to "whisper read" prompts. Teach children how to whisper read—reading so quietly only your partner can hear you—prior to doing the activity. Each student draws a line by the last word read at the end of 1 minute.
5. Partners reread their prompts one at a time to each other out loud. The listening partner may correct any misread words.
6. Both partners again read in a whisper (at the same time) while the teacher times 1 minute. Each student draws a line by the last word read at the end of 1 minute. Compare progress since first reading.
7. Repeat one or two more times, starting at step 5.

With practice, this fluency drill should take no longer than 8–10 minutes. The teacher should follow up on this process. Listen to individuals read their passage and record data (WCPM and errors).

● ● ● ● ●

Paired Repeated Reading

Pair two readers, one stronger than the other. The first student reads a short passage three times and gets feedback, then they switch roles. To pair students for alternate reading, the following suggestions are offered:

(continued)

(continued)

1. Rank order your students from strongest to weakest reader.
2. Divide the list into two columns (half being the highest performing, the other half being the lowest performing).
3. Pair the top reader in column 1 with the top reader in column 2.
4. Continue this process until all of the students are paired (e.g., student 1 with student 11, student 2 with student 12).

Sight Words

Here are some ideas for providing multiple exposures to and learning experiences with sight words.

Rainbow Writing

Each student will need folded paper and crayons. Depending on the age of the student, write the sight word or have the student write the word on the paper with a dark crayon providing a dark visual. Fold the paper over the word so it will *ghost* through paper. Have the student trace while saying the letters, then the whole word. Repeat several times, each time with a different color to achieve the rainbow effect!

Air Writing

Use large arm movements from the shoulder with extended index and middle fingers to write letters in the air while saying the word. Provide background visual of the letter or word for added visual connection while air writing.

Salt Box

Line a shallow box or tray with bright paper and a thin layer of salt. Students can use their index finger to write letters and words while saying the sounds or letter names. Gentle back-and-forth shaking "erases" so the students can write the word again.

Wikki Stix

Students enjoy using these waxy pipe cleaners to bend and form letters, trace raised shapes, and say sounds or letter names to learn sight words.

Touch Arm and Spell

Have students begin at the shoulder, moving down to their wrist and hand, then tapping with the other hand as words are spelled and blended.

Trace and Say

This is the most common form of multisensory instruction. Letters and words are written, then the student traces and says them. While this activity has been done during whole-class instruction at students' desks on paper or on wipe-off boards, it is also effective in small-group instruction. The teacher asks the students to come up individually and, using large motor skills, trace over the word

(continued)

(continued)

written on the board five times. The student says the letters as he or she traces, then the whole word (e.g., "w–h–a–t, what"). Next, the student erases the word, tries to write from memory, looks at the word on his flashcard to "check" for accuracy, and then writes the word in a sentence. Younger students can copy a sentence the teacher has provided. Students' sight word flashcards can be saved in individual boxes for daily review and practice.

Raised Letters

Glitter glue is great for creating cards of raised letters for students to trace with their index fingers and say. Students write sight words on index cards, as well as a sentence using that word on the back of the card. Students keep their collection in an index card box. Create categories for the words depending on how quickly students read the words (e.g., turtle words, bird words, car words).

Speed Drills for Sight Words

Speed drills are another way to build automaticity in sight word recognition. Use a grid like the one in Figure 5.7 and include words you have taught recently from your instant word list. Use the new or target words several times for multiple exposures. First, ask the students to read over the page, to "practice," and then let you know when they are ready to be

timed. Time the students, record their time, and chart their progress on Figure 5.8. Students enjoy keeping track of their progress, watching their growth, and earning a reward for their accomplishments!

Sight Word
Speed Drill

Name: _____   Date: _____

Figure 5.7.   Sight Word Speed Drill.

Sight Word
Progress Chart

Name:_____   Date:_____

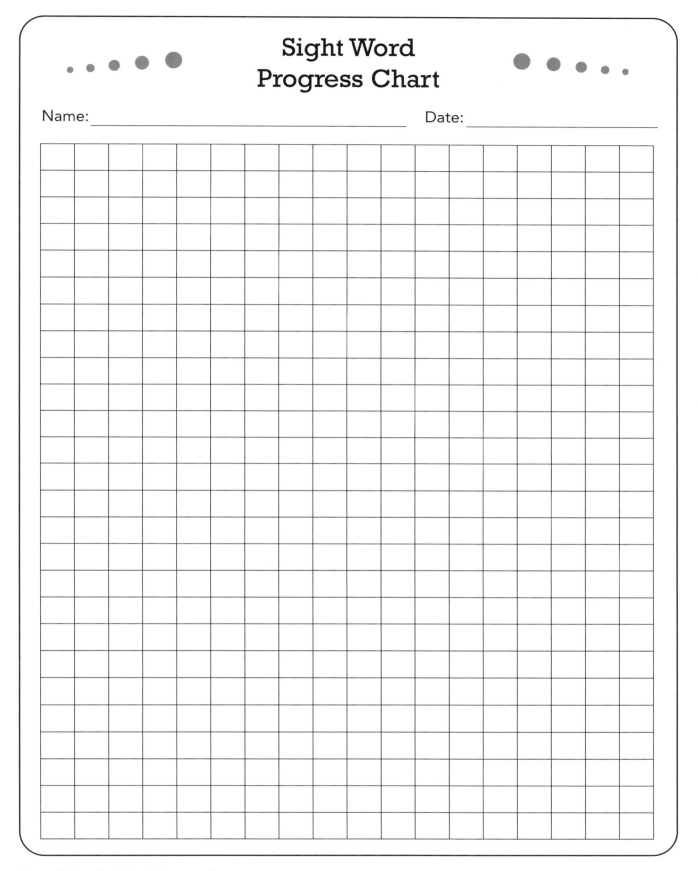

Figure 5.8.   Sight Word Progress Chart.

Next STEPS in Literacy Instruction: Connecting Assessments to Effective Interventions by Susan M. Smartt and Deborah R. Glaser

Reading Fluency

Fluency is improved by repeated reading of passages, phrases, words, syllables, and even letters and sounds.

• • • • •

Reading Phrases

Depending on the student's level or stage of reading development, it may be appropriate to provide Dolch (1948) sight word phrases or several phrases from the *1000 Instant Word List* (Fry, 1994). Examples from both lists are provided in Table 5.2. Have the student "scoop" the phrase with his or her pencil and/or two pointing fingers as he or she reads.

Table 5.2. Phrases for practice: A comparison of Fry Instant Words and Dolch sight word phrases and examples of "scooping"

Fry Instant Words	Dolch sight word phrases
He has it.	A big horse
What were we called?	The little dog
I like him.	A big house
The two went down.	The old man
She will sit.	A new hat
Each had one.	The funny rabbit
Write it down.	A pretty home
Look down there.	A pretty picture
Two said so.	The new coat
What will you see?	The small boat
Come to them.	
Would he write two?	Examples of scooping
Did you find that?	• The cat ran • after the rat. •
Who called about him?	
You are up and down.	• The happy baby • jumped up and down. •
Each day is long.	
That was about people.	• The white dog • took a walk • with a man. •
That number is two.	
They said to sit now.	
Their water is up.	
Have you been there?	
Which part is first?	

Sources: Dolch, 1948; Fry, 1994.

• • • • •

Involving Parents in Fluency Training

Instruct parents to provide a shared reading time each day with their child to improve reading fluency. Provide these steps for parents:

1. The parent reads a brief poem or paragraph (written at the child's independent reading level) to the child as the child follows along.
2. The parent and child read it again, together, several times (three times is best).
3. The child reads it to the parent independently.
4. The parent gives the child authentic praise for a job well done.

ORAL READING FLUENCY NORMS

ORF norms for Grades 1–8, as compiled by Hasbrouck and Tindal (2005), are presented in Figure 5.9. Teachers can use this chart to compare their students' performances on 1-minute ORF measures (in words correct per minute [WCPM]) with national norms at the various percentile levels and to set long-term fluency goals for their struggling readers. Notice how the norms change across the school year (see average weekly improvement column), which is an indication of growth that teachers can expect from students if they are to be on track and proficient on end-of-year, high-stakes tests. *Average weekly improvement* refers to the average words per week growth to expect from a student. It was calculated by subtracting the fall score from the spring score and dividing the difference by 32, the typical number of weeks between the fall and spring assessments. For Grade 1, because there is no fall assessment, the average weekly improvement was calculated by subtracting the winter score from the spring score and dividing the difference by 16, the typical number of weeks between the winter and spring assessments.

Although teachers can use the DIBELS or AIMSweb progress monitoring passages to assess students' rates of growth in fluency, they may also do a 1-minute probe on their own by selecting a short passage from the reading program at the student's instructional (yet a bit challenging) reading level (90% word recognition or better), asking the student to read for 1 minute and marking any errors the student makes on a teacher's copy. Count the number of words read correctly. Compare the number of words read correctly with the appropriate grade and time of year on the norms chart in Figure 5.9. According to Hasbrouck and Denton (2005), any student scoring below the 50th percentile in reading fluency, even after fourth grade, should continue receiving fluency training.

Grade	Percentile	Fall WCPM	Winter WCPM	Spring WCPM	Avg. weekly improvement
1	90		81	111	1.9
	75		47	82	2.2
	50		23	53	1.9
	25		12	28	1.0
	10		6	15	0.6
2	90	106	125	142	1.1
	75	79	100	117	1.2
	50	51	72	89	1.2
	25	25	42	61	1.1
	10	11	18	31	0.6
3	90	128	146	162	1.1
	75	99	120	137	1.2
	50	71	92	107	1.1
	25	44	62	78	1.1
	10	21	36	48	0.8
4	90	145	166	180	1.1
	75	119	139	152	1.0
	50	94	112	123	0.9
	25	68	87	98	0.9
	10	45	61	72	0.8
5	90	166	182	194	0.9
	75	139	156	168	0.9
	50	110	127	139	0.9
	25	85	99	109	0.8
	10	61	74	83	0.7
6	90	177	195	204	0.8
	75	153	167	177	0.8
	50	127	140	150	0.7
	25	98	111	122	0.8
	10	68	82	93	0.8
7	90	180	192	202	0.7
	75	156	165	177	0.7
	50	128	136	150	0.7
	25	102	109	123	0.7
	10	79	88	98	0.6
8	90	185	199	199	0.4
	75	161	173	177	0.5
	50	133	146	151	0.6
	25	106	115	124	0.6
	10	77	84	97	0.6

Key: WCPM = words correct per minute.

Figure 5.9. 2006 Hasbrouk and Tindall Oral Reading Fluency data. (From Davidson, M.R., Standal, T.C., Towner, J.C., Matsoff, J., et al. [2009]. *Reading fluency benchmark assessor: Teacher's guide* [p. 21]. Saint Paul: Read Naturally; adapted by permission. Reading Fluency Benchmark Assessor Copyright © 2009 Read Naturally, Inc.)

RESOURCES

Adams, G., & Brown, S. (2007). *The six-minute solution: A reading fluency program.* Longmont, CO: Sopris West. (This program comes in two levels: primary and intermediate. The program contains several graded passages for repeated reading practice and drill. It also includes automatic word lists for isolated word practice. Charts and fluency graphs are provided.)

Beck. R., Anderson, P., & Conrad, D. (2009). *Practicing basic skills in reading; One minute fluency builders series.* Longmont, CO: Sopris West Educational Services. (This set of practice sheets helps to build and maintain fluency [accuracy plus speed] in basic skills. It includes practice pages for pre-first through seventh grade in areas ranging from pre-reading language concepts, Dolch Words, vowels, blends, to sentences, passages and more)

Blevins, W. (2001). *Building fluency: Lessons and strategies for reading success.* New York: Scholastic Publishing. (This is a very helpful book for every teacher who wants a quick, friendly handbook of fluency strategies and lessons, intended for Grades 2–6.)

Fischer, P. (1995). *Speed drills from concept phonics.* Farmington, ME: Oxton House Publishers. (Contains words, phrases, and text readings that could be shared by several grade levels.)

Hasbrouck, J., & Denton, C. (2005). *The reading coach: A how-to manual for success.* Longmont, CO: Sopris West Educational Services. (This is an excellent resource not only for reading coaches, teachers, and administrators but also for anyone looking for a solid review of the current literature on reading instruction for struggling readers, time management, problem solving, and communication in schools.)

Hasbrouck, J., & Denton, C. (2009). *The reading coach 2: More tools and strategies for student focused coaches.* Longmont, CO: Sopris West. (Based on their extensive experience in working with reading coaches across the country since their first book, the authors have presented an impressive model for closing the gap between research-based practice and realistic, successful application in the classroom. They address RTI, team problem solving, designing both academic and behavioral interventions, adapting instruction to meet the varied needs of learners, and many more relevant topics for today's teachers and principals.)

Heibert, E.H. (2003). *Quick reads.* Glenview, IL: Pearson Scott Foresman. (This research-based fluency program improves both fluency and comprehension for Grades 2–6, or into middle and high school for remedial readers. The lesson takes approximately 15 minutes and includes short nonfiction passages, including both science and social studies topics. The passages have been carefully selected to support automaticity with high-frequency words, common phonics/syllable patterns, and multisyllabic words. Emphasis is placed on building background knowledge prior to the first reading in which the student reads the selected passage to himself or herself. For the second reading, the teacher reads or the student listens to an audio version, then answers a comprehension question afterwards. For the third reading, the student is asked to read as much as he or she can in 1 minute. Finally, the student is assigned a group of comprehension questions to reflect understanding of the passage.)

Honig, B., Diamond, L., & Gutlon, L. (2008). *CORE: Teaching reading sourcebook for kindergarten through eighth grade.* Berkeley, CA: Consortium on Reading Excellence. (This large book is an encyclopedia for teaching reading with a strong commitment to research-based practices. Chapter 7, on irregular word reading, provides a detailed explanation of why teachers should teach high-frequency (sight) words, and specific strategies for instruction is given. A list of the Educator's Word Frequency Guide [Zeno, Ivens, Millard, & Duvvuri, 1995] is included, which provides lists of words in sets of 25 from the most frequent to least frequent out of 160 words used in school and college textbooks; http://www.corelearn.com.)

Ihnot, C. (1991). *Read Naturally.* Minneapolis, MN: Read Naturally. (This program uses a strong research base, combining teacher modeling, repeated reading, retelling, and progress monitoring. The student begins with 1-minute "cold" reading to the teacher or computer, then practices three or four times while listening to a recorded fluent model. The student then practices independently without the model/recording. Finally, the student reads to the teacher or computer again, getting feedback, and time is charted; http://www.readnaturally.com.)

Neuhaus Education Center. (2003). *Practices for developing accuracy and fluency.* Bellaire, TX: Author. (This manual contains 30 passages for reading levels ranging from 1.0–5.0, as well as 30 rapid word recognition charts with high-frequency irregular words. The word charts are used to preview the words in a passage before reading. The student is timed on the words and on the passage; http://www.neuhaus.org.)

Rasinski, T.V. (2003). *The fluent reader: Oral reading strategies for building word recognition, fluency, and comprehension.* New York: Scholastic Publishing. (A very practical, ready-to-use manual for all teachers in Grade 1–8; with some modification, can be used in kindergarten.)

Comprehension

COMPREHENSION MEASURES

	DIBELS	AIMSweb	TPRI	FAIR
Kindergarten	NA	NA	Listening Comprehension (Inventory)	Listening Comprehension
Grade 1 (mid-year)	Retell Fluency* DORF (with retell component)**	Maze CBM	Word Lists, Reading Accuracy, Reading Comprehension (explicit, implicit, vocabulary questions) (Inventory)	Oral Reading Fluency
Grade 2	Retell Fluency* DORF (with retell component)**	Maze CBM	Word Lists, Reading Accuracy, Reading Comprehension (explicit, implicit, vocabulary questions) (Inventory)	Oral Reading Fluency
Grade 3	Retell Fluency* DORF (with retell component)**	Maze CBM	Word Lists, Reading Accuracy, Reading Comprehension (explicit, implicit, vocabulary questions) (Inventory)	Oral Reading Fluency
Grade 4	Retell Fluency DORF (with retell component)** Daze (DIBELS maze)**	Maze CBM		Oral Reading Fluency
Grade 5	Retell Fluency DORF (with retell component)** Daze (DIBELS Maze)**	Maze CBM		Oral Reading Fluency
Grade 6	Retell Fluency DORF (with retell component)** Daze (DIBELS Maze)**	Maze CBM (through grade 8)		Oral Reading Fluency (through Grade 12)

*DIBELS (Sixth Edition; Good & Kaminski, 2002)
**DIBELS Next (Seventh Edition; Dynamic Measurement Group, in press)

Comprehension is the goal of reading. Reading is a lifeline to advanced educational opportunities and increased economic potential. People read to learn and find out how to accomplish new tasks and to enjoy vicarious experiences and places they might not otherwise experience.

Reading comprehension is a complex task and involves the ability to derive meaning from text. It is an active process that requires connecting background knowledge, vocabulary, word recognition, and fluency along with the ability to make inferences and to integrate information as it is being read. According to the RAND Reading Study Group (2002), there are three major elements in reading comprehension: the text, the reader, and the activity. When designing reading comprehension instruction, master teachers weave these elements together with the knowledge that if they are able to teach their students to engage in the reading process through discourse actively and to employ research-based reading strategies consistently, successful reading comprehension will follow.

DESCRIPTIONS OF MEASURES OF COMPREHENSION

What Is Retell Fluency?

The DIBELS Retell Fluency measure assesses comprehension. Immediately after reading passages from the DIBELS Oral Reading Fluency (DORF) measure, students are asked to retell all they can remember.

What Is Maze?

Maze, designed to assess comprehension on AIMSweb and DIBELS Daze (7th ed.), is a multiple-choice cloze task that students complete while reading silently. The first sentence of a 150- to 400-word passage is left intact. Thereafter, every seventh word is replaced with three optional words in parentheses. One of the words is the exact one from the original passage. Science-based research has shown that this procedure provides a reliable and valid measure of reading comprehension, especially in Grades 4 and higher (Fuchs & Fuchs, 1991, 2004).

How Is Reading Comprehension Measured on the TPRI?

The TPRI uses three types of tasks to assess comprehension in Grades 1 through 3: word lists, reading accuracy, and reading comprehension questions. The primary purpose of the timed word list reading is for correct story placement. Once the correct story is selected for accurate placement in a passage (i.e., the level of story is matched to the student's reading level), the student is timed while reading a 100-word passage. WCPM is then calculated as a fluency rate. Next, five different comprehension questions are given to the student, including literal, inferential, and vocabulary questions:

- *Literal questions* typically refer to information that is stated directly and presented in a very straightforward fashion. Literal comprehension items cover facts and details and relationships between ideas (e.g., comparison, contrast, sequence of events, cause and effect) that are stated clearly in the passage.

- *Inferential questions* are often referred to as those in which the reader must "read between the lines." Using background knowledge or prior information combined with the text information at hand to make connections or inferences is essential in order to answer inferential types of questions.

- *Vocabulary questions* require the reader to identify the meanings of words as they are used in the passage. Integration of skills is employed. For example, readers must utilize context clues and maintain a general understanding of the passage. It is helpful to have an overall knowledge of common Greek or Latin roots, prefixes, and suffixes as well.

How Is Comprehension Measured on the FAIR?

Three key reading comprehension components are assessed on the FAIR: comprehension placement word list, reading comprehension (accuracy and fluency) and vocabulary (see Chapter 7). A listening comprehension task is given to students in the beginning and middle of kindergarten.

- *Comprehension placement word list:* The primary purpose of this task is to determine which passage is the best grade-level fit for students and allows for an accurate measure of comprehension, accuracy, and fluency. The student reads approximately eight words. The number of words read correctly determines which passage to administer.

- *Reading comprehension (accuracy and fluency):* On this task, the student reads a selected passage based on the results of the comprehension placement word list. Both fluency and word accuracy scores are calculated. The student then responds to comprehension questions that measure explicit, implicit, and vocabulary knowledge.

Why Do We Measure Comprehension?

ORF (now called DORF in the 7th edition of DIBELS NEXT) can predict a student's comprehension ability. The correlation between a student's ability to read fluently and accurately and comprehension has been demonstrated to be as high as 0.91 (Fuchs, Fuchs, & Maxwell, 1988). If students are reading words correctly per minute at benchmark levels on a measure of ORF, then teachers can be pretty confident that they also have a positive indication of students' comprehension. Retell Fluency and Maze are then backup measures used to identify those students for whom ORF is not indicative of adequate reading comprehension skill. Most often, these will be students with low language skills or ELL students.

With the addition of more in-depth, focused assessments of learning, teachers can grasp the relationship between assessment and classroom learning. This increasingly transparent connection allows teachers to make more effective decisions and provide focused, differentiated instruction, thus resulting in improved literacy skills for struggling readers.

For many years, educators thought that comprehension occurred as a natural outcome of the ability to read. However, this is not the case. Formal instruction through specific strategy instruction and other means strengthens the reader's ability to gain information from the text, expands learning beyond the text, and builds an appreciation for combining meaning from several sources (Cain & Oakhill, 2007). Specifically, educators have learned

- A teacher's overt modeling of comprehension behaviors is an effective tool in the classroom, one that improves students' use of comprehension strategies.
- Asking and assisting students to tell you about what they have read sends a message that what they are reading is important and helps them dig deeper for meaning.
- Prompting or questioning before, during, and after reading can lead students to deeper text understanding.
- Using more complex strategies that teach students to organize and summarize text produces higher levels of comprehension as students get older.

Listening Comprehension Sets the Upper Limit for Reading Comprehension

Reading comprehension, according to Gough and Tunmer (1986), is the product of decoding and listening comprehension. Since their *Simple View of Reading* was proposed, research has identified language skills as a major contributor to literacy and reading ability (Mehta, Foorman, Branum-Martin, & Taylor, 2005). Reading comprehension requires the presence of *both* decoding and well-developed language abilities to make meaning. Listening comprehension requires solid language abilities—vocabulary, syntax, background knowledge, and verbal reasoning—to connect personal context to sentence context in order to make meaning and allow students to comprehend a variety of text structures. Students whose language skills are deficit require direct instruction in those missing or weak oral language skills before successful comprehension can be achieved. For further discussion, see Chapter 7.

What Does This Simple View of Reading Mean to Teachers?

Right from the start, young students need to become aware of phonemes and learn the code of written language, graphemes, and speech sounds for those graphemes, so they can become proficient decoders. Thus, teachers need to teach decoding. Teachers also need to build listening comprehension. While students are learning to decode simple words and reading decodable books, teachers should read to them regularly from more sophisticated texts. These texts will provide exposure to longer complex sentence structure and unique vocabulary within multiple fictional and nonfictional settings. In the process, students should be engaged in discussion during and after reading, provided with word study that focuses on meanings of words, invited to share stories and experiences, and asked to explain "phenomena" in the classroom (e.g., growth of seeds, care of a guinea pig).

According to Carlisle and Rice, the more "talk (i.e., extended discourse) there is in the classroom, the greater the likelihood that students will be able to read complex texts with understanding from the late elementary years on" (2002, p. 158).

Teachers should model the comprehension thinking of proficient readers. During read-alouds, teachers may stop and model thinking about what they are reading. A teacher might say, "I wonder why polar bears have black skin. This is really hard to understand, so I better slow down and read that again."

Teachers should engage young students in thinking aloud during read-alouds by asking critical thinking questions. The teacher may say, "Tell me what you think about his decision to go home. What makes these children's lives different from ours?" Remind students to use think-alouds routinely. They may practice this strategy during their small-group instruction but forget to apply this strategy during independent reading. Teachers should take what good readers do implicitly or naturally and make it explicit for struggling readers. Readers need lots of supported practice before interaction with text at higher comprehension levels becomes automatic.

Most important, teachers should talk. Guided discussion is what teaching comprehension—both listening *and* reading comprehension—is all about. When building young students' listening comprehension, teachers are setting upper limits to where students' reading comprehension may grow once they have the decoding ability to read more complex material.

Retelling and Maze

DIBELS uses the process of *retelling* for Grades 1–6 as a comprehension indicator. AIMSweb and DIBELS use Maze, which is recommended for Grades 3–8. Both of these indicators help teachers identify students who may be at risk for academic difficulty and would benefit from focused comprehension instruction.

Retelling

Retelling is one way of measuring comprehension, but it is also an instructional method for creating awareness of comprehension, improving oral language, and facilitating the organization of information for recall. Some students with low language skills need to be taught how to retell what they have read. Teachers can model the elements of good retelling and then instruct students to practice retelling narratives and informational text. Teachers can assist students to improve retelling by teaching through the following stages to attain levels of complete retelling:

1. *Simple recall*
   - Retells beginning, middle, and ending events in order
   - Retells possible description of the setting

- States an initiating event and the solution of the problem
- Has a beginning, middle, and ending in order

2. *Multipart retelling*
- Sequences events and facts correctly
- Provides missing information through suitable inferences, such as character's emotions or cause and effect
- Includes reasonable explanations for basis of actions

3. *Most comprehensive retelling*
- Sequences actions and events correctly; tells main ideas
- Infers to supply missing information that explains actions; supplies details to support main ideas
- Explains the motivations behind the character's actions; adds personal inferences and interpretation to retell

Maze

Unlike retelling, Maze (AIMSweb and DIBELS Daze) is a method used for assessment only. Cloze, a once-popular method for teaching word identification and comprehension, is similar to Maze. Cloze passages relied upon asking students to guess words that would fit in the blanks of a passage. This practice has not withstood the empirical rigor of research. In fact, studies show guessing words produces inaccurate and faulty meaning and does not teach students to decode for accurate word reading (National Reading Panel, 2000). Only a small percentage of words can be guessed accurately based on context only. The cloze procedure is not recommended as a valid process for teaching reading.

Here is an example of a Maze passage:

> David and Mark wanted to go to a football game at the large new stadium. The game was five days away *(and, another, also)* they had to think of a *(walk, way, what)* to talk their parents into taking *(them, those, then)*. First, they developed a plan to *(hold, host, help)* convince their parents. Second, they planned *(some, a, those)* specific time to sit down and *(talk, sing, dance)* with them. Finally, the boys mapped *(in, out, over)* just what they wanted to say. It was now or never, the family talk must be tonight!

The Maze is an appropriate comprehension check for Grade 3 and up. Its technical validity increases as students get older, and it can be given in a group setting.

Comprehension Accomplishments

Like the other components of reading, comprehension appears to develop along a predictable continuum. The National Research Council (1998) recommended comprehension accomplishments by grade level. Teachers can use these lists of accomplishments, along with their state standards and Core reading program scope and sequence guides, to make sure they are teaching the necessary comprehension components at each grade level and that each child achieves his or her benchmarks. Teachers need to provide explicit comprehension instruction, making the internal thinking of comprehension visible. Use these accomplishments to direct planned learning opportunities through questioning and prompting, which will guide students to talk about what they have listened to and read.

Kindergarten

- Notices when simple sentences fail to make sense
- Connects information and events in text-to-life and life-to-text experiences
- Retells, reenacts, or dramatizes stories or parts of stories
- Listens attentively to books teacher reads to class
- Demonstrates familiarity with a number of types or genres of text (e.g., storybooks, expository texts, poems, newspapers, and everyday print such as signs and labels)
- Correctly answers questions about stories read aloud
- Makes predictions based on illustrations or parts of stories

First Grade

- Monitors own reading and self-corrects when an incorrectly identified word does not fit with the letter sounds in the word or the context surrounding the word
- Reads and comprehends both fiction and nonfiction that is appropriately designed for grade level
- Notices when difficulties are encountered in text, decoding, vocabulary, and complex sentence structure
- Reads and understands simple written instructions
- Predicts and justifies what will happen next in stories
- Discusses prior knowledge of topics in expository and narrative texts
- Discusses how, why, and what-if questions in sharing nonfiction texts
- Describes new information gained from texts in own words
- Distinguishes whether simple sentences are incomplete or fail to make sense; notices when simple texts fail to make sense
- Can answer simple written comprehension questions based on material read
- Engages in a variety of literary activities voluntarily (e.g., choosing books and stories to read, writing a note to a friend)

Second Grade

- Reads aloud with fluency and comprehension any text that is appropriately designed for grade level

- Reads and comprehends both fiction and nonfiction that is appropriately designed for grade level
- Rereads sentences when meaning is not clear
- Interprets information from diagrams, charts, and graphs
- Recalls facts and details from texts
- Reads nonfiction materials for answers to specific questions or for specific purposes
- Takes part in creative responses to texts such as dramatizations, oral presentations, and fantasy play
- Discusses similarities in characters and events across stories
- Connects and compares information across nonfiction selections
- Poses possible answers to higher order how, why, and what-if questions

Third Grade

- Reads aloud with fluency and comprehension any text that is appropriately designed for grade level
- Reads and comprehends both fiction and nonfiction that is appropriately designed for grade level
- Reads longer fictional selections and chapter books independently
- Takes part in creative responses to texts such as dramatizations, oral presentations, and fantasy play
- Can point to or clearly identify specific words or sentences that are causing comprehension difficulties
- Summarizes major points from fiction and nonfiction texts
- Distinguishes cause and effect, fact and opinion, main idea, and supporting details in nonfiction
- Asks how, why, and what-if questions in interpreting nonfiction texts
- In interpreting fiction, discusses underlying theme or message
- Uses information and reasoning to examine bases of hypotheses and opinions

The Importance of Discourse to Teaching Comprehension

The literature is full of resources and strategies for teaching comprehension. Therefore, comprehension lessons have become heavily strategy focused, sometimes removing the teacher and student from the rewards of deepening reading comprehension through discourse and dialogue. Current Core reading programs based on scientific research regularly attend to reading comprehension through daily lessons. Comprehension goals are provided, and prompts and queries guide teachers at critical junctures to engage students in discussion that leads to the realization of the content-related goals. Strategies are also included in these reading programs. It is the combination of teacher-directed rich discussion about content and strategies that truly teach reading comprehension skills to students.

Strong knowledge about the complexities of reading comprehension includes an understanding of how the text, the reader, the task, and the context all impact a student's ability to comprehend text. Teachers who use Core reading programs need little else in the way of strategies to accompany the reading program lessons. However, it is a good idea to have a few proven strategies to supplement instruction when students are not making the connections they need in order to strengthen and deepen understanding of what they are reading. The strategies and activities in this chapter are intended for that purpose. Above all else, teachers should engage students in *discourse* (conversation) and *writing* about what they have read and learned.

Additional Assessments and Instructional Tips

More information is often needed for planning instruction routines for students demonstrating comprehension weaknesses. The first question that teachers should ask is, "What components are necessary for comprehension?" Some of these components are discussed in previous chapters. This section separates comprehension into more detailed "chunks," including

- Reading accuracy and fluency
- Oral language
- Background knowledge
- Basic literal comprehension
- Inferential comprehension
- Understanding text structures (narrative and expository)
- Metacognitive skills

How can specific strengths and weaknesses in reading comprehension be identified or diagnosed? Both reading accuracy and fluency are measured with DIBELS, AIMSweb, TPRI, and FAIR. ORF Benchmark scores may be obtained by using the norms that accompany each test. The ORF Decision Tree (see Figure 5.1) may be used as a guide for determining additional assessment and instructional focus in areas of phonics, phonological awareness, sight word knowledge, and fluency. (More about the ORF Decision Tree in previous sections.)

Oral language can be assessed in a one-to-one setting by a qualified examiner using assessment instruments such as the TPRI, the Peabody Picture Vocabulary Test–Third Edition (PPVT-3; Dunn & Dunn, 1997), the Test of Word Knowledge (TOWK; Wiig & Secord, 1992), the Wechsler Individual Achievement Test (WIAT-II; Wechsler, 1992), the Texas Primary Reading Inventory (TPRI; Texas Education Agency, 1998), or the Iowa Test of Basic Skills (ITBS), to name a few.

Once oral language weaknesses are identified (or even when they are expected to be weak), many strategies and resources can be used for improving language skills. It is essential that teachers provide direct instruction in language skills along with language-rich environments, well-stocked classroom libraries, and abundant opportunities for language interaction. See the Activities in this chapter and in Chapter 7 for specific ideas for improving oral language development.[1]

Background knowledge can be assessed informally and formally through some of the more standardized vocabulary tests listed previously. However, because vocabulary knowledge tends to be text specific, it makes more sense to check students' background knowledge prior to reading a selection and provide the missing knowledge or information before reading. The prereading plan (PReP) strategy (Friend & Bursuck, 2006; Langer, 1984) allows teachers to do just that—identify what specific background knowledge is missing and decide what concepts to teach *before* starting a reading lesson. There are three steps to the PReP strategy:

1. The teacher prereads a section or story to be taught and chooses two or three key concepts to be taught.

2. The teacher holds a brainstorming session with students, telling them to verbalize anything that pops into their heads when they hear the key words. This gives the teacher a good idea of what the students may already know about the key words, and allows opportunities for clarifying any misunderstandings.

3. The teacher makes a determination of whether the students seem to have correct or accurate ideas of the key concepts or if additional hands-on multisensory elaboration and experience with the key concepts is needed. In some classrooms, only a few students may need the additional multisensory expansion; in other classrooms, the majority of the students may be unfamiliar with the new key concepts being introduced and large-group instruction may be warranted.

The PReP strategy is also recommended for use with English language learners. It provides an avenue for teaching vocabulary and oral language skills, both cornerstones of reading comprehension success.

Basic literal and inferential comprehension can be assessed informally with teacher-made tests, assessments that accompany core reading programs, or more traditional standardized measures typically administered by an approved examiner. Some of the standardized individually administered tests assessing literal and inferential comprehension include the following:

• The Gray Oral Reading Test–Diagnostic (GORT-D; Bryant & Wiederholt, 1991)

• The Test of Reading Comprehension–Third Edition (TORC-3; Brown, Hammill, & Wiederholt, 1995)

---

[1]*Note:* Before referring a student for a more formalized assessment of oral language, teachers may want to use the oral language screener (Carreker & Boulware-Gooden, 2009), provided in Chapter 7.

- The Woodcock Reading Mastery Test–Revised (WRMT-R; Woodcock, 1998)
- The Passage Comprehension Subtest in the Woodcock-Johnson Achievement Battery (AM WJ-III Achievement; Woodcock, McGrew, & Mather, 2000)

Most statewide achievement tests also include a measure of comprehension that is consistent with state reading standards. Teachers may use the scores from these tests as a general measure of comprehension as well.

Understanding narrative text structures is an often-missed component in assessment of reading comprehension instruction. In keeping with the understanding that struggling readers tend to be passive and not aware of text clues or aids that might assist them in both understanding and retaining what they read, it is important to assess students' knowledge of text structure in both narrative and expository texts. For young students, it is enough to expect them to become aware of the *wh* questions: *who, what, where, when,* and *why.* Carnine and colleagues (2004) suggest asking *wh* questions, such as the following, to determine how well young students comprehend them:

- Who is the story about?
- What is he or she trying to do?
- Where did the story take place?
- When did the event happen?
- Why did the character do what he or she did?

For older readers, Carnine and Kinder (1985) suggest assessing seven topics: theme, setting, character, initiating event, attempts, resolutions, and reactions. Teachers can create questions for each topic or ask the student to retell and evaluate the completeness of the student's retelling based on these seven elements.

The assessment form in Figure 6.1 can serve as an informal comprehension measure. Teachers may elect to use it as a retelling evaluation guide or as a basis for questioning and probing the student. It can be implemented as a progress monitoring tool to regularly evaluate the progress students are making toward complete understanding of the story grammar elements in their reading.

For students with expressive language weaknesses (i.e., those who may have particular difficulty expressing verbally what they know about a passage), teachers may consider some form of a performance assessment, a modified "hands-on" demonstration-type assessment. Historically, acting out or drawing a picture that reflects the mood or theme of a text has been considered an appropriate method to capture the student's knowledge, which might otherwise be obscured by language weaknesses. If expressive language skills are weak, however, use these opportunities to *teach* language skills. Model for students how to talk about what they have read through think-alouds. Provide sentence starters (e.g., "When Abby saw the bird…"), provide two possible answer choices as you prompt, and ask students to repeat the answer and add a little new information.

Assessing Essential
Story Grammar Knowledge

Story Grammar Elements	Sample Questions	Observed?
Setting	Where did it happen? When did it happen?	Yes/No
Character	Who is the story about? What is _____ like? Physical, Personality traits? Would you like to take his/her place?	Yes/No
Problem	What is _____'s problem? How did this get started? What does _____ need to try to do?	Yes/No
Sequence events	What did _____ do about _____? What will _____ do now?	Yes/No
Outcome	How did _____ solve the problem? How did _____ achieve the goal? What would you do to solve _____'s problem?	Yes/No
Reflection	How did _____ feel about the problem? Why did _____ do _____? How did _____ feel at the end? Why did he/she feel that way? How would you feel?	Yes/No
Theme	What is the major point of the story? What is the moral of the story? What did _____ learn in the end of the story?	Yes/No

Figure 6.1.   Assessment form for essential story grammar knowledge. (*Sources:* Bursuck and Damer, 2007; Carnine and Kinder, 1985.)

Next STEPS in Literacy Instruction: Connecting Assessments to Effective Interventions by Susan M. Smartt and Deborah R. Glaser

Expository text structure knowledge is assessed differently than narrative texts. When looking at an informational (expository) text with a student, teachers should

- Point to a bold chapter heading and ask, "Why is this writing in bold print?"
- Open to a page with pictures and ask, "Tell me how these pictures can help you understand what you read."
- Point to the text under the pictures and ask: "Why are these words here?"
- Open the book and say, "Show me where you could look to find out what a word means." (the glossary)
- Open the book and ask, "Where could you look to find out the name of a chapter?" (the table of contents)

Use the information gained to teach the major elements of expository text in a more concrete way.

After a student reads from an expository text with at least 95% accuracy (or after reading the text to the student), simply ask questions related to the content. For retelling, the teacher may instruct, "Tell me as much information as you can remember from the selection you just read" (Gunning, 2002; Klingner, 2004). If necessary, the teacher may add, "Can you tell me anything more?" When comprehension gaps are identified, teachers can use concept maps and other forms of graphic organizers to teach students how to organize expository text information by the most common text types:

- Compare and contrast
- Chronological sequence of events
- Point of view
- Problem/solution
- Process, cause, and effect

Metacognitive skills are a critical contributor to successful reading comprehension and are often a weakness for struggling readers. Metacognitive skills can be assessed by evaluating how well students are thinking about their reading as they read. For example, teachers can ask themselves, "How strategic are my students when they plan for reading and how well do they monitor during reading?" Although listening to students read aloud will give insight into reading behavior, it may be helpful to ask students directly, "What do you do while you're reading?" More specifically, teachers can ask, "What do you do before you read and to help make sure you understand what you read?" Ask the same questions during and after reading. For many students, this may be the first time they have thought about thinking about reading while they read!

At the end of the Comprehension Strategies section, there is a checklist of proficient reader behaviors for before, during, and after reading that can be used as an assessment tool, and also as an instructional and progress monitoring guide to lead students to being more active in their role as readers.

Sentence Comprehension

Before students can understand the meanings of paragraphs and entire passages, they must understand word meanings and sentence meaning. This may be the case for young children ages 3–5 or even for older students who have not, for whatever reason, developed age-appropriate oral language skills. Another prerequisite not commonly discussed in reading comprehension circles is the importance of the ability to retain verbal information in short-term memory. Although they master decoding and fluency, some students still struggle to comprehend what they read. Teachers may need to go back to the sentence level and assess the student's understanding of basic words and phrases in addition to short-term phonological memory.

Struggling readers with weaknesses in short-term memory may have difficulty repeating what they hear verbatim. School tasks, such as following directions or listening and keeping up with a story or lecture, require that students be able to retain information in short-term phonological working memory. According to Marzola (2005), "If individuals cannot retain the information in a sentence long enough to repeat it, they are unlikely to be able to recall the information needed from those sentences to answer simple questions." She recommended that students be able to repeat sentences containing five to eight words. The following scaffolded activity to increase students' ability to retain verbal input is recommended by Carnine and colleagues (2004) for 3–5 minutes of daily practice. Start with the *my turn–our turn–your turn* format and move to *my turn–your turn* as soon as students no longer need the *our turn* mediated support.

Teacher: "My turn, you listen: The car is red."

Teacher: "Our turn. Now we'll say the sentence together: The car is red."

Students and teacher in unison: "The car is red."

Teacher: "Your turn."

Students: "The car is red."

Teacher: "Good job! I like the way you listened very carefully to my words and repeated them back just the way I said them."

The teacher's voice will drop out as students' memory improves. Increase the length of each sentence (5–8 words), gradually providing practice with several sentences at the level that is most challenging for the students. Go back to shorter sentences when necessary. Drop out the *our turn* scaffolded step when students are more independent with the concept.

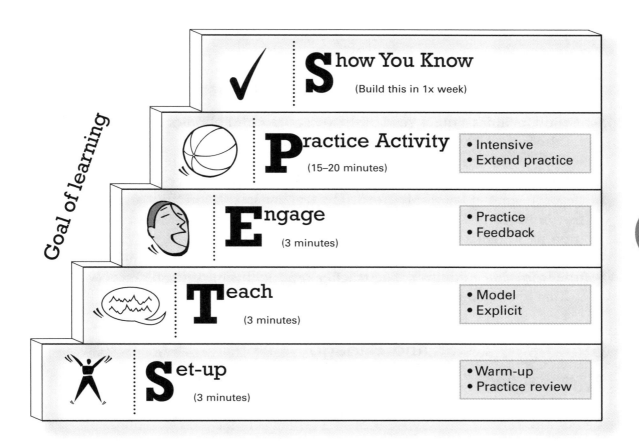

HERE WE GO: READY TO TEACH!

Inside a Real Classroom: A Comprehension Lesson Snapshot

Teachers at Reading Success Elementary school know that engaging students in dialogue about what they are reading is a powerful way to increase comprehension and teaches students how to think about text. They are working together to improve their use of prompts instead of questions that can be answered with simple recall responses. They are finding that this is not easy to do, so they often discuss the process with each other and help each other prepare prompts for shared reading selections at their grade-level meetings.

Mrs. Craft, a second-grade teacher, has been using graphic organizers to help students create summaries (see next section). This has been a helpful process that has produced higher level summaries in her class, but she realizes that she needs to engage in discourse about what the authors are saying. She wants her students to discover the "take aways" from their reading—the authors' intended theme-related goals.

As Mrs. Craft prepares for her lesson, she notes that the core program provides a couple of inferential questions to lead a discussion about the story, but none of them get at the theme or lesson that can be learned from reading the story. So she prepares a set of prompts to use during the next day's lesson. She will share these with her colleagues at their next meeting.

Set-up

Set-up includes a quick read of the vocabulary and phonics lesson words that are in the story. Mrs. Craft writes the words in a column on the board. She points to each word and gives a cue for students to read each word chorally. This is a review of phonics and vocabulary lesson words from the day before, in which the teacher leads a game of Guess My Word. The teacher says, "I am thinking of a word that is a musical instrument, one that you blow air into. Its sound is usually high notes." Students raise their hands as they figure out the answer, but no one says the word until Mrs. Craft calls on a student to respond. Then all students read the word *flute* in unison. The teacher repeats this meaning-based reading game with a few more words.

  Teach and Engage

The class begins to read *Zeke and Pete Rule!* (Dunlap, 2005).

Teacher:	"Today, while we are reading, I will ask you questions that will help us understand the author's message. I want everybody to have a turn to answer the questions. A lot of our talk about the story will be about what you think the story is about. Why do you think Zeke asked Pete to sit and stay with him?"
Student 1:	"Because he liked him."
Teacher:	"Yes, but what did we learn about Zeke on the first page of the story that can give us a different answer?"
Student 2:	"He was playing his music all alone."
Student 3:	"He didn't want to be alone."
Student 4:	"Zeke wanted friends."
Teacher:	"I am going to read the first page again. Let's see if your answer makes sense. [Teacher reads the first page again.] So, why do you think Zeke asked Pete to sit and stay with him?"
Student 5:	"Zeke didn't like to play alone and wanted a friend."
Teacher:	"Do we all agree with this thinking? Let's read on. [A couple more pages are read.] How did Zeke and Pete work together?"
Students:	[Suggest several answers to this question]
Teacher:	"So, why can working together be a good thing? [This question is the main question to get students to realize that when our friends are good at something and we are good at something, we can work together and share our talents to help each other. This strengthens friendships.] Will someone please restate what we just learned about friendship in this story?"

Student 6:   "It is good to have friends, and when we play and work with our friends and learn something from them, we can teach each other new things."

Teacher: "Turn to your partner and share what we learned about friendship in this story."

Practice Activity

After reading the story and repeating the comprehension goal outcome, students are asked to write two or three sentences about friendship based on what they learned from reading the story. The teacher provides a sentence starter for students to use if they wish, such as "Being a good friend means...."

Show You Know

The teacher instructs students to form their pairs and asks them to reread the story to each other. Each partner reads a page. While they are reading, Mrs. Craft monitors the reading, especially with her struggling readers, to make sure accuracy levels are high. At the end of the story, each partner tells the other partner what they learned from reading the story.

COMPREHENSION STRATEGIES

Comprehension instruction is most successful when students apply strategies they are learning *directly* to the reading material that they are given to read. Teachers should not teach comprehension strategies in isolation of reading, but rather should make comprehension real. The following comprehension strategies are developed from the key comprehension strategies listed below, supported by science (NICHD, 2000; Snow, 2002):

• Monitoring comprehension
• Using graphic and semantic organizers
• Answering questions
• Generating questions
• Recognizing story structure (and other text structures)
• Summarizing

Strategies

Monitoring Comprehension

Teach students to monitor their understanding during reading by asking, "Does this make sense? Do I need to slow down? Do I need to reread this?" The teacher's verbal modeling of monitoring is a well-proven strategy: "I wonder what the author wants me to learn here."

Armbruster, Lehr, and Osborn (2001) summarized key comprehension monitoring strategies recommended for students who do not automatically monitor what they read as they read. Teachers should model these strategies aloud for students:

1. Identify specifically *where* the difficulty occurs (e.g., "I don't understand the first paragraph on page 20.")
2. Identify what the difficulty is (e.g., "I don't get what the author is trying to say about his hometown.")
3. Restate the difficult sentence or passage in one's own words (e.g., "Oh, so the author is saying growing up in his hometown was different than in the city he lives in today.")
4. Look back through the text (e.g., "The author talked about other places he's lived in Chapter 2. I wonder how they are the same or different from his hometown.")
5. Look *forward* in the text for information that might help resolve the difficulty. (e.g., "The text says the author was born in Bayou Country, but I don't have any idea where Bayou Country is. Oh, if I read ahead, it may tell me…. The text says, 'Many parts of southern Louisiana are known as Bayou Country.' Oh, I know all about Louisiana because I went to visit my cousins there last summer." (Activating background knowledge)

Graphic and Semantic Organizers

Graphic organizers are visual presentations of ideas, concepts, facts, and details and their relationship or interactions in an organized structure. They can be especially beneficial for struggling readers who have some type of oral language weakness. Graphic organizers help students to visualize links between ideas or to think visually and retain information more efficiently. They can be used to facilitate class discussion and as a helpful aid for review of

(continued)

(continued)

material and concepts. Two of the most commonly used graphic organizers are semantic mapping and story mapping.

Graphic organizers are most effective when teachers complete a practice run prior to using them with students. Then, teachers are clear about the goals of learning, will have encountered and addressed any problem areas, and can guide students through the process, prompting for vocabulary and key knowledge. Use graphic organizers before reading to set a purpose, during reading to collect and confirm information, and after reading to summarize. Each student should have their own organizer to complete; however, group efforts occasionally can be used to promote cooperative learning. Examples of graphic organizers are provided in Figures 6.2 and 6.3.

Connect–Correct–Collect

Connect–Correct–Collect (CCC) is a before, during, and after comprehension process that was developed by Suzanne Carreker (2005). It is an alternative to the common method of know–want-to-find-out–learned–still-need-to-learn (KWLS). Both of these procedures are used to set a purpose for reading and stimulate background knowledge about a topic before reading, and to assess what new knowledge has been gained after reading. With the KWLS

process, teachers often end up with lots of unsubstantiated material gathered from students that has very limited usefulness (see Figure 6.4). The CCC process, however, gives the teacher a little more control over the discussion by leading students through prepared questions to elicit information that relates directly to what the students will be reading (see Figure 6.5). For example, when preparing to read a passage about ants with KWLS, the teacher may ask, "Tell me what you know about ants." With CCC, the teachers would preread the passage and ask questions that can be answered in the text, such as "There are different kinds of ants. Do you know what some of those kinds of ants are? What are some of the things that ants eat? Where do ants live?" Students' *connect* responses can be checked against the information in the text for accuracy, in order to *correct* and *collect* new information they learn.

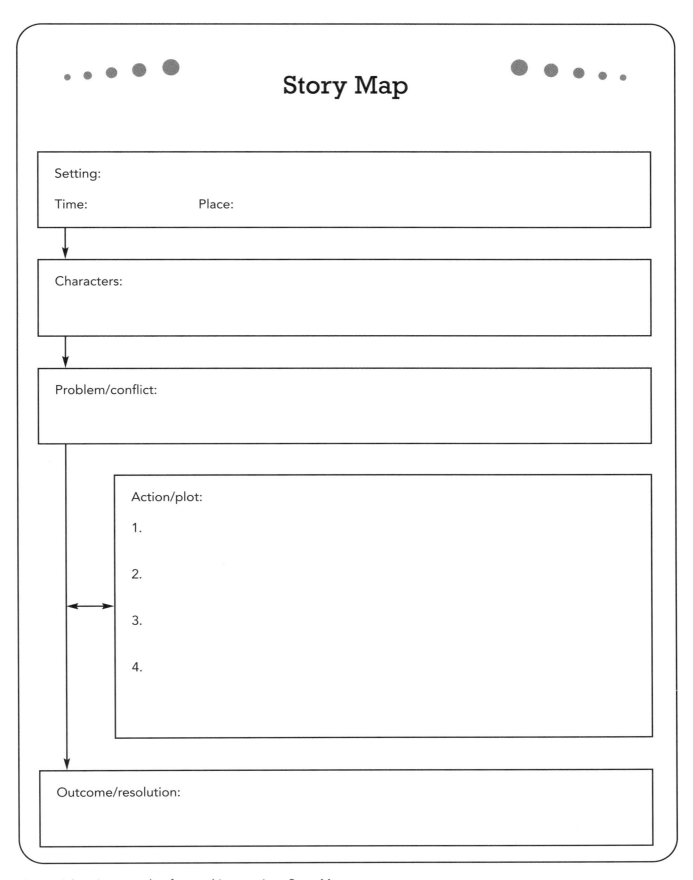

Story Map

Setting:

Time: Place:

Characters:

Problem/conflict:

Action/plot:

1.

2.

3.

4.

Outcome/resolution:

Figure 6.2.   An example of a graphic organizer: Story Map.

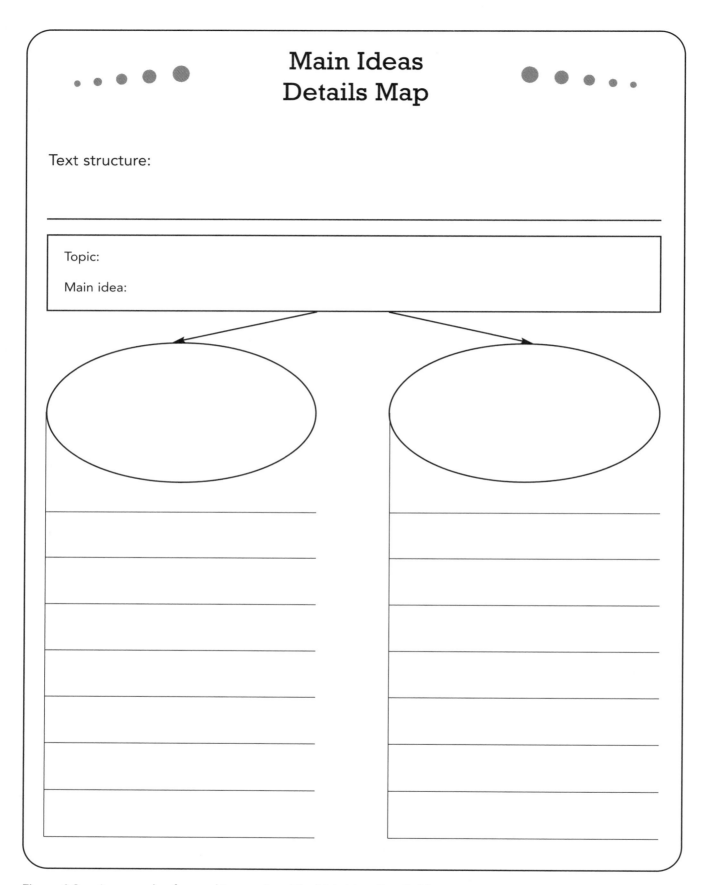

Figure 6.3. An example of a graphic organizer: The Main Ideas Details Map.

Reading Comprehension
KWLS Plus Strategy Sheet

K—Know	W—Want to Find Out	L—Learned	S—Still Need to Learn

Figure 6.4.   The Know–Want-to-Find-Out–Learned–Still-Need-to-Learn (KWLS) process.

Connect-Correct-Collect

Connect This is what I know.	Correct Do I need to correct anything?	Collect This is what I learned.

Figure 6.5. The Connect–Correct–Collect (CCC) process.

From Neuhaus Education Center. (2005). *Developing metacognitive skills* (p. 51). Bellaire, TX: Author, © 2005 by Neuhaus Education Center. Used with permission from Neuhaus Education Center, Bellaire, Texas. Permission to duplicate the forms for classroom use is granted.

 In *Next STEPS in Literacy Instruction: Connecting Assessments to Effective Interventions* by Susan M. Smartt and Deborah R. Glasser. (2010, Paul H. Brookes Publishing Co., Inc.)

Questioning

Well-prepared teachers know ahead of time when comprehension may break down in an assigned reading passage. Many times, the text presents complex sentence structure or the author does a poor job of connecting information or providing key background information. Prepare key questions that go deeper than simple recall and ask these at these critical points. Ask questions that begin with, "Why do you think…" or "Tell me what you learned here."

Generating Questions

Instruct students to generate questions from their reading material. Prepare them for this process by teaching them question–answer relationships (Raphael, 1986):

1. Prepare several questions about something that the students have read.
2. Make some of the questions recall, so that the answers are in the text (e.g., "What did the character do when he heard about the problem?").
3. Create a few complex questions that require critical thinking, judgment, and opinion, so that the answer is in the students' heads (e.g., "What would have happened if she had read the letter?").
4. Require students to identify if the answers to the questions are found in the text or if they are found in their heads.
5. Instruct students to create their own questions. Direct them to create some questions with answers that come from the text and some questions with answers that come from their minds.

Teachers may need to provide students with lots of help to create these types of questions. Exercises in which students classify questions may be appropriate before asking them to generate their own. Model and demonstrate what these kinds of questions are all about. Compare and contrast simple questions (e.g., "What happened next?") with complex questions (e.g., "Why do you think she left the party?"). Give students the *wh* question words to get them going: *who, what, where, when, why,* and *how.*

• • • • •

WH Questions

Sometimes teachers assume that young children know the meaning and understand the *wh* or question words. However, these words can be troublesome for many students. Before students can comprehend the meaning of sentences and answer complex questions, they need to be able to recognize different types of information and answer the basic questions of text:

- What happened?
- Who did the action?
- Where did it take place?
- When did the event occur?
- Why did it happen?

When teaching the *wh* words, introduce one new question word at a time and do not rush the process. Make sure the students have a solid understanding before introducing another *wh* word. Carnine et al. (2004) suggested teaching *who* and *what* questions first, *when* and *where* next, and *why* questions last. Teachers can use the following *my turn–your turn* approach for teaching *wh* words:

Teacher only,
modeling: "Mary skated down the street. *Who* skated down the street? Mary. *What* did Mary do? Skated down the street."

Teacher: "I'm going to make a statement, then ask you to answer a question. Is everyone ready? The boy ran fast. *Who* ran fast?"

Students: "The boy."

Teacher: "*What* did the boy do?"

Students: "Ran fast."

Continue the procedure as each *wh* word is introduced. For example, for *where* and *when* read the following sentences:

Teacher: "Johnny ran down the street early this morning. Say the sentence."

Students: "Johnny ran down the street early this morning."

Teacher: "*Where* did Johnny run?"

Students: "Down the street."

Teacher: "*When* did Johnny run?"

Students: "Early this morning."

(continued)

(continued)

PRACTICE ACTIVITY

Once students have been introduced to all five *wh* words (*who, what, when, where,* and *why*), the teacher provides each student with a set of the five *wh* word cards. The teacher reviews the meaning and use of each *wh* word by asking corresponding questions about a familiar topic. Students can also be directed to turn to their partner and take turns using the *wh* words: "Who went to the store? Why did he go? What did he buy?"

The teacher then reads a short two- or three-paragraph passage to students and asks questions that correspond to the *wh* question words. Students either hold up their card (against their forehead) to show they know what type of question was being asked or touch the correct card from the group of cards on their desks. Students may collaborate with their partners to see if they have compatible responses, as teacher glances across desks to monitor for correct responses.

Next, the teacher asks students to rearrange the *wh* cards on their desks into a specific order: *who, when, what, where,* and *why.* Instruction then transitions to more advanced learning of the elements of story grammar: characters (who), setting (where, when); action/outcome/event (what happened and why) (Carreker, 2005).

Writing to Improve Comprehension

Writing forces students to formalize what they know. Writing about what they have read, along with solid writing instruction, builds an understanding of how written language works and can improve sensitivity to syntax (word order), vocabulary, and more complex sentence structure (Graham & Perin, 2007). Avoid free journal writing when the focus for writing tasks is to improve reading comprehension. Prepare higher order and inferential questions to guide students' writing. Questions that begin with "What do you think..." can really get students involved with language use. Discuss answers through conversation *before* instructing students to write their answers. Of course, correct students' work for content, but also use the opportunity to evaluate spelling, sentence structure, mechanics, and vocabulary.

● ● ● ● ●

Reciprocal Teaching

In reciprocal teaching (Palencsar & Brown, 1984), students take turns leading discussions about the text in small groups. The prompts are prepared on cue cards for students to use. The teacher writes each of the following headings and questions on a separate card and places them on a small metal ring. The student who is the teacher holds the cards and asks the questions to lead discussion. This process works best if the real teacher trains students to use it by modeling the process beforehand.

PREDICT BEFORE EACH SECTION

Please get ready to read to_____ .
I predict this section will be about _____ because_____.

QUESTION GENERATING

Ask questions as you read: *who, what, where, when, why, how,* and *what if.*
Are there any ideas you found interesting or puzzling?

CLARIFY

Were there any words you did not understand?
Was there anything confusing to you?
Do you have any "I wonder" questions?

SUMMARIZE

This was about _____.
What do you think the author wants us to remember?

● ● ● ● ●

Recognizing Story Structure

Narrative text reflects a structure that young children understand. There is a beginning, middle, and ending to a story just like there is a beginning, middle, and ending to the child's day. Beyond this simple organization, there also exists setting, problem, important events, outcome and theme. Teach these elements of story structure using graphic organizers. Lead a discussion about

(continued)

(continued)

story content using the vocabulary of story structure: What is the problem in this story? What is the setting? Who is the main character? Use Figure 6.3 or a story map from any core reading program to assist with understanding narrative text organization.

● ● ● ● ● ●

Summarizing

Learning to summarize has its roots in the early comprehension work that teachers do with children. It is a complex skill that requires the abilities to categorize and find the main idea. "What was this paragraph about?" is a simple question that begins the teaching and learning process of summarizing. Students will initially provide a retell instead of a summary, including many details from the reading. If students are including too much information in their summaries, try a strategy called Sticky Ideas to help them clarify the main ideas of a passage.

Students are given two or three narrow sticky tabs. Students are guided while reading to mark the important ideas in a paragraph, page, or topic area with the tab as they come to them. The ability to find main ideas is one of the contributing skills to the ability to summarize. It is helpful to ask students to share with the group their main ideas and explain why they chose the ideas they did. This process is similar to one used by Hoyt (2008).

● ● ● ● ● ●

What Good Readers Do: Learn from the Pros

Research tells us that good readers are actively engaged as they read and that struggling readers tend to be more passive. The following strategies are to be used before, during, or after reading. They may be referenced for ideas to help readers become more engaged in thinking about the texts. Post the headings on a bulletin board. Add the strategies under the headings as they are taught. Model the strategies openly and explicitly for students. Reference the board frequently as a reminder to apply these "good reader strategies."

(continued)

(continued)

What Good Readers Do

Before reading, good readers...	During reading, good readers...	After reading, good readers...
☑ Set a goal, a purpose	☑ Monitor their understanding as they read	☑ Reflect on their comprehension
☑ Preview the text; become familiar with its organization	☑ Compare what they read to their own personal experiences and knowledge	☑ Revisit the set purpose for reading the material
☑ Predict what the text will say	☑ Restate ideas into their own words	☑ Consider the new learning in light of what they anticipated learning
☑ Connect their background experience, information, attitudes, and feelings	☑ Identify the big picture ideas, the main ideas	☑ Determine the most important connections to remember
☑ Try to develop some interest in the topic; make up some "I wonder" questions that will be answered in the text	☑ Slow down, monitor, reread, and repair comprehension	☑ Attempt to clarify vague ideas through rereading, discussion, and other means
	☑ Note unknown vocabulary and seek the meaning of words	☑ Review material periodically
	☑ Paraphrase/summarize passages	☑ Evaluate their learning
	☑ Create visual images while reading	

(continued)

(continued)

Harris and colleagues (2008) translated these before, during, and after reading strategies into a new acronym, TWA:

- THINK before reading
- Think WHILE reading
- Think AFTER reading

We suggest adding a discussion element to each of these statements:

- Think and discuss with a partner *what you will be reading about.*
- Think and be ready to answer questions *while* you are reading.
- Think and discuss with the group what you thought about the reading *when you finish.*

Teachers should create a poster outlining each of the TWA steps and post it in the room as a reminder for both teachers and students!

RESOURCES

Birsh, J. (2005). *Multisensory teaching of basic language skills.* Baltimore: Paul H. Brookes Publishing Co. (In a chapter titled "Teaching Comprehension from a Multisensory Perspective" by Margaret Taylor Smith, the importance of not waiting until decoding skills are developed to initiate comprehension instruction is discussed. Listening comprehension instruction should take place along with decoding instruction. There is ample information about how to direct instruction of comprehension for struggling readers.)

Cain, K., & Oakhill, J. (2007). *Children's comprehension problems in oral and written language: A cognitive perspective.* New York: Guilford Press. (This edited text investigates reading comprehension through the lens of language skills. It identifies which skills contribute to reading comprehension at what phase of reading development to guide our instruction.)

Carnine, D.W., Silbert, J., Kame'enui, E.J., Tarver, S.G., & Jungjohann, K. (2004). *Teaching struggling and at-risk readers a direct instruction approach.* Glenview, IL: Pearson Scott Foresman. (This book has explicit guidelines and even scripts for teaching comprehension. Unlike other books designed to remediate reading problems, this resource provides specific suggestions for strategies to use when initial strategies are unsuccessful. When addressing comprehension, the authors start with an overview defining comprehension at both the beginning and later primary stages. Then they proceed to give concrete suggestions of how to teach comprehension across various levels of development with the research-based connections carefully identified.)

Carreker, S. (2005). *Developing metacognitive skills: Vocabulary and comprehension.* Bellaire, TX: Neuhaus Education Center. (This book includes lessons to teach listening comprehension for three reading and language skill levels. Graphic organizers, instructional tips, and scaffolded lessons prepare teachers to teach and students to gain metacognitive comprehension skills.)

Harris, K.R., Graham, S., Mason, L.H., & Friedlander, B. (2008). *Powerful writing strategies for all students.* Baltimore: Paul H. Brookes Publishing Co. (This book is a virtual "how-to" manual for teaching writing strategies, especially for students who struggle to write. Furthermore, since the overlap between students who struggle to read and those who struggle to write is significant, the strategies provided in this book are remarkably similar to those metacognitive strategies used by many reading teachers, such as self-monitoring and goal setting. This book focuses on self-regulated strategy development as a writing strategies approach with over 2 decades of supportive research. Writing improves reading comprehension and vocabulary development. Teachers will find this book a strong resource for integrating the two.)

Honig, B., Diamond, L., & Gutlon, L. (2008). *CORE: Teaching reading sourcebook for kindergarten through eighth grade.* Novato, CA: Arena Press. (This mammoth book is a true encyclopedia of teaching reading, with a strong commitment to research-based practices. It contains solid descriptions of comprehension strategies and examples for use in the classroom for both expository and narrative texts. It provides many helpful hints for working with the English language learners; http://www.corelearn.com/resources)

Hults, A. (2004). *Reading first: unlock the secrets to reading success with research-based strategies.* Huntington Beach, CA: Creative Teaching Press. (The comprehension section of this book focuses on teaching text strategies. It includes many graphic organizers and semantic maps, question-generating activities, strategies for summarizing, and comprehensive ways for students to self-monitor comprehension. A cognitive strategies checklist included in this book may be especially helpful. It is designed to help students focus on reflecting, predicting, checking, connecting, and clarifying as they read; http://www.creativeteaching.com)

Klingner, J., Vaughn, S., & Boardman, A. (2007). *Teaching reading comprehension to students with learning difficulties.* New York: Guilford Press. (This book is a comprehensive source for a solid overview of reading comprehension and various ways to assess reading comprehension along with vocabulary instruction. It provides a clear description of how to teach comprehension strategies starting with text structure; before, during, and after reading strategies; reciprocal teaching; and collaborative strategic reading. This book contains many helpful tables and charts listing supplementary materials and tests.)

Mathes, P.G., & Torgesen, J.K. (2005). *SRA Early Interventions in Reading Comprehensive.* McGraw-Hill SRA, Columbus, OH. (This is a supplemental early reading program with a strong focus on comprehension. Levels 1 and 2 are described as an intensive intervention program designed to be used along with a core reading program for struggling readers in Grades 1 and 2. Ideally, the program is provided for 120 lessons lasting about 45 minutes each session. The classroom teacher, resource teacher, or a paraprofessional can be trained to deliver the intervention. Although the fundamental components of early reading are included in this program, it differs from most because it integrates all of the research-based elements of teaching such as error correction, pacing, scaffolding, immediate corrective feedback, and specific praise, among others. The teacher's manual is teacher friendly, with clearly stated objectives and lists of teaching materials. Screening and placement tests are included if needed. Comprehension skills are typically developed through activities that stimulate students' receptive and expressive vocabulary. Students are taught to self-monitor and use story grammar to help in understanding what they hear or read. Finally, this program has a uniquely strong research base of support; learn more at http://www.sraonline. com/intervention_resources/recommended_programs/html/EIR.htm.)

Moats, L. (2009). *Language Essentials for Teachers of Reading and Spelling (LETRS)*. Longmont, CO: Sopris West Educational Services. (Modules 6 and 11 cover comprehension in this series of LETRS training manuals and are excellent research-based manuals for reading teachers. Professional development based on the LETRS modules is available through the publisher.)

Pauk, W. (2000). *Six-way paragraphs: 100 passages for developing the six essential categories of comprehension*. New York: Jamestown Publishers. (These student books come in three levels: introductory [reading levels 1–4 with 25 passages at each level], middle [4–8], and advanced [8–12]. The books feature high-interest, factual content designed to build both reading level and informational background knowledge. They focus on six questions, with the main idea being the primary focus. Other questions involve subject matter, supporting details, conclusions, clarifying devices, and vocabulary in context. A diagnostic chart is included to enhance the process of identifying which types of questions are more difficult or easier for students and areas that need more work; http://www.glencoe.com/gln/james town/index.php4.)

Snow, C. (Ed.). (2002). *Reading for understanding: Toward an R&D program in reading comprehension*. Washington, DC: RAND Corporation. (This book is the result of a study conducted by the RAND Reading Study Group, made up of 14 experts in reading who were charged with proposing strategies for improving long-term research and development programs supporting the development of improved reading comprehension. The book contains definitions of reading that include four parts: the reader, the text, the activity, and the context. It also summarizes what we already know and what we need to know about reading comprehension.)

Vaughn, S., & Linan-Thompson, S. (2004). *Research-based methods of reading instruction, grades K–3*. Alexandria, VA: Association for Supervision and Curriculum Development. (This book contains suggested activities and strategies for teaching all five of the essential components of reading, and reading comprehension is particularly strong. The authors make sure all strategies in this book are research based; http://www.ascd.org)

7

Vocabulary

VOCABULARY MEASURES

	DIBELS	AIMSweb	TPRI	FAIR
Kindergarten	NA	None currently	Listening Comprehension	Listening Comprehension
Grade 1	Word Use Fluency**	None currently	(Vocabulary of print-related concepts)	Expressive Vocabulary
Grade 2*	Word Use Fluency**	None currently	Word Reading (Understanding of words in context)	Expressive Vocabulary
Grade 3*	Word Use Fluency**	None currently	Word Reading (Understanding of words in context)	Expressive Vocabulary (vocabulary embedded within reading comprehension questions; through Grade 12)

*Neuhaus Oral Language Screening: Grade 2–Grade 5
**DIBELS (Sixth Edition, Good & Kaminski, 2002; *Note:* DIBELS Next, Seventh Edition, does not include Word Use Fluency.)

• • • • •

FORMATIVE ASSESSMENTS FOR VOCABULARY SKILLS

Vocabulary skills can be measured through DIBELS Word Use Fluency (WUF), TPRI Listening Comprehension Tasks, FAIR Expressive Vocabulary, the Neuhaus Oral Language Screening Tool (Carreker & Boulware-Gooden, 2009), and other informal and standardized assessments.

DIBELS Word Use Fluency

DIBELS provides a measure of oral language and vocabulary knowledge through Word Use Fluency. A student is given a word orally and asked to use the word to show that they know the meaning. The number of words the student uses in response, along with an appropriate conveyance of word meaning, is used to score vocabulary knowledge. An indication of a student's verbal skills is also gathered by this measure. Word Use Fluency (WUF) is not included in DIBELS Next.

TPRI Listening Comprehension Tasks and FAIR Expressive Vocabulary

Both TPRI and FAIR provide a listening comprehension measure for nonreaders, specifically kindergarten students who are not yet reading text independently (i.e., beginning and middle of the year). Students listen to a passage read aloud and respond to five comprehension questions, both literal and implicit.

On FAIR, an Expressive Vocabulary Task is given in kindergarten through Grade 2 at both the beginning and the end of the year to students whose performance is in the at-risk categories or in "the yellow and red success zones," as referred to by some who use graphs to chart student progress. Students are asked to look at picture cards and identify the name, action, or attribute represented and to respond to a question, with or without a prompt. For example, the teacher may say, "What is this?" or "What is this person doing?" or "Tell me another word for ___ [e.g., *sad*]."

Standardized or normative measures of vocabulary knowledge can also be used to establish vocabulary levels. Common measures are the Peabody Picture Vocabulary Test (Dunn & Dunn, 2007), the Expressive One-Word Picture Vocabulary Test (Brownell, 2001a), and the Receptive One-Word Picture Vocabulary Test (Brownell, 2001b). In addition, many teachers find the CORE Vocabulary Screening test (Diamond & Thorsnes, 2008), a measure of reading vocabulary for Grades 1–8, to be easily accessible and efficient.

The Neuhaus Oral Language Screening Tool

The Neuhaus Oral Language Screening Tool has been validated for Grades 2–5. The purpose of this screener (see Figure 7.1) is to alert teachers to readers who may lack language proficiency to the point that it may negatively affect reading comprehension. With this expanded knowledge, teachers are then in a strong position to provide additional language support and supplemental services to the student.

The Neuhaus Oral Language Screening Tool

Student name: _____   Teacher name: _____   Date: _____

Procedure: The student names items from four different categories (see below). He or she names items in each category for 30 seconds. Use hash marks to record the number of items. Count repeated items once. Do not count items named that are out of the category. Record the final number. Total the final number of all four categories and divide by two. This number represents the number of items named in 1 minute.

Directions: *You are going to name items in categories. When I give you the category or group, you will name items or things until I say, "stop."*

Ready? Name things that you find in a classroom. Begin.
Time the student for 30 seconds as he or she names *things in a classroom.*
Record items named with hash marks: _____
After 30 seconds, say, "Stop." Record the number of items: _____

Ready? Name fruits and vegetables. Begin.
Time the student for 30 seconds as he or she names *fruits and vegetables.*
Record items named with hash marks: _____
After 30 seconds, say, "Stop." Record the number of items: _____

Ready? Name animals. Begin.
Time the student for 30 seconds as he or she names *animals.*
Record items named with hash marks: _____
After 30 seconds, say, "Stop." Record the number of items: _____

Ready? Name states in the United States. Begin.
Time the student for 30 seconds as he or she names *states in the United States.*
Record items named with hash marks: _____
After 30 seconds, say, "Stop." Record the number of items: _____

Total for all four categories: _____
Divide by 2 ____

Benchmarks:
2nd grade: 14 items per minute
3rd grade: 15 items per minute
4th grade: 18 items per minute
5th grade: 22 items per minute

Figure 7.1.   The Neuhaus oral language screening tool.

From Carreker, S., & Boulware-Gooden, R. (2009). *Neuhaus Oral Language Screening.* Bellaire, TX: Neuhaus Education Center, © 2009 by Neuhaus Education Center. Used with permission from Neuhaus Education Center, Bellaire, Texas.
Permission to duplicate the forms for classroom use is granted.
In *Next STEPS in Literacy Instruction: Connecting Assessments to Effective Interventions* by Susan M. Smartt and Deborah R. Glaser. (2010, Paul H. Brookes Publishing Co., Inc.)

The Neuhaus Oral Language Screening Tool was developed around the premise of the simple view of reading (Gough & Tunmer, 1986; Hoover & Gough, 1990). Traditionally, of the two components that make up the simple view of reading—decoding and language comprehension—decoding has been the easier to evaluate and teach. The language comprehension component is more difficult to unpack for assessment and instruction because comprehension of written text is an amalgam of decoding and fluency as well as oral language, world knowledge, syntax, working memory, attention, and motivation. Reading comprehension assessments often measure only one aspect of the whole. The Neuhaus Oral Language Screening Tool measures the language comprehension component of reading comprehension.

Oral language is the foundation on which literacy is based, and reading comprehension depends on oral language skills. If the reader knows the meanings of most of the words on a printed page, the likelihood of the reader understanding the text improves (National Institute of Child Health and Human Development, 2000). In addition, the reader's oral language discourse skills contribute to reading comprehension. The screening, given individually, is intended for use during the first 4 weeks of a new school year; however, it may be given as needed. Here is a brief summary of the tool:

1. The student names items in a given category for 30 seconds.
2. The number of items named in each of the four categories is tallied.
3. The total numbers of all items named in all categories are added together and divided by two.
4. The resultant number is the number of items the student named in 1 minute.

The benchmarks for the different grade levels are listed at the bottom of the screening tool.

A student at a given grade level who meets the appropriate benchmark is most likely at or above an average standard score for that grade level in reading comprehension and vocabulary. If a student reaches the benchmark on the Oral Language Screening Tool at his or her grade level, but is exhibiting (or begins to exhibit) difficulties in reading comprehension, a screening of word recognition should be given to determine if reading comprehension is hindered by inaccurate or slow decoding. A student who does not meet the designated benchmark at his or her grade level will benefit from activities such as naming, semantic webs or maps, and story retelling (see Chapter 6).

A promising validation base is already established for this tool. However, the authors believe it would be beneficial for any test results collected from school districts using the screener to be shared with them.

Other Informal and Standardized Assessments

Some teachers assess vocabulary and general comprehension by using their own listening comprehension tests. These measures are developed first by the teacher selecting passages from graded books, then reading the passages to the students or having the students listen to a recorded version. After listening to the text being read to them, the students are asked a variety of comprehension questions ranging from literal to more complex, inferential, and experiential questions requiring higher order critical thinking skills. The students listen and answer orally; thus, no reading or writing is required by the student. Usually no more than five to eight comprehension questions are included, depending on the length of the passage. Students' listening comprehension and vocabulary are assessed through the teacher's informal judgment of their use of language and the accuracy of the students' answers.

Teachers working with students for whom English is not their first language need to know their students' English language levels. Language assessments that include vocabulary measures can provide this information and help determine the levels of language exposure and growth that their students will need. The Peabody Picture Vocabulary Test (Dunn & Dunn, 2007) is a common assessment for this purpose.

How Are Comprehension and Vocabulary Related?

Comprehension and vocabulary go hand in hand. Strong, well-developed vocabulary knowledge sets the stage for strong and efficient reading comprehension. Both skills rely on the presence and use of oral language. Each skill supports the development of the other. Therefore, vocabulary instruction can be combined with comprehension instruction. Consider the following interconnectedness of decoding, vocabulary, comprehension, and fluency: If a word is decoded and pronounced, but the word meaning is unknown, comprehension will be impaired. If a word is not decoded automatically and fluently, reading slows down and comprehension may also be impaired. Knowing a word's meaning assists with accurate and fluent word decoding and recognition (Kamil & Hiebert, 2005).

Vocabulary is a powerful predictor of reading comprehension. Studies by Jordan, Snow, & Porche (2000) concluded that vocabulary size in kindergarten predicts reading comprehension in intermediate and middle school. The often reported "reading slump" in fourth grade is attributed to below-grade-level vocabulary knowledge. Orally tested vocabulary at the end of first grade predicts reading comprehension 10 years later (Cunningham & Stanovich, 1997).

With this understanding of the critical role vocabulary plays in reading comprehension and word reading, vocabulary should be a focus of instruction all day, every day! Through conversation and shared discussion using the words that students will see in print when they read, teachers can increase students' vocabulary and comprehension. This requires purposeful and thoughtful preparation on the teacher's part.

What Do We Know About Improving Vocabulary Skills in the Classroom?

Students come to us with a vocabulary reflective of their oral language experiences in early childhood. Some children emerge from environments where language experiences were rich and advantageous to the development of extensive vocabularies, whereas others have had limited exposure to language and experience in the world; they may bring very limited language understanding and ability to the classroom (Hart & Risley, 1995).

Vocabulary levels vary widely in classrooms where students bring discrepant background and oral language experiences and increasingly speak languages other than English. Estimates tell us that with explicit teaching, students learn about 400 words per year (Beck, McKeown, & Kucan, 2002). However, by listening to and reading moderately challenging material, students can learn nearly 3,000 words per year (Nagy & Anderson, 1984).

Vocabulary Is Learned Through Implicit and Explicit Means

Vocabulary is learned incidentally (indirectly by exposure to language through reading and being read to) and through planned and explicit vocabulary instruction.

Indirect–Implicit Vocabulary Instruction

Teachers should expose students to language and lots of varied vocabulary. Teachers can weave these indirect methods for increasing oral language and vocabulary into daily routines in the following ways:

- *Read orally to students.* Choose texts that provide exposure to unusual, unique vocabulary, yet have utility in a student's life, while discussing familiar concepts. Discuss content using vocabulary from the text.

- *Lead and encourage discussions using vocabulary from the readings.* Say to students, "Tell me about the boy's decision and use the word *difficult*."

- *Include expository text choices for oral reading.* This is especially important in schools with high numbers of students with low socioeconomic status who have not had interaction with the wider world, and the resulting opportunities to develop the associated vocabularies and background knowledge.

- *Offer increasing opportunities for students to read on their own as their reading skills increase.* Remember, monitored oral reading is preferred to silent, unmonitored reading for students who are still mastering basic reading skills and are at some risk on their fluency measures. Monitored oral reading means that teachers choose reading material for students that is just right (not too hard and not too easy) and listen to students read. While listening, teachers provide feedback through correction, assisting with decoding, and checking for understanding. Young readers need multiple opportunities to read material with 100% accuracy, thus creating neural connections for correctly learned word recognition. Teacher-monitored oral reading facilitates this process.

- *Provide opportunities for students to listen to books on tape.* Follow up with teacher-led discussion about the content, use vocabulary from the story, and focus on predefined goals of learning about the content (vocabulary and comprehension).

Direct–Explicit Vocabulary Instruction

Explicit vocabulary instruction requires the selection of a set of words to teach. Comprehensive reading programs choose words from the reading selections and provide explicit teaching methods to teach those words during weekly lessons. Upon close scrutiny of those words, however, the teacher may discover that students are familiar with some of them or there may be words that have little or no usefulness in other contexts. It is helpful for teachers to understand how to choose words that, when learned, promote productive vocabulary development so as to strengthen vocabulary lessons.

Choosing words to teach is not an easy task. What words should you teach and how many? When should you stop once you begin choosing words? Word lists multiply quickly when previewing reading materials to identify vocabulary words to teach. It is not unusual for teachers to isolate 15 or 20 words in a story, but it is unreasonable to assume that students will truly learn that many new words. The amount of time it would take to teach all of those words may be the entire reading period! The following guidelines can help teachers choose the words to teach explicitly through the practice activities that follow. Vocabulary for instructional consideration can be classified as one of three types (Beck et al., 2002):

- *Tier I:* familiar words that students know and use, which are critical to the meaning of the text (e.g., *mother, house, play, cold*)
- *Tier II:* unfamiliar words that carry unique meanings, of which students have a concept and can express with a simpler common vocabulary term (e.g., *relative, habitat, recreate, frigid*)
- *Tier III:* unfamiliar words that are specialized within a context and that students will rarely encounter; they have low utility and can be taught through brief explanation within the context of the story (e.g., *platypus, biserial, sachet*)

Generally, Tier II words should be chosen for instruction. These words are useful terms, which students can use to relate to and discuss their own experiences. Teachers should choose three to five Tier II words per reading selection. These are the words that will expand students' vocabularies. English language learners may require attention to Tier I words as they are learning English.

Any text or conversation provides opportunities to teach or strengthen new vocabulary, either implicitly or explicitly. Teachers can use the following steps when teaching new vocabulary words:

1. *Begin with a routine.* Say the word, then have the student say the word. Always ask students to say the word. This engages the phonological components of the brain and begins establishing neural connections for remembering the word.
2. *Provide a definition of the word.* Make the definition simple and connect the meaning and word's use to something the children have experience with.

3. *Connect the meaning of the word to the context* in which it is used in the reading selection or conversation.

4. *Remind students to use the word often.* Model the use of the word for students. Celebrate when students use their new words. Post the words in the room to remind you and the students to use the words in conversations and writing.

When their awareness is heightened, teachers may realize that they are regularly confronted with unusual vocabulary. Consider sources such as community events, news stories, television programs, or advertisements. Choose general words that may not be present in the situation or text but can be used to discuss the content (e.g., use the word *devastating* when discussing a tornado). Over time, teachers develop a sensitive awareness to increasing their own vocabulary and opportunities to model vocabulary use in conversation and instruction with their students. The goal is for teachers to increase their own vocabularies and model use of unusual words in their conversations with students.

HERE WE GO: READY TO TEACH!

We've discussed elements of effective vocabulary instruction and the connection between vocabulary knowledge and reading comprehension. Now it is time to look in on Mr. Hudson's classroom and observe a real vocabulary lesson being taught with the STEPS Lesson Plan format as the guide.

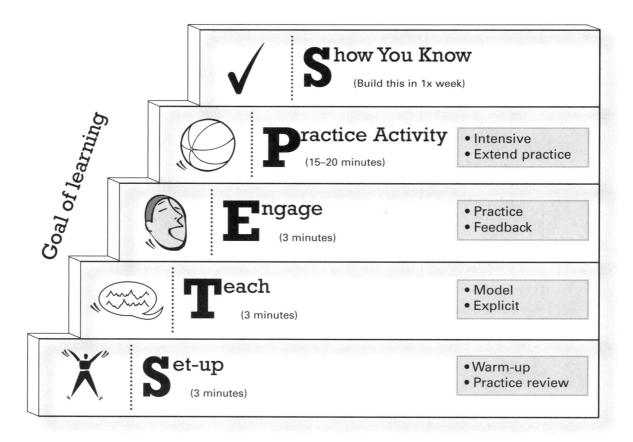

Inside A Real Classroom: A Vocabulary Lesson Snapshot

Mr. Hudson is a third-grade teacher. He has been working to improve his verbal interaction skills in the classroom because he knows how closely correlated language skills are to literacy skills. His goal is to increase student talk and decrease teacher talk while boosting his and his students' vocabulary levels. Four of his students are English language learners. He knows that the benefits of these targeted skills will include improved language skills for all of his students.

Mr. Hudson chooses an assortment of vocabulary words from the core reading program selection and from content area and read-alouds to use in discussion and to teach explicitly every day. He revisits the words often and over time, minimally for 1 week. Here is a brief snapshot of his vocabulary lesson during the reading period.

 Set-up

Set-up includes a review of previously learned vocabulary. The class is divided into small groups. Mr. Hudson writes three words from the previous week's vocabulary lesson on index cards. He gives one card to each of three small groups of students. Each group takes a turn to play Act It Out for their word (see Activities section). Students raise their hands when they know the word. One group is chosen to guess. When the word is determined, two other students in the group must use the word in a sentence to show they know the meaning. Points are awarded to teams.

  Teach and Engage

Mr. Hudson demonstrates, shows, and models the meanings of words and uses them in a variety of contexts. Students are engaged, too, connecting the words and meanings to their own experiences. Several words from the week's reading lesson are written on the board. Mr. Hudson guides students to decode each word and then directs the students to say each word after him. Once students have decoded and repeated each word in the list, he focuses on three words for direct instruction.

Teacher:	"Great job reading these words. They will be used in the story we read this week, *The Long Road Home*. [Points to word.] This word is *ashamed*. Say it."
Students:	"Ashamed."
Teacher:	"*Ashamed* means feeling badly about something you did. In the story, Rebecca feels ashamed—bad and sad—about something she did to her

friend. Sometimes we use this word *ashamed* when we are talking about feeling guilty or wishing you didn't do something you did. When would you use the word *ashamed*?"

Student: "When I take something from my little sister and make her cry, I feel ashamed."

Teacher: "Nice job making that connection and using *ashamed.* Anyone else know a time when you would use this word?"

Another student volunteers a context from her experience and uses the word. The teacher repeats the process with the other two words.

 ## Practice Activity

Students work with the teacher to complete a graphic organizer for one of the vocabulary words. They complete graphic organizers for the other words over the next 2 days. Graphic organizers are often included in reading programs. See the Activities section for some examples. The teacher may say, "Let's work together to fill in this organizer for our new word *ashamed.* Write it in the middle circle." The teacher then creates the graphic organizer on a piece of chart paper as the students create theirs. Students work together to verbalize a definition for *ashamed* and write it; brainstorm synonyms and antonyms for *ashamed;* and take turns verbally sharing contexts in which *ashamed* can be used. They are then directed to write sentences or draw a picture for one of the contexts. The teacher instructs students to add additional context sentences and pictures during extra activity time.

 ## Show You Know

After reading the story, students are asked to turn to their partner and use the vocabulary words in a discussion about the story. The teacher says the word, the students say the word, and then they engage in Talk a Word (see Activities). The teacher monitors the discussions for accurate use of the words.

Activities

Teach Individual Words

The following explicit, teacher-directed activities are categorized according to four guidelines established for effective vocabulary instruction (Graves, 2004):

Teach Individual Words

Provide Children with Frequent, Extensive, and Varied Experiences with Language

Teach Students Strategies for Learning Words Independently

Foster Word Consciousness

Talk a Word

Place students into groups of two and say a vocabulary word that the students have learned. Students should be instructed to share a discussion with their partner using the provided word. Each student must say at least one sentence using the word that tells about a personal experience, the story, or other observation. Ask individual students to share their discussion, again using the target vocabulary word. Repeat the process with another word.

   Note: The teacher should monitor the discussions and praise correct use of the word or provide support and correction when needed.

Vocabulary Word Diary

Provide students with their own individual vocabulary diary. Instruct students to write target vocabulary words in their diaries. Younger students can then illustrate their words and older students can write sentences using the vocabulary words. Provide time to review these diaries often, sharing sentences and asking younger students to describe their illustrations using the target words.

Display Words

Create a bulletin board or exclusive place on a wall to post vocabulary words. Refer to them often when talking with students. Ask students to use the words

(continued)

(continued)

as a reference when writing and speaking. Continue to add new words as they are taught. Remove words once students are using them regularly, demonstrating that they own the words. Display these words in another location, indicating, "We Know and Use These Words!" Reward the students for using these words during the school day. Students can write their name on a sticky note and place it on the words they use.

● ● ● ● ●
Match Word

Make two lists of words and display them in two columns. The students must think of something that a word from the first list has in common with a word in the second list. When they think of a match, they may come to the front of the room, draw a line to connect the two words they are thinking about, and tell what the words have in common. Words like these could be used with second graders, and might be taken from a common core reading program:

List 1	List 2
harbor	*applaud*
extraordinary	*protection*
entire	*uncertain*
miracle	*extravagant*
hesitate	*scare*

Explaining the connections is perhaps even more valuable than making the connections. During the explanation, students verbalize the higher level thinking that leads to increased levels of oral language ability.

Note: Younger students will require support. Teachers may need to connect two words and ask, "How do these words go together?"

● ● ● ● ●
Act It Out

Small groups of students act out a target word's meaning and classmates guess the word. Verbs work well with this activity. Post the words in the room for students to reference when guessing.

● ● ● ● ●

Word Bee

Small groups of students work together to define a target word and present definitions to classmates. Give students a definition template, such as

A [noun] is a _____ that _____.

To [verb] is a way of _____ that _____.

● ● ● ● ●

Word Substitution

Teammates replace a target word in a sentence with another word that means the same thing. Remembering to provide children with frequent, extensive, and varied experiences with language can be a challenge. Finding out about well-research approaches that incorporate the principles of effective language instruction for young children can be even more difficult. In the next section, you will learn more about one strategy that meets all of these requirements; is research-based, extensive, and can be used frequently with children in Grades K–2.

Provide Children with Frequent, Extensive, and Varied Experiences with Language

The following activities will help give children exposure to language.

● ● ● ● ●

Shared Storybook

This oral language and vocabulary targeted intervention is easy to implement with little preparation and planning needed. It provides frequent, extensive, and varied exposure to vocabulary. Directions are provided here, but it is recommended that the process be reviewed in the original publication (Baumann & Kame'enui, 2004). Students should have at least six exposures to the target storybook vocabulary over 6 days. Plan to use two storybooks per week, which will each be read two times. Read the first storybook on Monday and

(continued)

(continued)

Wednesday, and read the second storybook on Tuesday and Thursday. An overview of the shared storybook routine is provided in Figure 7.2.

Monday	Tuesday	Wednesday	Thursday	Friday	Monday
Read book 1	Read book 2	Read book 1	Read book 2	Story retell	Review all words
Introduce target words. Define them during reading.		Use target words to preview/review the book.		Talk about the story using target words and illustrations to help retell.	Use cloze procedure with the words. Read new book to begin process again.
Use target words in comprehension questions and discussion.		Students produce the definitions.		Use synonyms in Guess the Word game.	Play the What Am I Talking About? game.

Figure 7.2. An overview of the shared storybook routine. From Bauman, J.F., & Kame'enui, E.J. (2004). *Vocabulary instruction: Research to practice* (p. 41). New York: Guilford Press; adapted by permission.

DAYS 1 AND 2

First, introduce target words. Choose three words from the text that are important to understanding the story and likely to be unfamiliar to students. Write them on index cards or sentence strips. Display the words one by one, reading each one to the students and asking the students to repeat the words. Tell students, "When you hear this word in the story, raise your hand." When the words are read and students raise their hands, stop and say the word and then give a simple definition of the word.

Tip: Practice giving a simple definition beforehand. Sometimes it's not so easy!

Reread the sentence with the target word and continue reading. If students do not raise their hands when one of the target words is read, say, "Did anyone hear one of our words?" and read the sentence again. Proceed to then give the definition and continue reading. Then, use the word in comprehension questions and discussion. After reading the story, ask one comprehension question per word. Ask a question that can be answered using a target word. Direct students to use the words. Ask students to rephrase their answers, using the target word if necessary (e.g., "Why was Harry digging furiously?").

DAYS 3 AND 4

Use target words to preview and review. Prior to rereading the story, show students pictures from the book that illustrate the target words. Talk about the

(continued)

(continued)

picture and story using the target words in the discussion. Have students produce definitions. During the discussion, students should respond to teacher requests to tell what the target words mean:

Teacher: "In the story, the children see a strange dog. What is *strange*?"

Student 1: "*Strange* is something or someone that you do not know."

Student 2: "*Strange* is what Harry was when he was all dirty!"

DAYS 5 AND 6

Talk about words with illustrations. Show a picture from the story that illustrates a target word. Talk briefly about the picture. The teacher may say, "Harry put his scrubbing brush in the ground and covered it with dirt. What is our special word for that? Yes, *buried*." Then play Guess the Word by providing opportunities for students to choose a synonym for the target word. The teacher may say, "What word goes with furiously? *Wildly* or *calm*?"

Use the cloze procedure to present target words within a different context than the story. Use a sentence with the target word missing. Students provide the target word to fill in the blank:

Teacher: "The seeds were put in the ground and covered with dirt. The seeds were…."

Students: "Buried!"

You can also play the What Am I talking About? game.

Teacher: "See if you can tell me what I am talking about. We went to the circus and saw many monkeys in a cage. They were very wild, playing and jumping all over the cage. When we threw peanuts into them, they went wild in a fast way. What is our special word for how the monkeys acted?"

Students: "Furiously!"

If students need help, give them a choice (e.g., "Did the monkeys act calmly or furiously?").

● ● ● ● ●

Concept Picture Sorts (Grades K–1)

One of the ways that students store words in their brains is by grouping them with other words that have similar meanings. Therefore, categorizing

(continued)

(continued)

words, pictures, and concepts strengthens semantic connections and assists with recall of those words. Here is an activity to start with:

1. Choose a concept or category (e.g., animals, things that make noise, things with legs).
2. Introduce the concept and help students brainstorm items that belong to the category (e.g., "Name some things that are alive").
3. Assist students with contrasting the concept to items that do *not* fit the category (e.g., "Name some things that are not alive").
4. Provide pictures for students to sort into the categories that were introduced or direct students to find pictures in magazines for sorting.

Another variation on the concept sort is to give a selection of pictures to students and instruct them to find all of the pictures that fit a given category. Students can also be instructed to group the pictures according to their own categories and tell about their grouping. Extend the vocabulary by offering synonyms for common words (e.g., the horse gallops and trots, a cat pounces).

● ● ● ● ●

Word Mapping (Synonyms, Antonyms, Contexts)

This activity is effective, extensive, and varied in the exposure it provides for students. The graphic organizer is an all-purpose tool that helps students to organize information. In this case, students will be organizing words and concepts associated with those words, which compare and contrast in meaning. Instruct students to create their own graphic organizer along with the teacher. Graphic organizers are more effective when students are actively involved in creating their own. Teachers need to "rehearse" the word mapping prior to the exercise to be prepared with words and various contexts they want students to learn through the exercise.

1. Present the word to be mapped (e.g., *appear*).
2. One by one, create webbed categories off of the main word (see Figure 7.3). Ask students to contribute words to the given category. Always begin with synonyms, then antonyms. Add the other categories dependent on the lesson goals and student skill levels. Help students define contexts and experiences illustrating when the word can be used.
3. Provide clues as needed to help students discover more words.

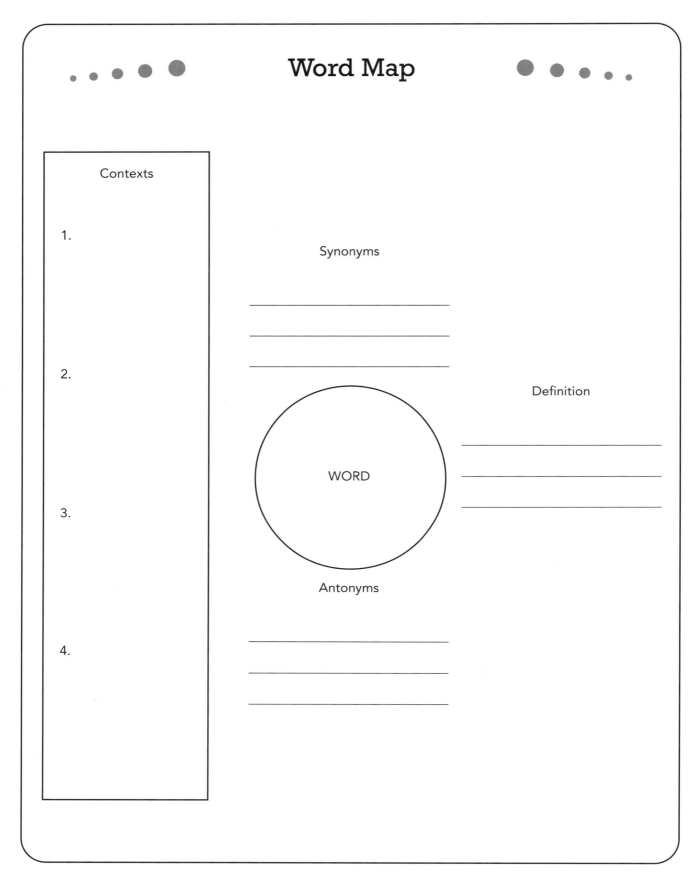

Word Map

Contexts

1.

2.

3.

4.

Synonyms

_____

_____

_____

WORD

Definition

_____

_____

_____

Antonyms

_____

_____

_____

Figure 7.3. Word Map Template.

Teach Students Strategies for Learning Words Independently

Teachers can only teach so many words to students. After fourth grade, as students become fluent readers, the major work of learning new words gradually becomes more the students' task. Prepare students to be word conscious, recognizing when they come across a new word in their reading and what to do with the word to make it their own.

● ● ● ● ●

Dictionary Skills

The method of using the dictionary to look up lists of words and write the definitions has been replaced with a clearer understanding of how to better use the dictionary to promote long-term vocabulary learning. It is important for students to know how to use dictionaries. Dictionaries should be an essential staple in all classrooms, used often by both teachers and students. Teachers should model dictionary use. Refer students to dictionaries to answer questions about words and confirm meanings.

Dictionaries are useful for checking the definitions of words. When students encounter a new word, they should first surmise the meaning based on the context, then look it up to check for confirmation of the meaning. Definitions are most useful if there is an existing basic understanding of the word's use and meaning beforehand. Urge your student to try to explain the word in everyday language and give examples.

One way to learn new vocabulary is to learn the word in relation to another word. The synonym, antonym, category, and descriptions of new words help students to remember and recall those words. Provide explicit instruction to help students understand simple definitions with the *Collins Cobuild* (2005) dictionary. First, model the process of using the *Cobuild* to define unfamiliar words. Next, do it with the students. Then, direct students to use the dictionary independently.

The *Cobuild* dictionary was initially developed for English language learners as a simplified definition dictionary. It focuses on how the word is used, with easily understood wording. Words are rated by the frequency of their use in the English language. This dictionary is also a helpful tool for deciding which words to teach based on frequency of use in everyday English language exchanges. Several levels are available: student, beginner, regular, and advanced.

• • • • •

Word Parts: Roots and Affixes

Teaching morphemes through roots and affixes leads to productive vocabulary instruction, in which learning one word facilitates the learning of several words. For example, teaching the morpheme *-struct*, which means "to build," along with a few affixes can lead to learning many words (e.g., *construct, instruct, instruction*). Learning roots provides visual and meaningful patterns that make it easier to learn. See Resources for programs to help teach word parts.

• • • • •

Create a Word

Write prefixes or suffixes on index cards, one per card. On another set of cards, write root or base words. Instruct students to combine roots or bases with the prefixes to make new words. Students present their words to the rest of the class, give definitions, and use the words in sentences. List the new words on the board for reference. Use Tables 7.1–7.5 as references for teaching word parts.

Table 7.1. Most frequently used prefixes

Prefix	Meaning	Key word	Origin
anti-	against	antifreeze	Latin
de-	opposite	defrost	Latin
dis-	not, opposite of	disagree	Latin
en-, em-	cause to	encode, embrace	Latin
fore-	before	forecast	Latin
in-, im-	in	infield	Latin
in-, im-, il-, ir-	not	injustice, impossible	Latin
inter-	between	interact	Latin
mid-	middle	midway	Latin
mis-	wrongly	misfire	Latin
non-	not	nonsense	Latin
over-	over	overlook	Anglo-Saxon
pre-	before	prefix	Latin
re	again	return	Latin
semi-	half	semicircle	Latin
sub-	under	submarine	Latin
super-	above	superstar	Latin

(continued)

(continued)

Prefix	Meaning	Key word	Origin
trans-	across	*transport*	Latin
un-	not	*unfriendly*	Anglo-Saxon
under-	under	*undersea*	Anglo-Saxon

From White, T.G., Sowell, J., & Yanagihara, A. (1989, January). Teaching elementary students to use word-part clues. *The Reading Teacher, 42*(4), 302–308. Reprinted with permission of the International Reading Association. www.reading.org

Table 7.2. Most frequently used suffixes

Prefix	Meaning	Key word	Origin
-able, -ible	can be done	*comfortable*	Latin
-al, -ial	having characteristics of	*personal*	Latin
-ed	past-tense verbs	*hopped*	Anglo-Saxon
-en	made of	*wooden*	Latin
-er	comparative	*higher*	Anglo-Saxon
-er, or	one who	*worker, actor*	Anglo-Saxon
-est	comparative	*biggest*	Anglo-Saxon
-ful	full of	*careful*	Anglo-Saxon
-ic	having characteristics of	*linguistic*	Latin
-ing	verb form/present participle	*running*	Latin
-ion, -tion, -ation, ition	act, process	*occasion, attraction*	Latin
-ity, -ty	state of	*infinity*	Latin
-ive, -ative, -itive	adjective form of a noun	*plaintive*	Latin
-less	without	*fearless*	Anglo-Saxon
-ly	characteristic of	*quickly*	Anglo-Saxon
-ment	action or process	*enjoyment*	Anglo-Saxon
-ness	state of, condition of	*kindness*	Anglo-Saxon
-ous, -eous, -ious	possessing the qualities of	*joyous*	Latin
-s, -es	more than one	*books, boxes*	Anglo-Saxon
-y	characterized by	*happy*	Latin

From White, T.G., Sowell, J., & Yanagihara, A. (1989, January). Teaching elementary students to use word-part clues. *The Reading Teacher, 42*(4), 302–308. Reprinted with permission of the nternational Reading Association. www.reading.org

Table 7.3. Most frequent affixes in printed school English (ranked)

Rank	Prefix	Percent of all prefixed words	Suffix	Percent of all suffixed words
1	*un-*	26	*-s, -es*	31
2	*re-*	14	*-ed*	20
3	*in-, im-, il-, ir-* (not)	11	*-ing*	14
4	*dis-*	7	*-ly*	7

(continued)

(continued)

Rank	Prefix	Percent of all prefixed words	Suffix	Percent of all suffixed words
5	en-, em-	4	-er, -or (agent)	4
6	non-	4	-ion, -tion, -ation, -ition	4
7	in-, im- (in)	3	-able, -ible	2
8	over-	3	-al, -ial	1
9	mis-	3	-y	1
10	sub-	3	-ness	1
11	pre-	3	-ity, -ty	1
12	inter-	3	-ment	1
13	fore-	3	-ic	1
14	de-	2	-ous, -eous, -ious	1
15	trans-	2	-en	1
16	super-	1	-er (comparative)	1
17	semi-	1	-ive, -ative, -tive	1
18	anti-	1	-ful	1
19	mid-	1	-less	1
20	under- (too little)	1	-est	1
All	other	3	other	7

From White, T.G., Sowell, J., & Yanagihara, A. (1989, January). Teaching elementary students to use word-part clues. *The Reading Teacher, 42*(4), 302–308. Reprinted with permission of the International Reading Association. www.reading.org

Table 7.4. Common Latin roots

Root	Meaning	Key word	Root	Meaning	Key word
aud	hear	audible	man	hand	manual
bene	well, good	benefit	mem	mind	memory
centi	hundred	centipede	migr	move	migrate
contra	against	contrary	miss	send	missile
cred	believe, trust	credible	ped	foot	pedal
dict	say, speak	dictate	pop	people	popular
duct	lead	conduct	port	carry	porter
equi	equal	equitable	rupt	break	erupt
extra	outside	extravagant	sign	mark	signal
fac	make	factory	spect	look	inspect
fig	form	figure	sta/stat	stand	statue
flec	flex, bend	flexible	struct	build	construct
form	shape	formulate	trac/tract	pull	tractor
fract	break	fracture	urb	city	suburb
init	beginning	initial	vid/vis	see	video/visible
ject	throw	reject	voc	voice	vocal
junct	join	junction	volv	roll	revolve

From White, T.G., Sowell, J., & Yanagihara, A. (1989, January). Teaching elementary students to use word-part clues. *The Reading Teacher, 42*(4), 302–308. Reprinted with permission of the International Reading Association. www.reading.org

(continued)

(continued)

Table 7.5. Common Greek roots

Root	Meaning	Key word	Root	Meaning	Key word
amphi	both	amphibian	micro	small	microscope
aster	star	asterisk	mono	single	monorail
auto	self	automatic	ology	study of	biology
biblio	book	bibliography	opt	eye	optical
bio	life	biology	para	beside	parallel
chron	time	chronic	phil	love	philosophy
geo	earth	geology	phon	sound	phonograph
graph	write, record	photograph	photo/phos	light	photograph
hemi	half	hemisphere	pod	foot	podiatrist
hydr	water	hydraulic	psych	mind, soul	psychic
hyper	over	hyperactive	scope	see	microscope
ist	one who	dentist	sphere	ball	hemisphere
logo	word, reason	logic	syn	together	synonym
macro	large	macrobiotic	tele	from afar	telephone
mech	machine	mechanic	therm	heat	thermometer
meter	measure	altimeter			

From White, T.G., Sowell, J., & Yanagihara, A. (1989, January). Teaching elementary students to use word-part clues. *The Reading Teacher, 42*(4), 302–308. Reprinted with permission of the International Reading Association. www.reading.org

Foster Word Consciousness

The following activities will build word consciousness or awareness.

● ● ● ● ●

Word Wizards

In this activity (Stahl & Stahl, 2004), the teacher introduces target words. Words are displayed and discussed in context, and definitions are given. When children hear or see these words throughout the day or class period, they tell the teacher. The teacher then puts a sticky note or draws a star after a student's name each time he or she recognizes the target words. When children get five notes or stars, they are designated as Word Wizards.

Word Awareness Framework

Graves and Watts-Taffe (2008) proposed a framework with six categories for fostering word consciousness:

1. *Create a word-rich environment.* Do students see items labeled all around the classroom? Are there engaging, accessible books of all sizes and shapes within easy reach? Do they hear amusing, stimulating, captivating words spoken by the teacher and their fellow students? Do they use sophisticated, impressive words in their own interactions both verbal and written?

2. *Recognize and promote skilled and appropriate use of vocabulary.* Are there plenty of positive vocabulary role models in your classroom to demonstrate precision and variety in their choice of words? Do you provide frequent read-alouds followed by discussions for rich vocabulary enhancement? Preschool and primary age students successfully learn the meanings of many sophisticated words when teachers incorporate repeated readings accompanied by direct focus on specific words during discussions (Beck & McKeown, 2007).

3. *Promote word play.* Do your students see you enjoying the mystery and excitement of learning new words? Young children (K–3) enjoy the I Spy book series (Marzollo & Wick, n.d.), in which they are required to match crazy pictures with words and rhyming riddles. Older students always enjoy idioms and puns (see http://www.punoftheday.com). Some students find that illustrating puns and idioms using their artistic skills is a refreshing medium for understanding multiple meanings of words.

4. *Foster word consciousness through writing.* Do your students make careful choices of the words they select when writing, particularly during the revision process? Do they consider if they have chosen the best word to express their meaning (e.g., precise enough, too difficult, used too frequently)?

5. *Involve students in original investigations.* Is the vocabulary unique to specific situations, professions, regions, and settings? How has the vocabulary changed over time (e.g., from grandparents' to students' favorite expressions)?

6. *Teach students about words.* Do students know that some words have more than one meaning (e.g., *flight*), are interrelated (e.g., *flower, tulip, rose, garden, vase*), and are learned incrementally? Word learning tends to take place on a continuum moving from unknown (never having seen the word) to known (knowing and remembering the word; Nagy & Scott, 2000).

Dale (1965) developed a chart like the one in Figure 7.4 to help teachers assess the extent of a student's knowledge about words. When teachers know

(continued)

(continued)

before they present a lesson which words are familiar and unfamiliar to their students, they are in a better position to select words for instruction and specific activities for enhancing word knowledge. Teachers are able to analyze the extent of word knowledge in this way. As students come across unfamiliar words repeatedly, over time their knowledge of the words is increased. Students then move up the levels of word knowledge to the goal of "having a full and precise meaning" (Graves and Watts-Taffe, 2002). The levels of word knowledge are defined as follows:

1. Have never seen or heard the word before
2. Have seen or heard the word before but do not know what it means
3. Vaguely know the meaning of the word; can associate it with a concept or context
4. Know the word well; can explain it and use it

● ● ● ● ● ●

Support for English Language Learners

All of the teaching advice and activities in this chapter are appropriate and excellent considerations for English language learners (ELLs). Keep in mind that some students who are raised in homes where English is spoken nonetheless may be ELLs because they have had limited exposure to the language. Reflect on these additional ideas:

- Provide additional support before and after school. Make time to have conversations with children and model the use of new vocabulary words. When students have difficulty finding the words to express themselves, answer questions for them, asking the students to repeat after you.
- Preteach essential vocabulary and background knowledge. Prepare students ahead of time for lessons with unfamiliar words and contexts.
- Emphasize meaning rather than pronunciation.
- Use pantomime, pictures, and graphic organizers to help students organize and remember materials.
- Apply flexible grouping and smaller group sizes in response to students' varying language levels.

Students learn from each other too, so include more-verbal students in groups with less-verbal students, especially when monitoring discussions.

Levels of Word Knowledge Chart

Words	Never seen or heard word before 1	Have seen or heard word before but don't know what it means 2	Vaguely know the meaning of word; can associate it with a concept or context 3	Know the word well; can explain it and use it 4

Figure 7.4. Levels of Word Knowledge Chart. (Sources: Dale, 1965; Graves & Watts-Taffe, 2002)

RESOURCES

Baumann, J.F., & Kame'enui, E.J. (2004). *Vocabulary instruction: Research to practice.* New York: Guilford Press. (This is an edited text in which authors contribute their expertise organized around three themes: teaching specific vocabulary, teaching vocabulary-learning strategies, teaching vocabulary through word consciousness, and language play.)

Beck, I.L., & McKeown, M.G. (2002). *Text talk.* New York: Scholastic. (*Text Talk* engages teachers and students in robust vocabulary instruction tied closely to comprehension. This early reading program was developed by leading vocabulary researchers who have done prolific work in the field, and this program has been proven effective in scientific research.)

Beck, I.L., McKeown, M.G., & Kucan, L. (2002). *Bringing words to life: Robust vocabulary instruction.* New York: Guilford Press. (This book adheres to a research-based framework and contains practical strategies for teaching vocabulary in kindergarten through high school. Topics include: how to select words for instruction, creating meaningful learning activities, and sample classroom dialogues. An appendix lists vocabulary words.)

Diamond, L., & Gutlohn, L. (2006). *CORE vocabulary handbook.* Berkeley, CA: Consortium on Reading Excellence. (This book focuses on the three critical components of exemplary vocabulary instruction: teaching specific words, teaching independent word-learning strategies, and promoting word consciousness. It is teacher friendly and has sample lesson plans that are helpful in boosting vocabulary instruction in any reading program; http://www.corelearn.com.)

Honig, B., Diamond, L., & Gutlon, L. (2008). *CORE: Teaching reading sourcebook for kindergarten through eighth grade.* Berkeley, CA: Consortium on Reading Excellence. (This oversized book is a true encyclopedia of teaching reading with a strong commitment to research-based practices. It contains a detailed chapter with many practical suggestions for teaching vocabulary by grade level and is careful to include information for English language learners; http://www.corelearn.com.)

Hults, A. (2003). *Reading first: Unlock the secrets to reading success with research-based strategies.* Huntington Beach, CA: Creative Teaching Press. (This book provides a concise summary of the National Literacy Council's *Put Reading First* report, with instructional activities in all five critical components of reading instruction: phonemic awareness, phonics, fluency, vocabulary, and comprehension. Vocabulary activities are divided by topics, such as directing instruction of individual words, discussing a vocabulary word in context, and providing repeated exposure to new words; http://www.creativeteaching.com.)

Stahl, S., & Kapinus, K. (2001). *Word power: What every educator needs to know about teaching vocabulary.* Washington, DC: National Education Association. (This relatively short, friendly, 36-page book covers the basics of teaching vocabulary: encouraging wide reading, deciding which words to teach, how to teach words, vocabulary activities, word parts, and instructional strategies.)

Instructional Resources for Intermediate Students

Bebko, A.R., Alexander, J., & Doucet, R. (2001). *Language! Roots.* Longmont, CO: Sopris West Educational Services. (This morphologically based vocabulary supplement contains more than 250 reproducible masters in a sturdy binder. The reproducible materials move students from sound-letter correspondence to understanding words as units of meaning and provide access to the rich vocabulary of the English language. The activities expand student vocabulary by employing roots, prefixes, and suffixes from Latin and combining forms from Greek. Although designed to be used with the *LANGUAGE!* curriculum, it can also be used on its own, particularly for test preparation.)

Ebbers, S. (2004). *Vocabulary through morphemes: Suffixes, prefixes, and roots for intermediate grades.* Longmont, CO: Sopris West Educational Services. (Systematic, structured lessons explicitly teach students the meanings of the building blocks of language so that they can grasp new words and their meanings. Flexible lessons increase vocabulary, teach antonyms and synonyms, and help students make connections using word families.)

Ebbers, S., & Carroll, J. (2010). *Daily oral vocabulary exercises.* Longmont, CO: Sopris West Educational Services. (A teacher and student friendly source for expanding academic vocabulary in grades 4 through 12. Includes ample review and practice along with both English and Spanish cognates for ease of use with ELL students.)

Mountain, L., Fifer, N., & Flowers, N. (1990). *Vocabulary from classic roots: Strategic vocabulary instruction through Greek and Latin roots.* Cambridge, MA: Educators Publishing Service. (This book is ideal for students in Grades 4–11 who are transitioning from the learning-to-read to the reading-to-learn phase and who would benefit from a better understanding of how content-area multisyllabic words work. By learning a few Greek and Latin roots, students will be surprised at how quickly they can read and understand words that were previously unfamiliar.)

Electronic Resources for All Students

Wordsift (http://www.wordsift.com). (Developed at the Stanford University, this free online resource allows students to type in a word and access the Visual Thesaurus. Students are provided visual images of words, superb graphics, and even video clips that can facilitate their ability to understand abstract word meanings and to see relationships between words and ideas. More effective than memorizing definitions, teachers and students can talk about word meanings and look at pictures to jumpstart discussions that relate to real-life experiences.)

Dr. Anita Archer's Strategic Literacy Instructional Video Series (http://www.scoe.org/pub/htdocs/archer-videos.html). (From the Sonoma County Office of Education, these videos can also be downloaded from iTunes (http://www.itunes.com). All videos represent interactive, engaging literacy instruction.)

Resources for the Classroom (http://www.scoe.org). (The Sonoma County Office of Education posts many helpful instructional ideas and research updates for educators on their web site. Updates often include videos of expert teachers teaching vocabulary and comprehension.)

Weaving It All Together

8

Weaving Elements Together for a Lifetime of Reading

Gardeners, artists, chefs, musicians, and accountants all have specialized tools, without which the achievement of their intended and desired results would not be possible. These professionals' tools assist with the development of unique individual and combined components, elements and parts in isolation, and when finished, produce a completed handiwork. So it is for teachers of reading.

Next STEPS in Literacy Instruction: Connecting Assessments to Effective Interventions provides multiple specialized tools for teachers that isolate the critical and necessary skills that students need to be fluent, comprehending readers. These skills have been clearly identified. Fluency measures can assess those skills so that teachers can recognize which students may be at risk for future difficulty and which skills are contributing to the difficulties students display. When teaching struggling readers, teachers need to know which skills to teach and how to best teach those skills, while choosing from a variety of effective and proven tools.

Each skill in *Next STEPS*—phoneme awareness, decoding, fluency, vocabulary, and comprehension—is dependent on the others in order for students to read fluently with comprehension. These skills are taught early in isolation and with older struggling readers because students must develop strengths and automaticity in each skill area. However, it is critical that teachers understand the reciprocal and interrelated nature of these skills. One of the tools in *Next STEPS* is to teach small groups of students in order to focus on the development of identified skills. When teachers do this, it is essential to the success of the profession to weave the components together to strengthen the reading process as a whole.

The concept of separate yet interconnected skills, which are dependent on each other, informs the practice of *Next STEPS* (see Figure 8.1). Weaving the components during reading instruction can be done in any of the following ways:

- Follow a lesson on phoneme segmentation by teaching students the letter-sound connections (*weaving phoneme awareness and decoding*)
- As a part of a decoding lesson with isolated words, provide practice with reading those words in sentences and stories and model comprehension strategies (*weaving phoneme awareness, decoding, fluency, and comprehension*)
- Following a vocabulary lesson, guide students to decode those words, discuss the words in the context of their own experience and of the story, and then read and reread the text (*weaving phoneme awareness, decoding, fluency, vocabulary, and comprehension*)

Stop and think about it: There are opportunities to teach reading all day, every day! Teachers need to check their weaving ability every day by asking, "Did I weave the skill components today? Did I teach the *indicated* skills, identified through assessment, and then *combine* the skills to strengthen my students' learning?" *Next STEPS* teachers know how to assess and teach reading skills, and then weave the processes for a lifetime of reading!

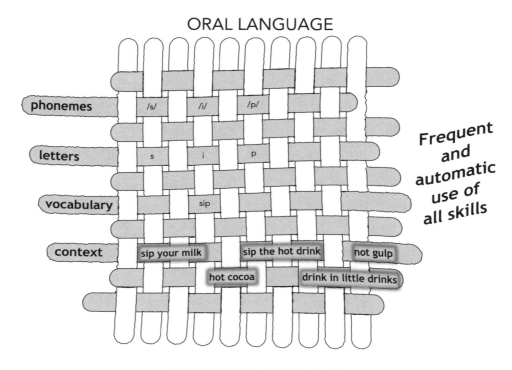

Reading: Martin came inside stamping the snow from his boots. His smiling face was rosy red from the cold and a sip of hot chocolate sounded delicious.

Figure 8.1.   The concept of interweaving separate yet interconnected skills, such as those involving phonemes, letters, vocabulary, and context, leads to frequent and automatic use of skills.

References

Adams, M. (1990). *Beginning to read: Thinking and learning about print.* Cambridge, MA: MIT Press.

Adams, M.J., Foorman, B.R., Lundberg, I., & Beeler, T. (1998). *Phonemic awareness in young children: A classroom curriculum.* Baltimore: Paul H. Brookes Publishing Co.

Armbruster, B.B., Lehr, F., & Osborn, J. (2001). *Put reading first: The research building blocks for teaching children to read.* Washington, DC: National Institute for Literacy.

Baumann J.F., & Kame'enui, E.J. (2004). *Vocabulary instruction: Research to practice.* New York: Guilford Press.

Bear, D., Invernizzi, M., Templeton, S., & Johnston, F. (2008). *Words their way: Word study for phonics, vocabulary, and spelling instruction* (2nd ed.). Upper Saddle River, NJ: Prentice Hall.

Beck, I.L., & McKeown, M.G. (2007). *Different ways for different goals, but keep your eye on the higher verbal goals.* In R.K. Wagner, A. Muse, & K. Tannenbaum (Eds.), *Vocabulary acquisition: Implications for reading comprehension* (pp. 182–204). New York: Guilford Press.

Beck, I.L., McKeown, M.G., & Kucan, L. (2002). *Bringing words to life.* New York: Guilford Press.

Berninger, V., & Wolf, B. (2009). *Teaching students with dyslexia and dysgraphia: Lessons from teaching and science.* Baltimore: Paul H. Brookes Publishing Co.

Blevins, W. (2006). *Phonics from A to Z: Grades K–3.* New York: Scholastic.

Breznitz, Z. (2006). *Fluency in reading: Synchronization of processes.* Mahwah, NJ: Lawrence Erlbaum Associates.

Brown, V.L., Hammill, D.D., & Wiederholt, J.L. (1995). *Test of Reading Comprehension–Third Edition (TORC-3).* Austin, TX: PRO-ED.

Brownell, R. (2001a). *Expressive One-Word Picture Vocabulary Test.* Novato, CA: Academic Therapy.

Brownell, R. (2001b). *Receptive One-Word Picture Vocabulary Test.* Novato, CA: Academic Therapy.

Bryant, B.R., & Wiederholt, J.L. (1991). *Gray Oral Reading Tests–Diagnostic (GORT-D).* Austin, TX: PRO-ED.

Bursuck, W.D., & Damer, M. (2007). *Reading instruction for students who are at risk or have disabilities.* Glenview, IL: Pearson Scott Foresman.

Cain, K., & Oakhill, J. (2007). *Children's comprehension problems in oral and written language: A cognitive perspective.* New York: Guilford Press.

Carlisle, J.F., & Rice, M.S. (2002). *Improving reading comprehension: Research-based principles and practices.* Timonium, MD: York Press.

Carnine, D., & Kinder, D. (1985). Teaching low-performing students to apply generative and schema strategies to narrative and expository material. *Remedial & Special Education, 6,* 20–30.

Carnine, D.W., Silbert, J., Kame'enui, E.J., & Tarver, S. (2004). *Direct instruction reading* (4th ed.). Upper Saddle River, NJ: Merrill Prentice Hall.

Carnine, D.W., Silbert, J., Kame'enui, E.J., Tarver, S.G., & Jungjohann, K. (2006). *Teaching struggling and at-risk readers: A direct instructional approach.* Glenview, IL: Pearson Scott Foresman.

Carreker, S. (2004). *Developing meta-cognitive skills: Vocabulary and comprehension.* Bellaire, TX: Neuhaus Education Center.

Carreker, S. (2005). Teaching spelling. In J.R. Birsh (Ed.), *Multisensory teaching of basic language skills* (2nd ed., pp. 217–256). Baltimore: Paul H. Brookes Publishing Co.

Carreker, S., & Boulware-Gooden, R. (2009). *Neuhaus Oral Language Screening.* Bellaire, TX: Neuhaus Center.

Chall, J. (1996). *Learning to read: The great debate* (3rd ed.). Fort Worth, TX: Harcourt Brace.

Chard, D.J., Vaughn, S., & Tyler, B. (2002). A synthesis of research on effective interventions for building fluency with

elementary students with learning disabilities. *Journal of Learning Disabilities, 35,* 386–406.

Collins Cobuild Student's Dictionary. (2005). New York: HarperCollins.

Cunningham, A.E., & Stanovich, K.E. (1997). Early reading acquisition and its relation to reading experience and ability ten years later. *Developmental Psychology, 33,* 934–945.

Dale, E. (1965). Vocabulary measurement: Techniques and major findings. *Elementary English, 42,* 895–901.

Davidson, M.R., Standal, T.C., Towner, J.C., Matsoff, J., et al. (2009). *Reading fluency benchmark assessor: Teacher's guide.* Saint Paul: Read Naturally.

Deno, S.L. (1985). Curriculum-based measurement: The emerging alternative. *Exceptional Children, 52,* 219–232.

Deno, S.L., Fuchs, L.S., Marston, D., & Shinn, J. (2001). Using curriculum-based measurement to establish growth standards for students with learning disabilities. *School Psychology Review, 30,* 507–524.

Deno, S.L., Marston, D., Shinn, M.R., & Tindal, G. (1983). Oral reading fluency: A simple datum for scaling reading disability. *Topics in Learning and Learning Disabilities, 2*(4), 53–59.

Denton, C., & Hocker, J. (2006). *Responsive reading instruction: Flexible intervention for struggling readers in the early grades.* Longmont, CO: Sopris West.

Diamond, L., & Thorsnes, B.J. (2008). *Assessing reading: Multiple measures* (2nd ed.). Novato, CA: Arena Press.

Dolch, E.W. (1948). *Problems in reading.* Champaign, IL: Garrard Press.

Dowhower, S.L. (1987). Effects of repeated reading on second-grade transitional readers' fluency and comprehension. *Reading Research Quarterly, 22,* 389–406.

Dunlap, L. (2005). *Zeke and Pete Rule!* New York: Houghton Mifflin.

Dunn, L.M., & Dunn, L.M. (1997). *Peabody Picture Vocabulary Test–Third Edition (PPVT-III).* Circle Pines, MN: American Guidance Service.

Dunn, L.M., & Dunn, D.M. (2007). *PPVT-4 Form A: Peabody Picture Vocabulary Test* (4th ed.). Minneapolis, MN: NCS Pearson.

Dynamic Measurement Group. (2011). *DIBELS Next* (7th ed.). Eugene, OR: Author.

Eaker, R., DuFour, R., & DuFour, R. (2002). *Getting started: Recruiting schools to become professional learning communities.* Bloomington, IN: National Educational Service.

Elliott, J., Lee, S.W., & Tollefson, N. (2001). A reliability and validity study of the Dynamic Indicators of Basic Early Literacy Skills–Modified. *School Psychology Review, 30,* 33–49.

Florida Department of Education. (2009). *Florida Assessments for Instruction in Reading.* Tallahassee, FL: Author.

Foorman, B.R., Francis, D.J., Schatschneider, C., & Mehta, P. (1998). The role of instruction in learning to read: Preventing reading failure in at-risk children. *Journal of Educational Psychology, 90,* 37–55.

Friend, M., & Bursuck, W.D. (2006). *Including students with special needs: A practical guide for classroom teachers.* Boston: Allyn & Bacon.

Fry, E. (1994). *1000 instant words.* Westminster, CA: Teacher Created Materials.

Fry, E.B., Fountoukidis, D.L., & Polk, J.K. (1985). *The new reading teacher's book of lists.* Englewood Cliffs, NJ: Prentice Hall.

Fuchs, D., & Fuchs, L.S. (2005). Peer-assisted learning strategies: Promoting word recognition, fluency, and reading comprehension in young children. *The Journal of Special Education, 39,* 34–44.

Fuchs, D., Fuchs, L.S., Mathes, P.G., & Simmons, D.C. (1997). Peer-assisted learning strategies: Making classrooms more responsive to diversity. *American Educational Research Journal, 34,* 174–206.

Fuchs, D., Fuchs, L.S., Thompson, A., Al Otaiba, S., Yen, L., Yang, N.J., et al. (2001). Is reading important in reading-readiness programs? A randomized field trial with teachers as program implementers. *Journal of Educational Psychology, 93,* 251–267.

Fuchs, L.S., & Fuchs, D. (1991). Curriculum-based measurements: Current applications and future directions. *Preventing School Failure, 35,* 6–11.

Fuchs, L.S., & Fuchs, D. (1992). Identifying a measure for monitoring student reading progress. *School Psychology Review, 21*(1), 45–58.

Fuchs, L.S., & Fuchs, D. (2004). *Using CBM for progress monitoring* [PowerPoint slides]. Retrieved December 1, 2009, from http://www.studentprogress.org/library/Training/CBM%20Reading/UsingCBMReading.

Fuchs, L.S., Fuchs, D., Hosp, M., & Jenkins, J.R. (2001). Oral reading fluency as an indicator of reading competence: A theoretical, empirical, and historical analysis. *Scientific Studies of Reading, 5,* 239–256.

Fuchs, L.S., Fuchs, D., & Kazdan, S. (1999). Effects of peer-assisted learning strategies on high-school students with serious reading problems. *Remedial and Special Education, 20,* 309–319.

Fuchs, L.S., Fuchs, D., & Maxwell, L. (1988). The validity of informal measures of reading comprehension. *Remedial and Special Education, 9,* 20–28.

Gillon, G.T. (2004). *Phonological awareness: From research to practice.* New York: Guilford Press.

Good, R.H., & Kaminski, R.A. (Eds.). (2002). *Dynamic Indicators of Basic Early Literacy Skills* (6th ed.). Eugene, OR: Institute for Development of Educational Achievement.

Gough, P.B., & Tunmer, W.E. (1986). Decoding, reading, and reading disability. *Remedial and Special Education, 7,* 6–10.

Grace, K. (2005). *Phonics and spelling through phoneme-grapheme mapping.* Longmont, CO: Sopris West Educational Services.

Graham, S., & Perin, D. (2007). *Improving writing of adolescents in middle and high schools.* Washington, DC: Alliance for Excellent Education.

Graves, M.F. (2002). *Vocabulary instruction.* Minneapolis: University of Minnesota. Paper prepared for the Minnesota Reading Excellence Act project.

Graves, M.F., & Watts, S.M. (2002). The place of word consciousness in a research-based vocabulary program. In S.J. Samuels & A.E. Farstrup (Eds.), *What research has to say about reading instruction* (3rd ed., pp. 140–165). Newark, DE: International Reading Association.

Graves, M.F., & Watts-Taffe, S. (2008). For the love of words: Fostering word consciousness in young readers. *The Reading Teacher, 62,* 185–193.

Gunning, T.G. (2002). *Assessing and correcting reading and writing difficulties* (2nd ed.). Boston: Allyn & Bacon.

Harris, K.R., Graham, S., Mason, L.H., & Friedlander, B. (2008). *Powerful writing strategies for all students.* Baltimore: Paul H. Brookes Publishing Co.

Hart, B., & Risley, T.R. (1995). *Meaningful differences in the everyday experience of young American children.* Baltimore: Paul H. Brookes Publishing Co.

Hasbrouck, J., & Denton, C. (2005). *The reading coach: A how-to manual for success.* Longmont, CO: Sopris West.

Hasbrouck, J., & Denton, C. (2010). *The reading coach 2: More tools and strategies for student-focused coaches.* Longmont, CO: Sopris West.

Hasbrouck, J., & Tindal, G. (2005). *Oral reading fluency: 90 years of measurement* (Tech. Rep. No. 33). Eugene, OR: University of Oregon, College of Education, Behavioral Research and Teaching.

Heckelman, R.G. (1969). A neurological-impress method of remedial reading instruction. *Academic Therapy Quarterly, 4*(4), 277–282.

Hintze, J.M., Callahan, J.E., III, Matthews, W.J., Williams, S.A.S., & Tobin, K.G. (2002). Oral reading fluency and prediction of reading comprehension in African American and Caucasian elementary school children. *School Psychology Review, 31,* 540–553.

Hintze, J.M., Ryan, A.L., & Stoner, G. (2003). Concurrent validity and diagnostic accuracy of the Dynamic Indicators of Basic Literacy Skills and the Comprehensive Test of Phonological Processing. *School Psychology Review, 32,* 351–375.

Honig, B., Diamond, L., Gutlon, L. (2008). *CORE: Teaching reading sourcebook* (2nd ed.). Novato, CA: Arena Press.

Hoover, W.A., & Gough, P.B. (1990). The simple view of reading. *Reading and Writing, 2,* 127–160.

Hosp, M.K., Hosp, J.L., & Howell, K.W. (2007). *The ABCs of CBM: A practical guide to curriculum-based measurement.* New York: Guilford Press.

Hoyt, L. (1999). *Revisit, reflect, retell: Strategies for improving reading comprehension.* Portsmouth, NH: Heinemann Press.

Hudson, R.F., Lane, H.B., & Pullen, P.C. (2002). Reading fluency assessment and instruction: What, why, and how. *Reading Teacher, 58*(8), 702–714.

Individuals with Disabilities Education Improvement Act (IDEA) of 2004, PL 108-446, 20 U.S.C. §§ 1400 *et seq.*

Jordan, G.E., Snow, C.E., & Porche, M.V. (2000). Project EASE: The effect of a family literacy project on kindergarten students' early literacy skills. *Reading Research Quarterly, 35,* 524–546.

Kame'enui, E.J., Carnine, D.W., Dixon, R.C., Simmons, D.C., & Coyne, M.D. (2002). *Effective teaching strategies that accommodate diverse learners.* Columbus, OH: Merrill Prentice Hall.

Kamil, M.L., & Hiebert, E.H. (2005). Teaching and learning vocabulary: Perspectives and persistent issues. In E.H. Hiebert & M.L. Kamil (Eds.), *Teaching and learning vocabulary: Bringing research to practice.* Mahwah, NJ: Lawrence Erlbaum Associates.

Klingner, J.K. (2004). Assessing reading comprehension. *Assessment for Effective Intervention, 29,* 59–70.

Langer, J.A. (1984). Examining background knowledge and text comprehension. *Reading Research Quarterly, 14,* 468–481.

Lavoie, R. (1998). *How difficult can this be? The F.A.T. City Workshop* [video]. Retrieved July 24, 2009, from http://www.learningstore.org/we1001.html

Learning First Alliance. (2000). *Every child reading: A professional development guide.* Retrieved May 21, 2009, from http://www.learningfirst.org

Marzollo, J., & Wick, W. (n.d.). *I Spy* book series. New York: Scholastic.

Mathes, P. (2005). *SRA early interventions in reading.* New York: MacMillan/McGraw-Hill.

Mathes, P.C., Torgesen, J.K., & Allor, J.H. (2001). The effects of Peer-Assisted Literacy: Strategies for first-grade readers with and without additional computer-assisted instruction in phonological awareness. *American Educational Research Journal, 38,* 371–410.

McMaster, K.L., Fuchs, D., Fuchs, L.S., & Compton, D.L. (2005). Responding to non-responders: An experimental field trial of identification and intervention methods. *Exceptional Children, 71,* 445–463.

Mehta, P.D., Foorman, B.R., Branum-Martin, L., & Taylor, W.P. (2005). Literacy as a unidimensional multilevel construct: Validation, sources of influence, and implications in a longitudinal study in grades 1 to 4. *Scientific Studies of Reading, 9,* 85–116.

Moats, L.C. (1999). *Teaching reading is rocket science: What expert teachers of reading should know and be able to do.* Washington, DC: American Federation of Teachers.

Moats, L.C. (2004). Relevance of neuroscience to effective education for students with reading and other learning disabilities. *Journal of Child Neurology, 19,* 840–845.

Morgan, P.L., Fuchs, D., Compton, D.L., Cordray, D.S., & Fuchs, L.S. (2008).

Does early reading failure decrease children's reading motivation? *Journal of Learning Disabilities, 41,* 387–404.

Nagy, W., & Anderson, R.C. (1984). The number of words in printed school English. *Reading Research Quarterly, 19,* 304–330.

Nagy, W.E., & Scott, J.A. (2000). Vocabulary processes. In M.L. Kamil, P. Mosenthal, P.D. Pearson, & R. Barr (Eds.), *Handbook of reading research* (Vol. III, pp. 269–284). Mahwah, NJ: Lawrence Erlbaum Associates.

National Institute of Child Health and Human Development. (2000). *Report of the National Reading Panel. Teaching children to read: An evidence-based assessment of the scientific research literature on reading and its implications for reading instruction* (NIH Publication No. 00-4769). Washington, DC: U.S. Government Printing Office.

National Research Council. (1998). *Preventing reading difficulties in young children.* Washington, DC: National Academies Press.

Neuhaus Education Center. (2005). *Developing metacognitive skills* (p. 51). Bellaire, TX: Neuhaus Education Center.

No Child Left Behind Act of 2001, PL 107-110, 115 Stat. 1425, 20 U.S.C. §§ 6301 *et seq.*

Norton, E., & Wolf, M. (2008). *The relationship of morphological skills to decoding and reading fluency: Insights from beginning and struggling readers.* Presented at the meeting of the International Dyslexia Association, Seattle, WA.

O'Connor, R.E., Notari-Syverson, A., Vadasy, P.F. (2005). *Ladders to literacy: A kindergarten activity book* (2nd ed.). Baltimore: Paul H. Brookes Publishing Co.

O'Shea, L.J., Sindelar, P.T., & O'Shea, D.J. (1987). The effects of repeated readings and attentional cues on the reading fluency and comprehension of learning disabled readers. *Learning Disabilities Research, 2,* 103–109.

Palencsar, A.S., & Brown, A.L. (1984). Reciprocal teaching of comprehension monitoring activities. *Cognition and Instruction, 1,* 117–175.

Pikulski, J.J., & Chard, D.J. (2005). Fluency: Bridge between decoding and comprehension. *The Reading Teacher, 58,* 510–519.

RAND Reading Study Group. (2002). *Reading for understanding: An R & D program in reading comprehension.* Santa Monica, CA: RAND Corporation.

Raphael, T. (1986). Teaching question answer relationships, revisited. *The Reading Teacher, 39,* 516–522.

Rasinski, T.V. (2004). *Assessing reading fluency.* Honolulu, HI: Pacific Resources for Education and Learning.

Scammacca, N., Vaughn, S., Roberts, G., Wanzek, J., & Torgesen, J.K. (2007). *Extensive reading interventions in grades K–3: From research to practice.* Portsmouth, NH: RMC Research Corporation.

Shaywitz, S. (2003). *Overcoming dyslexia.* New York: Knopf.

Shefelbine, J., & Newman, K. (2004). *SIPPS: Systematic instruction in phoneme awareness, phonics, and sight words* (2nd ed.). Oakland, CA: Developmental Studies Center.

Shinn, M.R., Good, R.H., Knutson, N., Tilly, W.D., & Collins, V.L. (1992). Curriculum-based measurement reading fluency: A confirmatory analysis of its relation to reading. *School Psychology Review, 21,* 459–479.

Simmons, D.C., & Kame'enui, E.J. (2000). *Overview of the big ideas in beginning reading.* Institute for the Development of Educational Achievement. College of Education, University of Oregon. PowerPoint presentation.

Sindelar, P.T., Monda, L.E., & O'Shea, L.J. (1990). The effects of repeated readings on instructional and mastery level readers. *Journal of Educational Research, 83,* 220–226.

Smartt, S.M., & Reschly, D.J. (2007, June). *Barriers to the preparation of highly qualified teachers in reading.* Presented at the meeting of the National Comprehensive Center for Teacher Quality, Washington, DC.

Snow, C. (2002). *Reading for understanding: Toward an R&D program in reading comprehension.* Santa Monica, CA: RAND Reading Study Group.

Stahl, S., & Kapinus, B. (2001). *Word power: What every educator needs to know about teaching vocabulary.* Washington, DC: National Education Association.

Stahl, S.A., & Stahl, K.A. (2004). Word wizards all! Teaching word meanings in preschool and primary education. In J.F. Baumann & E.J. Kame'enui (Eds.), *Vocabulary instruction: Research to practice* (pp. 59–78). New York: Guilford Press.

Stanovich, K. (1986). Matthew effects in reading: Some consequences of individual differences in the acquisition of literacy. *Reading Research Quarterly, 21,* 360–407.

Stanovich, K.E. (1991). Word recognition: Changing perspectives. In R. Barr, M.L. Kamil, P. Mosenthal, & P.D. Pearson (Eds.), *Handbook of reading research* (Vol. 2, pp. 418–452). New York: Longman.

Texas Education Agency. (1998). *Texas Primary Reading Inventory.* Austin, TX: Author.

Torgesen, J.K. (2000). Individual differences in response to early interventions in reading: The lingering problem of treatment resisters. *Learning Disabilities Research and Practice, 15,* 55–64.

Torgeson, J.K. (2004, Fall). Preventing early reading failure. *American Educator.*

Torgesen, J.K., & Hudson, R. (2006). Reading fluency: Critical factors for struggling readers. In S.J. Samuels and A. Farstrup (Eds.), *What research has to say about fluency instruction* (pp. 130–158). Newark, DE: International Reading Association.

Torgesen, J.K., & Miller, D.H. (2008). *Using assessment to improve academic literacy instruction for adolescents.* Portsmouth, NH: RMC Research Corporation.

Traub, F., & Bloom, N. (2003). *Recipe for reading.* New York: Walker & Company.

Vaughn Gross Center for Reading and Language Arts. (2005). *Introduction to the 3-Tier Reading Model: Reducing reading difficulties for kindergarten through third grade students* (4th ed.). Austin, TX: The University of Texas at Austin.

Wechsler, D. (1992). *Wechsler Individual Achievement Test.* San Antonio, TX: Harcourt Assessment.

White, T.G., Sowell, J., & Yanagihara, A. (1989). *Teaching elementary students to use word-part clues. The Reading Teacher, 42,* 302–308.

Wiig, E.H., & Secord, W.A. (1992). *Test of Word Knowledge.* Ontario: Psychological Corporation.

Woodcock, R.W. (1998). *Woodcock Reading Mastery Test–Revised–Normative Update*

(WMRT-R/NU). Circle Pines, MN: American Guidance Service.

Woodcock, R.W., McGrew, K.S., & Mather, N. (2000). *Woodcock-Johnson III: Complete Battery.* Itasca, IL: Riverside.

Zeno, S.M., Ivens, S.H., Millard, R.T., & Duvvuri, R. (1995). *The educator's word frequency guide.* Brewster, NY: Touchstone Applied Science Associates.